Cinema and Colour

Cinema and Colour

The Saturated Image

Paul Coates

A BFI book published by Palgrave Macmillan

In memoriam Krzysztof Kieślowski

First published in 2010 by
PALGRAVE MACMILLAN

on behalf of the

BRITISH FILM INSTITUTE
21 Stephen Street, London W1T 1LN
www.bfi.org.uk

There's more to discover about film and television through the BFI. Our world-renowned
archive, cinemas, festivals, films, publications and learning resources are here to inspire you.

Palgrave Macmillan in the UK is an imprint of Macmillan Publishers Limited, registered in
England, company number 785998, of Houndmills, Basingstoke, Hampshire RG21 6XS.
Palgrave Macmillan in the US is a division of St Martin's Press LLC, 175 Fifth Avenue,
New York, NY 10010. Palgrave Macmillan is the global academic imprint of the above
companies and has companies and representatives throughout the world. Palgrave® and
Macmillan® are registered trademarks in the United States, the United Kingdom, Europe
and other countries.

Cover design: Mark Swan
Cover images: *Le Mépris* (Jean-Luc Godard, 1963), Rome-Paris Films/Films Concordia/
Compagnia Cinematografica Champion; *Two or Three Things I Know About Her* (Jean-Luc
Godard, 1967), Anouchka Films/Argos-Films/Films du Carrosse/Parc Film; *The Wizard of
Oz* (Victor Fleming, 1939), Loew's Incorporated
Designed by couch
Set by Cambrian Typesetters, Camberley, Surrey
Printed in China

This book is printed on paper suitable for recycling and made from fully managed and
sustained forest sources. Logging, pulping and manufacturing processes are expected to
conform to the environmental regulations of the country of origin.

British Library Cataloguing-in-Publication Data
A catalogue record for this book is available from the British Library
A catalog record for this book is available from the Library of Congress
10 9 8 7 6 5 4 3 2 1
19 18 17 16 15 14 13 12 11 10

ISBN 978–1–84457–314–1 (pbk)
ISBN 978–1–84457–315–8 (hbk)

CONTENTS

A : THEORY AND HISTORY

1 Introduction: Theorising Colour and Ambivalence

LIBERATION AND AMBIVALENCE: GIOTTO'S JOY, MUNCH'S DEPRESSION

Moments of liberation are ambiguous, even before the revolution begins to consume its children: divesting objects of the contexts that first lent them meaning cannot dispel completely the shadows of old ones. For an incalculable time objects shimmer between different orders of signification. Where one is acknowledged consciously, the other lives an unconscious afterlife, even if only haunting the unconsciousness known as habit. Meaning may then depend on beholders, or their moods. Consequently, such revolutionary moments as the 'breakthrough into colour' of early twentieth-century visual art or 1960s art cinema breathe an ambiguity that feeds polysemy. One example, chosen arbitrarily, can render this clearer. Thus, on the one hand, the primary association encoded within the blue of Krzysztof Kieślowski's *Trois couleurs: bleu* (*Three Colours: Blue*) (1993) would seem to accord with a cultural one linking it to depression, 'the blues': after all, a car crash widows its protagonist in its opening minutes. However, when I suggested this to Kieślowski, he retorted 'on the other hand in Spain – or perhaps Portugal, I'm not sure – it's quite the reverse: their age-old traditions identify blue with something vital and full of energy. … I've met numerous people from various parts of the world – and even from our cultural sphere – who have explained that there are vastly different relations with these colours.'[1] Julia Kristeva, meanwhile, reads blue as the colour of joy in Giotto's frescoes at Assisi and Padua. This association with joy is also traditional and allegorical, blue being the appropriate colour of sublimity – all the more so, of course, given the costliness of blue pigments when the frescoes were painted. However, her assertion that '[a] narrative signified cannot constrain the signifier'[2] modernistically acknowledges the slipperiness of colour's location, its readiness to inhabit multiple contexts and traditions. The colour of Giotto's joy can also exude depression, and blue can also be claimed by Edvard Munch. Consider, for example, Peter Watkins' discussion of the prevalence of blue in his *Edvard Munch* (1974):

> We did a series of tests and discovered that filming outdoors with an interior lighting stock produces a blue bias to the colour. We decided that we liked this look, especially as it helped to de-saturate the colours and looked less like Hollywood and more like the lighting in Oslo homes in the last century. I had already experimented with indirect lighting in *Privilege* [1976], with Peter Suschitzky as cameraman. Now I wanted to go further, especially as colour had meant so much to Edvard Munch as well. He also had a 'blue' period in his work – notably when he first moved to France in 1889, when he referred to blue as the colour symbolizing death to the ancient Greeks.[3]

Not surprisingly, blue figures frequently in Munch's deliberations on his art, which the film's dialogue quotes. The decision to shoot *outdoors* using an *interior* stock itself mixes visual systems towards a possible ambivalence.

If the signifier 'blue' oscillates between joy and depression, a similar range is available to all other colours. The oscillation is inherent in their functioning within any signifying system – and not just in the ambiguity-laden modernity documented by Munch – as colour names themselves entertain uncertain relations with the realities they designate, varying from culture to culture. Their relationship with referents is often loose. Even at its closest, there is no tight fit; rather, colour shifts around a meaning to which it has been tethered artificially and temporarily, like a ship bobbing at anchor.

BETWEEN COLOUR SYMBOLISM AND COLOUR PSYCHOLOGY

What is sometimes called 'the psychology of colour' may overlap with, and partially motivate, colour symbolism, but it is not identical with it. After all, symbolism is culture-specific, whereas human psychology, or some portion of it, may be seen as universal. Whereas culture-specific symbolism is accessed consciously as part of belief systems or ideologies, 'colour psychology' appears to be rooted in physiological and in a sense unconscious reactions and mood changes in persons exposed to particular colours. The degree to which such unconsciousness might correspond to, say an individual (Freudian?) unconscious, or a more collective (Jungian?) one, is moot. In any case, some psychologists align these reactions with a culture-neutral signifying system, for instance on an arc of pleasure running from colours deemed more pleasant and grouped around the wavelength designated 'blue' (blue, blue-green, green, purple-blue, red-purple and purple) to less pleasurable ones grouped around the 'yellow' one (yellow, green-yellow and red-yellow), with red in an intermediate position.[4] Because such physiological, cross-cultural reactions are inflected and sometimes subverted by expectations enshrined explicitly in the colour symbolism of cultures or subcultures (for instance, in a descending scale of particularity: of religions, nations, football teams or street gangs), colour experience displays considerable potential for ambiguity. Moreover, if, as tests by Tom Porter appear to suggest, children under seven usually have red as a favourite colour, whereas eight- and nine-year-olds prefer blue,[5] ambivalence and ambiguity might result from an embedding at different developmental stages of preferences for colours often conceptualised as incompatible. In any case, ambiguity may be particularly endemic in cinema, which is both a sign-system and an experience, and whose darkening of the auditorium invites fantasies with varying degrees of proximity to the unconscious and to the dream Freud declared the royal road to it. (Film theorists' tendency to simplify matters by situating it only at one end of this continuum is regrettable. See, for instance, Carroll[6] for a mapping of cinema almost entirely in the realm of the conscious, Baudry[7] for its grounding in the oneiric.)

The extent of the potential disparity of views concerning colour meaning can be gauged by some early twentieth-century remarks by the Canadian *Women's Journal* on the subject of that most 'stereotypically female' colour, pink. (Correctional facilities have been known to paint walls Baker-Miller pink to 'reduce aggression' in the males who populate them disproportionately.) The *Journal* declared pink a strong colour, more suitable for boys, with the 'delicate and dainty' blue being girlish.[8] Another measure of the divergence of views on this subject may be found in Adrian Nestor and Michael J. Tarr's studies of perceptions of the relationship between colour and gender in Caucasian faces. Although respondents to a question about colour-gendering predicted men's faces would be more green and women's red, in actuality the colouring, detectable through computer analysis of photographs (Tarr used 200), averages out as the reverse: men's faces are slightly redder, and women's greener.[9] Although Tarr suspects that women's purchases of rouge may reflect their pull towards the masculinity with which it may therefore unconsciously be associated, one can only speculate about the significance of the widespread modern Occidental cultural links (facial, and in attire) between women and red. Freudians and Lacanians might see a red-clad woman (red clothing being far more common among western women than western males) as seeking to render herself more masculine, tapping the denied power signified by the phallus, particularly should the quotient of red be enhanced by the wielding of a significantly shaped lipstick; Platonists might evoke an individual yearning for the other half-self lost when an originally androgynous entity split into two sexes; while evolutionary biologists might speak of a desire to attract male attention (psychoanalysts might add: on the basis of male narcissism) to ensure selection for mating. Such speculations, of course, only scrape the surface of colour's deep cultural lability, its openness to variable readings.

This book foregrounds films that prompt such speculations. They do so by employing colour in the deliberately complex, multivalent, poetic and cross-cultural manner that seems to me most interesting, as well as most apt to our globalised, multicultural times. If they are signed in the main by directors usually termed 'European auteurs', this is because the relatively high quotient of freedom preserved within their production situations (often ones that now no longer obtain) allows a loosening of culturally programmed bonds between colours and meanings. Thus the colour usage of a Bergman, an Antonioni, a Kieślowski, a Tarkovsky or a Godard would not only be less predictable than that of mainstream American cinema, be it the Technicolor policed by a Natalie Kalmus or the one that takes colour simply as an unremarkable part of the workaday business of filming. It would also go beyond the usual practices of a Zhang Yimou, whose long-standing interest in colour is evident and exhilarating, but who uses it less for ambiguity than for spectacle. The meaning of the raising of the red lantern is unmistakable (broadcasting the favour bestowed upon a particular concubine, marking the shifts in power between the four 'sisters'). It galls the other women with its lack of ambiguity. Because colours can evince considerable slippage in their moorings to objects, somewhat disconcertingly (though this would not have surprised André Bazin, who lauded neo-realism for its perceived adequacy to 'the ambiguity of reality'[10]), where colour is concerned the ambiguity usually deemed characteristic of modernist texts infiltrates realism also. Is this ambiguity one reason why Film Studies has paid colour little attention, fearful perhaps of its capacity to trouble the widespread investment in realisms not prone to foreground questions of form? Meanwhile, if an image's colours are conceived as not merely necessary features of a realistic illusion, but rather as possibly all signifying, *yet unpredictably*, that combination of excess and arbitrariness of meaning can overload the spectatorial mental circuitry. Since the most interesting colour films appear to require habits of reception associated with a modernism widely considered passé or elitist, this too can be disconcerting in a largely postmodern climate, though charges of elitism may be subverted by postmodernity's possession of its own means of unseating realism (to be discussed shortly): those of fantasy.

The somewhat randomly selected examples of colour ambiguity given above are simply basic forms of the more complex colour multivalence immanent within and potentially issuing from them. Colour's attractiveness for modernists (a feature of modernism to be examined in Chapter 2, which will also sample the debate over the definition of this movement) lies, initially, in the opportunities it offers to *épater le bourgeois* by inverting customary expectations, assigning 'the wrong' colours to objects. However, this attraction deepens as expected codings cease to be simply inverted, and in a sense reinforced through inversion, but are discarded, in a 'revaluation of values' involving an openness to a range of other codings. Difference goes beyond the status of an exoticism used to dislodge the familiar, as familiarity itself subsides. Instead, that difference acquires validity in its own terms. In other words: colour as implicit polemic modulates into colour as a source of reverie, fantasy. This potential for fantasy may be exploited most fully in the works of such European auteurs as the ones named above, but such multivalence characterises various types of works that abjure realism. Realism may be denied either through strategies usually termed 'modernist', or by building fantasy worlds (the possible compatibility of these strategies being shown by their co-presence in the paintings of Gauguin). Similarly – to name two films seldom mentioned together – both *Viskningar och rop* (*Cries and Whispers*) (1973) and *The Wizard of Oz* (1939) resist constraints upon the meaning of their colours, albeit by very different means. For all the differences, this commonality justifies the conjunctions of European and American films found in the sixth and seventh chapters of this book in particular.

Modernist or fantastic, therefore, denials of realism may be seen as responding to the inherent multivalence of colour, whose foregrounding becomes a key agent of realism's unseating. The variety of possible fits between colours and objects – the possibility of alienating colours from the things in which they seem rooted – generates a world that is no longer self-evident. (Is Miss Gulch *really*, or only metaphorically, a witch?) The new world is that of Robert Musil's *Möglichkeitsdenken* (thinking in possibilities): one where things could always be different. At the same time, this anti-realism is nevertheless a form of 'realism' inasmuch as it presupposes a sober, if implicit acknowledgment of the break-up of the object effected by industrialisation and colonialism (processes to be discussed further in Chapter 2), as the 'drifting away' of fantasy may accompany or prompt the adjective's – the property's – separation from the noun that is the object. Fantasy is of course also an inevitable response to the difficulty of reading increasingly displaced things and people in the midst of modernity.

If mainstream narrative film-making aims to 'harness the technicolour rainbow' (to quote the title of Scott Higgins' fine account of the phased development of Technicolor across the 1930s[11]), the most interesting uses of colour unharness it. Where Godard's encounter with colour unfolded in stages reminiscent of Higgins' segmentation of Technicolor's progress through the 1930s – from demonstration and assertion to restraint – inklings of colour's potential haunt Antonioni long beyond the mid-1960s, culminating in the visionary prefigurings of contemporary digital manipulations in *Il mistero di Oberwald* (*The Oberwald Mystery*) (1981). Meanwhile, Kieślowski's reservation of explicit encounter with colour to the finale of his career suggested a belief that long apprenticeship was needed to prepare for an exceptionally demanding aesthetic challenge. All three might have sympathised with Carl Dreyer's analysis of the state of colour film in 1955:

> This year it is twenty years since the first feature film in color came out. Hundreds of color films followed, but when we look back, how many of them do we remember for the aesthetic pleasure they gave us. Two – three – four – five? Maybe five, but probably not more.[12]

Dreyer's enumeration of the paucity of aesthetically convincing colour films may spark demands for recipes for better achievement. Dreyer himself recommends the addition of a painter – not just a colour technician – to the film crew: John Huston's *Moulin Rouge* (1952), he comments (perhaps superfluously), would have benefited considerably from the presence of Toulouse-Lautrec himself.[13] Whatever one's recipe, its cardinal ingredient would surely be one that enhanced spectatorial attention to colours functioning not as automatic, indifferent adjuncts of a realistic tracing of the surfaces of things, but as keynote signifiers.

The European directors named above, like most of those considered in this book – many of them not European – conceptualise colour as moving fluidly along open frontiers, shifting meaning and sites, ricocheting between persons and objects, submerging and surfacing across images and narratives. Unlike Higgins, none would criticise the colour use of the intriguing *Pleasantville* (1998) because 'though [it] strongly demonstrates digital colour manipulation, few of its effects are suited to conventional production. Digital production is harnessed to narrative, but obviously so.'[14] Rather, they would deem that 'obviousness' one version of the quasi-modernist foregrounding of the device that prevents unquestioning business as usual. Their multivalent texts continually disclose new dimensions, eluding the closure whose efficient message-delivery primes progression to another throw-away product.

In other words: such films seek to build colour systems independent of, or in dialogue with, conventionalised cultural ones. Just how unconventional and personal these can become is seen in Vittorio Storaro's account of his allegorical colour palette for Bernardo Bertolucci's *The Last Emperor* (1987) – where red represents Pu Yi's memory, on seeing the blood of his slit veins, of having burned as an emperor; orange signifies 'the warm colour of the family'; yellow, identity; and green, the knowledge that enters the Forbidden City with the green bike of his tutor. The challenge in analysing cinematic colour systems lies in their mutual interference with a rippling multiplicity of extra-textual belief systems, subsystems and fragmentary impulses, only some of which are deemed 'natural'. Such interference often frustrates precise determination of the point at which a colour's permissible significations stop and start reverberating. Is the film's system sufficiently robust to resist spectators' desires to impose the better-known meanings they may find more comfortable? Are film-makers themselves necessarily comfortable with allowing meaning a somewhat free play within their structures (a Kieślowski would be; others might not)? Such undecidability piquantly spices their works' fascination with a certain frustration. In other words: the ambiguity not only can, but perhaps should, yield a certain ambivalence, some of whose roots will be considered below.

SOME ROOTS OF AMBIVALENCE?

Writing of some of the meanings that orbit yellow, Goethe – that key theoretician of colour – states that 'a slight and barely perceptible change' suffices to transform 'the beautiful impression of fire and gold … into one not undeserving the epithet foul'.[15] It may seem both remarkable and enigmatic that so small a divergence should exert so large and devastating an effect. Nevertheless, the various transformations of colour meanings into their opposites discussed by Sergei Eisenstein (e.g., with regard to the colour green, for instance, 'a number of contradictory interpretations evolved. The color of hope was also the color of hopelessness and despair'[16]), like Sigmund Freud's analogous tracking of the ambivalence of varieties of words he terms 'primal',[17] arguably mirror the interaction of mechanisms of naming and dualistic thought.

First, naming. As Rudolf Arnheim notes, naming colour is extremely difficult. Thus,

[i]f, for example, we look at the chart complied by Hiler from different sources for the name of the color corresponding to 600 millimicrons, we find that it has been described by various authors as Orange Chrome, Golden Poppy, Spectrum Orange, Bitter Sweet Orange, Oriental Red, Saturn Red, Cadmium Red Orange, or Red Orange.[18]

The difficulty in naming threatens the perception of a colour's purity and integrity. If such purity is obviously essential in the case of the gold whose sullying would threaten its status as the currency of currencies, the same applies to all other colours. Rather than recognise that no colour exists in a state of purity corresponding to that of its concept, we may perceive it as not entirely 'itself', as in fact in the process of turning into another. The imperceptibility of the point at which one colour may be said to become another can engender a paranoid fear that none is what it seems. The safest option, therefore, locking in restless movement round a colour circle now become vicious, is to assume that in fact they are not.

Dualistic thought, for its part, is sufficiently widespread among human communities to lend structuralism a continued relevance, for all the protestations of a post-structuralism with a vested (Oedipal) interest in declaring it passé. Insofar as thought-systems founded on absolute distinctions may be held to preserve a religious absolutism, declarations of their outmodedness rest upon theses concerning the growing secularisation of society in modernity; however, those theses themselves overlook the polarisation of fundamentalisms and political parties even within declared democracies. The emblem of the longevity of such habits within philosophical thought may be Raphael's contrast, in *The School of Athens*, between the figure of Plato pointing heavenwards as Aristotle holds out his own hand towards earth. To the extent to which signification per se is cemented by linguistic systems of difference, thinking 'height', for instance, inevitably entails thinking its counterpart. If imagining one pole of a binary entertains an afterimage of its opposite, the result, however semi- or even unconscious, can be a pathological suspicion either that the latter preserves a conspiratorial identity with the primary one, or that its merely partial occupation of the field of being renders its separate status the merely apparent one of a shadow.

The conjunction of these two conceptual habits generates a sense of ambivalence vis-à-vis the phenomenal. Confronted with something called 'high', one may wonder whether it fully exemplifies, and hence completely deserves, this designation. If something else might be higher, is the one in question truly high? One attempted resolution lies in the Platonic dislocation of generality from the particular (of abstract sign system from concrete experience) known as the doctrine of the Forms: the Chair of Chairs is distinct from every individual copy of its Idea. Thus Plato ontologises a distinction that is both linguistic and psychological. Applied to colour, this prevents any gold being Gold; any yellow, Yellow. (The painter, however, might view the colours on his palette as just such Ideas, as long as they stayed there, and the palette as the prototype of the abstract.) If the world is a painting, its colours drip ambivalence.

Where cinema is concerned, the slow pace of colour's march towards universal acceptance, which Stephen Watts memorably likened less to the 'thunderclap' of sound's adoption than 'the gradual appearance of a rainbow, creeping steadily across the sky, until its arc is complete',[19] suggests widespread scepticism regarding the possibility of fully accurate reproduction in the realm of the visual. Whereas the condition of sound's acceptance was its ability rapidly to demonstrate, for all the jostling of sound systems, a reasonably precise alignment with the world's soundscape, the divergences between colour film stocks and processes imply a final impossibility of alignment, rendering the coloured world's exact reproduction a Form always beyond reach, even beyond the horizon: a fata Morgana.

ANOTHER SOURCE OF AMBIVALENCE: BETWEEN PRIMARIES

Although for most the idea of primary colours evokes the triangle of blue, yellow and red, a passage on the topic by Ed Branigan indicates that the issue is not quite so simple. With admirable succinctness, he outlines some well-known distinctions: '[t]he physical or light primaries (which mix toward white light) are red, blue, and green. The pigment or painter's primaries (which mix down toward black) are red, blue, and yellow. The psychological primaries (which mix in vision toward gray) are red, blue, yellow, and green.'[20] The question of how many primaries there are, apparently absurdly easy to answer, thus becomes rather complex. For most readers, the primaries will be the painter's ones, which also mix into a series of secondary and tertiary colours located between them on a colour circle sliced up, somewhat arbitrarily, into twelve portions. The plotting of the relations of colours found in the colour circle of design textbooks, with its hierarchy of primaries, secondaries and tertiaries, is a pragmatic abstraction from what a true circle of the colours would look like: whereas in reality each and every colour should constitute a point (corresponding to a wavelength), here the three key points that can be mixed into other colours are accorded primacy, largely to facilitate such mixing, but also to conceal the difficulty involved in all colour nomination. For even such a circle of points, although corresponding more closely to the reality of colour relations, would simplify the dizzying multiplicity of their transitions: 'the true circle' seems to resemble a Platonic Form invisible to the naked human eye. Moreover, an arrangement based upon three primaries, although technically correct in terms of painterly procedures, is also vulnerable to criticism as limited by adherence to a three-term logic. Considered in terms of such maps of reality as the semiotic rectangle of A. J. Geimas or the quadrangular personality-types model of Carl Gustav Jung or – perhaps more relevantly in this context – the simultaneous display of four Leslie Carons in *An American in Paris* (1951), against backgrounds of red, green, blue and yellow, a list of four pre-eminent colours seems equally justified. This is why Arnheim glosses the words 'if we accept three basic colours' with the parenthetical remark that 'authorities do not agree on this subject'.[21] An arrangement of 'four primaries' may seem absurd from the purely technical perspective of a painter mixing colours, but it also reflects a sense that no reasonable world-view could omit green as one of its fundamental pillars. In any case, of course, only in subtractive colour systems are the primaries red, yellow and blue. In an additive one, comprising red, blue and green, yellow emerges only 'by default', through the intersection of red and green. Additive colour schemes mix coloured light (red, blue and green); subtractive ones mix pigments (red, blue and yellow). Irrespective of whether a film stock's technology is additive or subtractive, film lies at their intersection, employing both coloured light (lighting) and pigments (costumes, set decoration). The question of the relationship between filmic colour and sets of primaries has at best a double answer; at worst, an indeterminate one.

'COLOUR SUTURE' AND COMPLEMENTARITY

For Goethe, the sight of a single colour awakens a desire for the presence of its complement. In other words, here too the ambiguous nature of the apparently singular generates the ambivalence discussed earlier. As Goethe puts it in paragraphs 805 and 806 of his *Theory of Colours*:

805

When the eye sees a colour it is immediately excited, and it is its nature, spontaneously and of necessity, at once to produce another, which with the original colour comprehends the whole chromatic scale. A single colour excites, by a specific sensation, the tendency to universality.

806

To experience this completeness, to satisfy itself, the eye seeks for a colourless space next every hue (sic) in order to produce the complemental hue upon it.[22]

Paragraph 805 is borne out by a well-known experiment: if, after prolonged staring at a red object, one closes one's eyes, the brain spontaneously reproduces green, as if to 'cool down' the heat of the red wavelength. In terms of film studies, this property of colour perception is strikingly reminiscent of suture theory, according to which the reverse shot whose semi-circle matches the one covered by the previous shot demonstrates the work's desire to appear to encompass the totality of the visual field. It simulates scrupulous attention to 'reality', to the 'worldness' of a world whose filmic model matches its reality, the circle. As paragraph 806 indicates, however, Goethe conceptualises this urge to apprehend the universal as mediated through colourlessness. Philosophy's 'law of the excluded middle' is amended by the addition of a third term to the two-term operation suture theory describes. Goethe's theory reflects both his personal philosophical commitment to a dialectic of the individual and the universal, and the general Romantic belief in the capacity of the isolated genius to generate totality, which in this case would be the entire range of colours implicit within (in cinematic terms, projected onto) a colourless space. (The screen would be white, round and located at the centre of the colour circle.) Objections to this theory might define the world of colour as one of parts, each one separate from an impossible whole that in any case suffers immediate suppression by the automatic physiological movement from colour to complement. The adjacent colourless space becomes utopian, non-existent. The world of colour would then be centrifugal, perhaps Deleuzian. Nevertheless, even in this case, the idea of 'wholeness' might be preserved spectrally, not represented as a perceptible unity but implicit in the compositional balancing of contradictory parts (a 'classical' concern for symmetry resembling the 'classic Hollywood' visual vocabulary of suture theory).

However, when Goethe argues that 'nature tends to emancipate the sense from confined impressions by suggesting and producing the whole',[23] the implied synonymity of 'suggesting' and 'producing' is illusory. The emergence of a complementary colour may suggest the entirety of the colour circle, but it does not produce it. What it produces is not a circle but a line linking opposites. If the totality does indeed become graspable through complementary colours, it is because otherwise the potentially infinite number of potential stopping points located round the circle would arrest movement almost as soon as it started, the temporal freezing embodied in Zeno's paradox. Opposed colours hold the totality between them in tension, where the actualised totality of the circle drowns in an *embarras de richesse*.

Irrespective of possible objections, Goethe's theory is potentially variously productive. For instance, it helps explain why flags, those markers of very real, national spaces, sometimes lodge whiteness at their centre. This insertion of blanks would, of course, be overdetermined, probably serving initially to prevent an adjacence of dyes causing blurring along the line of their interference. (A similar problem – that of 'fringing' – bedevilled many early film colour technologies, becoming most evident at moments or points of rapid movement, as when red and green detach themselves from the flicking tails of excited beagles.) The history of flag-making, therefore, might be plotted as moving from a single colour's pairing with white (the crosses of St George and St Andrew, whose naming after saints indicates their 'primitive' nature), to two colours separated by a white band, to more complex modern flags employing dyeing technologies that easily juxtapose strong colours without smudging. If Goethe is right and a colour's route to its complement passes through a way-station of colourlessness, such whiteness is in a sense itself already the universal: a universal coded as potential, not the black whose universality is usually read as final, negative. (The Jewish Sabbath, which commences at sunset, inscribes an exceptional implicit theology of creation out of mystery and darkness, the *tohu bohu* of the start of *Genesis*.) And since both white and black encode totality, neither can ever be seen as embodying it.

COLOUR AND/AS KITSCH

A disquiet about colour that bases itself not upon the slipperiness of its object but upon the traditional art-historical opposition of colour and line or form, and fears to surrender a putatively more important, 'masculinised' line (and discipline) to the sensual attractions of colour, has been denounced as 'chromophobia' by David Batchelor.[24] A more justifiable unease concerning the use of colour in film was voiced by Rudolf Arnheim, whose 'Remarks on Color Film' identify form not with the lines within an image but with the very declaration that something has imagistic status (in other words: most important is not the line that appears *within* the image but the unseen one running *around* it). Radically different views of visual phenomena result, depending on whether or not they are classified as images.

> People of taste have considered the colors in color film atrocious; many have thought them unnatural. That can only mean that either the colors in film are as awful as they are in nature, or that they are beautiful in nature, but made horrible in film. If we make an experiment and place a young girl in the sun and look at her image on the frosted glass slide of the camera, what we see there looks remarkably like the images of color film. All tones seem exaggerated, inharmonious, the girl looks obtrusively made up, and the entire picture seems common and meaningless. Now consider a good painting in the same way – its result on the frosted glass is unaltered in its beauty. From which follows: the fault lies not, as is so often argued, with the color technicians (even when, as at present, they do not perfectly fulfil their task). The reason is not physical, but psychological: as soon as a piece of nature becomes an image, we view it with different eyes. (The reduction of the plastic into planes may have some bearing on this.) It seems that we consider it like a painting and, therefore, require different values.[25]

Arnheim's parenthesis worries lest the difference between the two reactions not be fully explicable. However, if the effect does indeed stem from the transformation of nature into an image, the probable cause lies not in the transposition of the plastic into the planar that is one feature of image-making, but in another of its features: the imposition upon nature of a frame.

Arnheim then burrows into the issue from another angle, doggedly seeking a solution. 'Nature is beautiful, but not in the same sense as art. Its color combinations are accidental and hence usually inharmonious.'[26] The accuracy of 'inharmonious' may be doubted, as the categorisation of an image as accidental, random and subject to change surely renders questions of harmony irrelevant. Accident makes no claim to possess harmony, represent deliberate form, or obey such criteria as balance, coherence or tastefulness. Walter Benjamin would probably have viewed the demand for harmony as attempting a reactionary reversal of the exemplarily distracted disposition of the modern spectator into the contemplativeness subtending earlier, auratic, pre-filmic art. Such Benjaminian objections might be met by emphasising – as Arnheim himself does earlier – that issues of harmony or discord do not arise in monochrome film, whose black, white and grey form a continuous scale; colour alone may be dogged by the question whether certain hues 'go together', and the potentially artistically stultifying effects of prioritising tastefulness as an answer. As instantiated in the work of Natalie Kalmus, Technicolor's expert fashioner of colour schemes to match scenes much as Classical Hollywood employed musical scores – for emphasis alone – mere tastefulness irritates Arnheim as much as it had Carl Dreyer.[27] Instead, both advocate an actual painter's involvement in a work's conception, rather than Technicolor's subsequent importation of technicians charged with selecting colours supposedly appropriate to the predetermined mood of a scene.

Open to classification as accidental, nature's appearances differ from those whose ingathering within a frame suggests the existence of meaningful relationships between them, as forcefields or constellations. Arnheim does not discuss the role of the frame. Recognition of its presence, however, acknowledges that the best means of dissolving inevitable visual discords may involve running colour film through a highly mobile camera, its continually shifting viewpoint preventing images being seen as deliberate compositions, and so revoking the desiderata of harmony. In this case, the art of film would imitate that of nature.

One possible example of such mimesis is the work of Robert Altman, with its wandering camera, slow zooming and commitment to accident in every sense. Altman's aesthetic of contingency might be called chromatic, by analogy with the Wagnerian subversion of harmony. After all, if the addition of colour can mean that of a distraction, since its potential enrichment of aesthetic experience simultaneously over-lays it with irrelevant questions of the degree of a colour's 'truthfulness-to-life', why not follow the explicit recommendations of Benjamin,[28] and the implicit ones of Altman, and embrace distraction? The drawback in this procedure might be its undermining not only of tastefulness (often an issue in Altman), but also of choice, seriousness and commitment. Batchelor may ironically dub seriousness 'a black-and-white issue',[29] but the irony recoils upon him, as conceptualising the world in black and white may well be the precondition of firm choice of a particular course of action. The muting of con-trast by colour – mentioned by Arnheim[30] – posits a reality devoid of the need for choice: a reality that may be called childish, endlessly consumerist, or even, in a 1960s sense, 'stoned'. (Colour here may be 'psychedelic' and favour the quality known as 'postmodernity'.) Its seduction offers the chimerical pos-sibility of 'having it all', as – sooner or later – everything will come to you. More appealingly, it also offers a utopia free of verdicts of taste, and the class assignments that dog them. Somewhat prematurely, post-moderns have declared a vanishing of the fear of colour.[31] Such an event would occur, however, only in a society free of fear of the *faux pas* of colour-mismatches: one which left unemployed the hordes of interior designers hired to silence clients' nagging, half-repressed fears of the possible social costs of exer-cising their new-found freedom of choice. The attraction exerted by such an 'interior design' aesthetic can be gauged by the success of the apologia for colour harmonisation informing Natalie Kalmus's defence of Technicolor, to be discussed later in this chapter.

NEGATIVE DIALECTICS: THE COLOUR CIRCLE IN PERMANENT REVOLUTION
Given their inherent ambiguity and proneness to slippage, colours are probably the most obviously dialectical of phenomena, their capacity to change with a change of neighbours[32] (not to mention vari-ations in brilliance or saturation) suggesting inherent mutability. How this dialectic can affect cinema emerges from Eisenstein's discussion of *Ivan Groznyy II: Boyarsky zagovor* (*Ivan the Terrible Part Two*) (1958), the only film on which he was able to use colour stock:

> At first all the colour themes are tied up in a knot. Then the red theme is gradually teased out, then the black, then the blue. What counts is that they are torn away from their original association with an object.[33]

This 'tearing away' offers a concise definition of Eisenstein's programme for the use of colour. In most narrative film, however, the detaching of objects from colours is seldom as complete as his characteristically violent metaphor implies. A dialectical tension persists between colour as object property and colour as independent entity (in a sense, between necessity and freedom, realism and the fantastic, verisimilitude and imagination). Narrative films assaying the complete separation Eisenstein advocates usually either do so briefly, and therefore possibly unsatisfactorily (my view of Michelangelo Antonioni's *Il mistero di Oberwald*, expounded below in Chapter 6), or interweave it persistently into a fabric of plot, like the same director's more powerful *Deserto rosso* (*Red Desert*) (1964), which drives this tension close to its limit, and further than Eisenstein had the chance to. It is hardly surprising, therefore, that Eisenstein himself should have located the prototype of colour liberation in the cartoon.[34] If animation fulfils his injunction to 'tighten it as far as you can', Antonioni's narratives take the next step the rest of Eisenstein's formula ('then release it a half-turn'[35]) appears to deem equally necessary. Is this the Leninist dialectic of 'two steps forwards, one step back', with the half-turn release constituting the narrative feature's required concession to the primacy of the reality privileged in Soviet aesthetics (however fantastic the realism of 'socialist realism')? And does this dialectic play itself out implicitly between Eisenstein's 'teased out' and his 'torn away': the former corresponding rather to the steady rhythm of continuous and typical action prevalent in realism; the latter, to the ecstatic, world-shattering moment of release?

For, understood in terms of colour, Eisenstein's earlier theory of the necessary explosion of the 'montage cell' that is the shot might be held to result from the precipitation of one key colour within it, the red that betokens imminent liberation and whose conceptual equivalent is the crowd's transformation into revolutionary collective subject by mechanisms akin to the ones of *ex-stasis* that preoccupy his *Nonindifferent Nature*.[36] For Andrei Tarkovsky, however, Eisenstein's respectful but determined adversary, a new level of consciousness dawns in the transition from the monochrome toil and slaughter of daily medieval life to the colour of Andrei Rublov's icons in that eponymous film. As the colour circle's permanent transition suggests permanent revolution, the withheld resolution marks its dialectic as 'negative', in the sense proposed by Theodor Adorno: as forbidding the synthesis Hegelian thought requires as the successor to thesis and antithesis. Such a synthesis would be utopian, the withheld messianic moment at which a colour would coincide fully with its concept or name. In the meantime, the only resolution, perhaps, occurs as the simulacrum of transcendence created when colours revolve so rapidly as to vanish in white; and yet, of course, as noted above, white's shadowing by black renders it no more than a representation of totality.

In Adornian terms, Goethe's two, mutually sustaining colours are halves that do not add up to a whole. In cinema, this is most evident in the historical and aesthetic fissure between monochrome and colour aesthetics. Their non-meshing reflects the uneven development and unfulfilled dialectic of our society, which certainly does not enact any planned teleology: the history of the advent of colour is a series of accidents with effects as unpredictable as those of the coming of sound mythologised so piquantly and self-servingly in *Singin' in the Rain* (1952). Any resolution is the optical illusion visited upon a beholder perennially distant from the apparent encounter of the mutually supporting parallel lines: for anyone actually 'there' (at the end of the technological rainbow that promises delivery of the gold of true colour?), they remain separate. Consequently, the most intriguing, even most technologically honest, films may be those that activate a monochrome-colour dialectic, be it explicitly, by alternating black-and-white and colour footage, or implicitly, by granting a strong visual presence, within a coloured *mise en scène*, to black or white or grey. They embody most fully the unresolved tension of the negative dialectic of colour and object, which is also one between sign systems that eschew, or clearly fall short of, any appearance of a full rendition of reality, and others apparently bent upon a pursuit of totality ('total cinema') – until the screen bites back, rebounding into the auditorium as 3D.

NATALIE KALMUS AND CONTRADICTION

Paradoxically, given its title, the obverse of a dialectically self-conscious theorisation of colour may well be 'Color Consciousness', Natalie Kalmus's landmark 1935 speech to the Technicans' Branch of the Academy of Motion Picture Arts and Sciences. The nearest thing to an aesthetic manifesto of colour to have emerged from within the mainstream industry, within which Kalmus would wield enormous power between the mid-1930s and 1948 as chief colour adviser for the Technicolor process devised by her husband Herbert,[37] its rhetoric gains adherents by mobilising a sufficient array of the conventional Occidental associations of particular colours to allow the singularity of each (in other words, its status as something controllable, like a colour on a palette) to fan out into the multiplicity of stories that could employ it. Combining reassuring certainty with flexibility, unity with diversity, Kalmus offers the apparent best of both worlds. Consider, for instance, the passage on red.

> For example, red calls to mind a feeling of danger, a warning. It also suggests blood, life and love. It is materialistic, stimulating. It suffuses the face of anger, it led the Roman soldiers into battle. Different shades of red can suggest various phases of life, such as love, happiness, physical strength, wine, passion, power, excitement, anger, turmoil, tragedy, cruelty, revenge, war, sin, and shame. These are all different, yet in certain respects they are the same. Red may be the color of the revolutionist's flag, and streets may run red with blood of rioters, yet red may be used in a church ritual for Pentecost as a symbol of sacrifice. Whether blood is spilled upon the battlefield in an approved cause or whether it drips from the assassin's dagger, blood still runs red. The introduction of another color with red can suggest the motive for a crime, whether it be jealousy, fanaticism, revenge, patriotism, or religious sacrifice. Love gently warms the blood. The delicacy or strength of the shade of red will suggest the type of love. By introducing the colors of licentiousness, deceit, selfish ambition, or passion, it will be possible to classify the type of love portrayed with considerable accuracy.[38]

In other words, this hypostasised 'red' is not limited: for all its singularity it has a wealth of 'shades', sustaining rhetorically a variety of story-elements. '*These are all different, yet in certain respects they are the same*' (my emphasis). The shades all exist within 'red', and are not allowed to shade off into, let alone become, other colours. Their separateness receives only lip service, therefore, as they subserve a uniform 'redness'. For all Kalmus's fervour, listeners may well have perceived hers as the voice of common sense, even science ('with considerable accuracy'), overlooking the overreaching bombast of the assertion that certain colours constitute invariant, well-known designators of licentiousness or ambition. And that – seduced audiences might think – is only one colour, a mere sample of the multifarious riches in the Technicolor coffers! They may not have suspected how illusory the proffered freedom would prove: how, for instance, the most committed colourist of mid-twentieth-century American cinema, Vincente Minnelli, would groan under the necessity to match the patterns mandated by Kalmus.

As Scott Higgins notes, the Kalmus project pursues contradictory aims:

Natalie Kalmus's was a set of long-standing aesthetic criteria for the proper use of color in motion pictures. It established that color was to be channelled toward the subtle expression of drama through careful harmony and co-ordination. At the same time, her literal chromatic vocabulary and her arguments for color's expressive power seem more in line with an aesthetic that emphasized color demonstration.[39]

Because Kalmus's advocacy is unconscious of its own contradictions, it can offer something for everyone unashamedly. Nevertheless, 'Color Consciousness' has a primary constituency, the practitioners of a motivated style that harnesses colour choice to story mood. Studios could accept an aesthetic that underscored the necessity of the interior shooting necessary to achieve total colour control. Colour becomes primarily a matter of *mise en scène*, humbly harmonised with a pre-existing screenplay and eschewing the montage that might juxtapose clashing colours. It is hardly surprising, therefore, that the Technicolor Kalmus promoted would later appear limited by its rooting in a studio system hostile to the unkempt open-air images disseminated by neo-realism after World War II. The limitations would become apparent with the stock's insensitivity to the subtler colours made available in the 1950s through the main rival stock, Eastmancolor.[40] Note for instance Jean Mitry's excoriation of the strong lighting required by Technicolor, which he maintained 'killed any relief or shading', belied the fact that 'color is never a uniform tone', and was fit only for lurid fantasy. On the other hand,

Eastmancolor brought out [the] authenticity and firmly established color as one of the resources of cinema's expressivity. Not only is the shading not killed by uniform lighting but the relief of the colours heightens the overall relief in the same way as the action of light and shade.[41]

When Jean-Luc Godard's *Une femme est une femme* (*A Woman is a Woman*) (1961) announces in its titles its use of Eastmancolor, it reveals implicitly why its heroine cannot achieve her desired status as Cyd

Une femme est une femme: an MGM–Rossellini co-production … the red and white of the lead actress's controlled colour scheme interlock (miraculously, randomly, momentarily) with red and white in a documented environment

Charisse in a musical with Gene Kelly: Godard's Rossellinian commitment to the outdoors, discontinuity and contingency – not to mention his less Rossellinian pursuit of play – resists the clear colour-meaning pairings of Technicolor's adjusted classical Hollywood style.

WHOLES AND HOLES

When discussing the colour harmonisation practices advocated by Natalie Kalmus, it is worthwhile considering Eric Rohmer's distinction between two kinds of 1950s colour films:

> On the one hand, those that we remember for their harmony, their general tonality, in which the director, the set designer, the costume designer, and the photographer wanted to create a work, if not of painters, at least of men sensitive to pictorial matters. … In the second category, on the other hand, color is occasionally, but then unquestionably in charge. These films haunt us not so much because of their overall climate as because of the power of certain details, of certain colored objects.[42]

Although the first category might seem to be exemplified by Technicolor, Rohmer has other pictures in mind, mentioning *Jigokumon* (*Gate of Hell*) (1953), *Romeo and Juliet* (1954) and *Lola Montès* (1955). Examples of the latter category are 'Harriet's blue dress in *The River* or the green one belonging to the "lonely heart" in *Rear Window*'.[43]

Rohmer prefers the latter variety, adjudging it more '*positive*', which appears to mean more 'filmic' (in the sense of less indebted to pre-existing aesthetic forms, such as paintings). Given his fascination by Hitchcock, whose *Rear Window* (1954) furnishes one of his examples – and perhaps also given his future directorial interest in studying girls much like the ones whose dresses are mentioned here – this is not surprising. More surprising may be the notion of Rohmer as essentially a Romantic figure, as his two categories match the traditional distinction between Classicism and Romanticism. Integration of all the elements of an image corresponds to a (Classical, Arnheimian) aesthetic of wholeness; that which permits a salience of single colours, to a (Romantic) one of the part. (In the case of Rohmer's own films, this might be the privileging of woman doubly inscribed in his works' engagement both with Catholicism, for which the Madonna is central, and traditions of courtly, i.e., Platonic or distant – frustrated – love.) Historically and logically, the aesthetics of the whole not only precede those of the part but form their precondition and continual point of reference. The Romantic work establishes its discontinuities by punching holes in a pre-established continuity, studding it with symbols, fragments, local intensities. Thus the 'Romantic' work is dialectically realist and Romantic: the 'realistic' simulation of a world defined as continuous sets the stage for its arresting rupture by colouristic bursts through which fantasy enters, like a high-pressure gas. These moments align with those of the Hitchcockian 'stain', as defined by Žižek.[44] If there is a dialectic within the Classical itself – something Rohmer is not drawn to define – it concerns a different continuity and discontinuity: not the contradiction between the part (the intense, often symbolically charged, single colour) and the background of an otherwise realistically rendered world, but rather an 'invisible', even 'repressed' split between a world that continues *beyond the frame* and the frame itself, whose 'painterly' quality entails a lack of internal contradiction. The Classical contradiction pits one whole – the image – against another, the world (the prioritisation of the idea of wholeness cannot be questioned; rather do world and image constitute two separate wholes): it resembles that between painting and scroll. And if Hollywood films of the mid-twentieth century are often termed

The River: Harriet's alignment with colour as a fruitless bid for attention

'classical', it is because – as Arnheim noted – the monochromatic image is in a sense always harmonious. The clash of black and white can never be as discordant as certain colour combinations.

COLOUR AND CHAOS

Chaos theory might well offer a useful guide to the complexity of colour films, and help define a fundamental difference between their organisation and that common in black-and-white ones. The interface of black and white is the attractor that orders normal dynamic systems, with which classic Hollywood monochrome may be aligned. Dynamic systems ending in a fixed point would have closure as their dominant; others, marked by repetition, would open themselves up explicitly to a sequel. Colour films, meanwhile, could be described as displaying an unstable equilibrium and as ordered more mysteriously, in non-linear fashion, by a 'strange attractor'. If this contrast holds, colour film would mandate a fractal structuration overridden by the cruder forms of colour systematisation and symbolisation found in mainstream cinema, and begun by Technicolor.

   Expressed in alliterative slogan form, 'Kieślowski not Kalmus' would be a formula for a colour use commensurate with the impossibility of assigning univocal meanings to any colour, with the chaotic unpredictability of colour effects. Whereas black and white have a clear, banal valence in the widespread codes aligning them conventionally with Evil and Good, no such transcendental anchor attaches to the colours of the spectrum: only politicians and sports fans are likely to identify, say, red/blue contrasts as ones of 'good' and 'evil'. In other words, where colour is concerned such identifications are merely local, parochial. In the cinematic colour world, not only do Good and Evil switch sides (Evil disguising itself sometimes as Good – like the white-clad Teutonic knights of Eisenstein's *Aleksandr Nevskiy* (*Alexander Nevsky* (1938)): they may not even exist. The structure is multi-polar, not bi-polar, less eschatological than everyday.

WHITE AND BLACK AND IDEOLOGIES OF RACE AND GENDER

If meditations on colour often begin with white, this may be reflective of white's frequent identification as the most classic starting point, the *tabula rasa*, and not just of racism. Nevertheless, the spectre of racism is inescapable. In his *The Mask of Art*, Clyde Taylor powerfully arraigns the association of whiteness with the ideal in the writings of such devotees of classical Greece as Winckelmann.[45] If Taylor's attack gains apparently incontrovertible force from such figures' ignorance of the original colouration of the Greek statues they admired, as well as from the feeding of a White Supremacist racism by such an association, some questions can be posed to it nevertheless. One may ask, for instance, whether the 'whiteness' of the 'white man' is the same as that of the statue. Assuming an identity between them risks enchaining separate phenomena in a possibly primarily linguistic linkage. Indeed, the statue might become 'ideal' through the disparity between its colouration and the flesh tones of real 'whites' who include the often 'dark' Mediterranean artists, such as the Italians who first idealised classical statuary in their (and its) Renaissance.

The degree to which an ideology of whiteness may be both utopian and extremely disturbing, and manifest itself in surprising places, becomes apparent from a passage from Béla Balázs, whom one would have thought sensitised by his Marxism to any hints of the presence of a colonialist mode of thought. In words both alarming and utopian, though, he envisages the future development of the new corporeal language of film:

> [h]ere lies hidden the first living germ of that white normal man [*Normalmensch*] who will one day
> emerge as a synthesis of the different races and peoples. The cinematograph is a machine which, in its
> own way, creates a living and concrete internationalism: *The sole and common psyche of the white race.*
> And, in addition to this: inasmuch as film suggests a unitary beauty ideal as the general goal of selective
> breeding, it will create a unitary type of the white race.[46]

These words mark the hidden intersection of the two dominant totalitarianisms of the twentieth century, as Soviet internationalism and National Socialist racism unite in their liquidation of difference. Only the oracular opacity of this 1924 anticipation of their confluence demonstrates the idealistic naïveté of Balázs himself, who did not know what spirit was speaking through him. He could not decipher the ideal, globalised face revealed by his beloved close-up as a mask of colonial conquest, the doubling of the *tabula rasa* of ideal revolutionary beginning in the colour-liquidating whiteness of death. (Es ist ein Blicker, der heisst Tod …)

Insofar as whiteness can be associated with an ideal through its conceptualisation as ante-colour, a *tabula rasa* of potentiality antedating the 'writing' that is creation, and also as light, the issue of gender, for its part, enters through Anne Hollander's identification of whiteness with a 'feminine radiance [that] invites the stain from life's dome of many-coloured glass, indeed already contains its essence'.[47] For her, 'the power of much white feminine dress has derived ... from the lust to take on color that white projects – perhaps even the lust to be marked with blackness, the pale yearning of the unwritten page'.[48] Whiteness thus attains an agency beyond the passivity conventionally ascribed and prescribed to the feminine, forfeiting the sexual innocence – note her references to lust – equally conventionally denoted by white. (Might this white be called 'passively aggressive'? And would, black – so often colour of male attire, after all – become a 'male' ante-colour, with white the 'female' one?) Similarly – in an example of particular piquancy for any student of cinema – binaries of whiteness and stain, potentiality and actuality, are subverted by the movie theatre photographs of Hiroshi Sugimoto. If black is seen to stain whiteness, that stain can wash itself out. Sugimoto's description of his method, like his images, is illuminating indeed:

> One evening while taking photographs [of dioramas] at the American Museum of Natural History, I had a near-hallucinatory vision. My internal question-and-answer session leading up to this vision went something like this: 'Suppose you shoot a whole movie in a single frame?' The answer: 'You get a shining screen.'[49]

At the heart of the images created by such two-hour, movie-length single-frame exposures is a bright white screen: containing 'everything', the screen appears to contain 'nothing'. Apparently bearing out the speculations of Heinrich von Kleist on the marionette theatre and the achievement of a second innocence at the end of time, the darkening flow of the signs of experience issues redemptively in a sign widely associated with innocence and beginning, white.

Since ideologies have histories, a primary commitment to whiteness need not always be ideological. In a society of compulsive consumption, viewing colours as secondary to whiteness can also become revelatory, subversively underlining how multiple coloured variants of one product seek to seduce as wide a variety of possible purchasers, to mask a fundamental sameness. If chromophobia is an ideology, so is chromophilia. Any celebration of the dwindling of colour hierarchies amid postmodernism's levelling of high and low should consider also the extent to which any such change enables a universal subjection to fashion, each colour the dominant of a season, each individual a mere 'consumer': the mesmerised, 'targeted' centre of a colour circle that itself reifies the flow of colour into a set of discrete (indentifiable, hence saleable) blocks.

NOTES

1. Paul Coates, '"The Inner Life is the Only Thing that Interests Me": A Conversation with Krzysztof Kieślowski', in Coates (ed.), *Lucid Dreams: The Films of Krzysztof Kieślowski* (Trowbridge: Flicks Books, 1999), p. 170.

2. Julia Kristeva, 'Giotto's Joy', in Kristeva, *Desire in Language: A Semiotic Approach to Literature and Art* (New York: Columbia University Press, 1980), p. 211.

3. Peter Watkins, 'Edvard Munch: A Self-interview with Peter Watkins' (New Yorker Video Booklet: *The Cinema of Peter Watkins: Edvard Munch*, 2005), p. 5.

4. Patricia Valdez and Albert Mehrabian, 'Effects of Colour on Emotion', *Journal of Experimental Psychology* vol. 123 no. 4 (December 1994), pp. 394–409. Cf. also Tom Porter's work, as summarised in Tom Porter and Byron

Mikkelides, *Colour for Architecture* (New York: Van Nostrand Reinhold Company, 1976), p. 93, which found that the order of cross-cultural colour preferences established by Eysenck in 1941 correlated closely with those of both Occidental subjects and ones in Botswana and Kenya in 1973.

5. Porter and Mikkelides, *Colour for Architecture*, p. 93.

6. Noël Carroll, *Mystifying Movies: Fads and Fallacies in Contemporary Film Theory* (New York: Columbia University Press, 1988), pp. 13–32.

7. Jean Louis Baudry, 'Ideological Effects of the Basic Cinematographic Apparatus', in Leo Braudy and Marshall Cohen (eds), *Film Theory and Criticism* (6th edn) (New York and Oxford: Oxford University Press, 1999), pp. 206–23.

8. 'The Colour Pink', *The Current*, CBC Radio One, 28 January 2009.

9. Adrian Nestor and Michael J. Tarr, 'Gender Recognition Using Colour', *Psychological Science*, <www.psychologicalscience.org/journals/ps/19_12_inpress/tarr_BN_final.pdf> (accessed 25 December 2008).

10. André Bazin, 'The Evolution of Film Language', in Bazin, *What is Cinema? Vol. I*, selected and trans. Hugh Gray (Berkeley, Los Angeles and London: University of California Press, 1967), p. 37.

11. Scott Higgins, *Harnessing the Technicolor Rainbow: Color Design in the 1930s* (Austin: University of Texas Press, 2007).

12. Carl Theodore Dreyer, 'Color and Colored Film', in Donald Skoller (ed.), *Dreyer in Double Reflection* (New York: E. P. Dutton, 1973), p. 169.

13. Ibid., pp. 172–3.

14. Higgins, *Harnessing the Technicolor Rainbow*, p. 215.

15. Johan Wolfgang von Goethe, *Theory of Colours*, trans. and notes by Charles Lock Eastlake (London: John Murray, 1840), p. 308.

16. Sergei Eisenstein, *The Film Sense* (Cleveland and New York: Meridian, 1963 (1942)), p. 137.

17. Sigmund Freud, 'The Antithetical Sense of Primal Words', in *Collected Papers Vol. IV*, authorised trans. under the supervision of Joan Rivière (London: Hogarth Press and the Institute of Psycho-Analysis', 1950), pp. 184–91. Freud's first example is 'In Latin, *altus* means high and deep, *sacer* holy and accursed' (p. 189).

18. Rudolf Arnheim, *Art and Visual Perception: A Psychology of the Creative Eye* (London: Faber, 1969), p. 348.

19. Stephen Watts, 'Editor's Note', in *Behind the Scenes: How Films are Made*, ed. Stephen Watts (London: Arthur Barker, 1938), p. 114, quoted in Eirik Frisvold Hanssen, *Early Discourses on Colour and Cinema: Origins, Functions, Meanings* (Stockholm: Stockholm University, 2006), pp. 90–1.

20. Edward Branigan, 'The Articulation of Color in a Filmic System: *Deux ou trois choses que je sais d'elle*', in Angela Dalle Vacche and Brian Price (eds), *Color: The Film Reader* (New York and London: Routledge, 2006), p. 173.

21. Rudolf Arnheim, 'Remarks on Color Film', in Dalle Vacche and Price, *Color*, p. 54.

22. Goethe, *Theory of Colours*, p. 317.

23. Ibid., pp. 319–20.

24. David Batchelor, *Chromophobia* (London: Reaktion, 2000), pp. 25–30 in particular.

25. Arnheim, 'Remarks on Color Film', p. 55.

26. Ibid.

27. Ibid., p. 46; Dreyer, 'Color and Colored Film', p. 172.

28. Walter Benjamin, 'The Work of Art in an Age of Mechanical Reproduction', in Benjamin, *Illuminations*, trans. Harry Zohn (London: Fontana, 1973), pp. 219–54.

29. Batchelor, *Chromophobia*, p. 30.

30. Arnheim, 'Remarks on Color Film', p. 54.

31. Wolfgang Ullrich and Juliane Vogel (eds), *Weiß* (Fischer Taschenbuch: Frankfurt, 2003), pp. 14–16.

32. This slippage is documented and theorised in Josef Albers' *Interaction of Color* (rev. and expanded edn) (New Haven and London: Yale University Press, 2006), for example, p. 71: 'This instability of value is extremely characteristic of color. … The purpose of most of our color studies is to prove that color is the most relative medium in art, that we almost never perceive what color is physically.'

33. Sergei Eisenstein, 'From Lectures on Music and Colour in *Ivan the Terrible*', in *Selected Works Vol. III: Writings*, ed. Richard Taylor, trans. William Powell (London: BFI, 1996), p. 326.

34. Sergei Eisenstein, 'On Colour', in *Selected Works Vol. II: Towards a Theory of Montage*, ed. Michael Glenny and Richard Taylor, trans. Michael Glenny (London: BFI, 1991), p. 255: 'The approximation of what has been *partially* achieved by animation … can only be fully realized in colour. And in that case, the filming of real objects will share all the advantages of the animated cartoon!' – Elsewhere, the privilege accorded the cartoon goes beyond that of an approximation: 'But to continue the discussion of colour. What can the "tightening up" be demonstrated on? How should we work in colour, so that the principle is taken to its limits? Where can you do the craziest things in colour? In what sort of Pictures?/Cartoons. To take the problem to its extreme, you have to make a cartoon' (Eisenstein, 'Lectures on Music and Colour', p. 335).

35. Eisenstein, 'Lectures on Music and Colour', p. 335.

36. Sergei Eisenstein, *Nonindifferent Nature*, trans. Herbert Marshall (Cambridge and New York: Cambridge University Press, 1987).

37. Natalie Kalmus, 'Color Consciousness', in Dalle Vacche and Price, *Color*, pp. 24–9.

38. Ibid., p. 26.

39. Higgins, *Harnessing the Technicolor Rainbow*, p. 47.

40. See Dudley Andrew, 'The Post-War Struggle for Colour', in Dalle Vacche and Price, *Color*, pp. 40–9, for a fine account of the ideological dimensions of the debate over the respective merits of Eastmancolor and Technicolor.

41. Jean Mitry, *The Aesthetics and Psychology of the Cinema*, trans. Christopher King (Bloomington and Indianapolis: Indiana University Press, 2000), pp. 225–6.

42. Eric Rohmer, 'Of Taste and Colors', in Dalle Vacche and Price, *Color*, p. 123.

43. Ibid.

44. Slavoj Žižek, *Everything You Always Wanted to Know About Lacan (But Were Afraid to Ask Hitchcock)* (London: Verso, 1992), pp. 235–40.

45. Clyde Taylor, *The Mask of Art: Breaking the Aesthetic Contract – Film and Literature* (Bloomington and Indianapolis: Indiana University Press, 1998), pp. 38–52.

46. Béla Balázs, *Schriften zum Film, Erster Band: >Der sichtbare Mench<, Kritiken und Aufsätze 1922–1926*, ed. Helmut H. Diederichs, Wolfgang Gersch and Magda Nagy (Budapest, Berlin and Munich: Carl Hanser, 1982), p. 58 (emphasis in original).

47. Anne Hollander, *Feeding the Eye: Essays* (Berkeley, Los Angeles and London: University of California Press, 1999), pp. 140–1.

48. Ibid., p. 140.

49. Quoted in Michael Fried, *Why Photography Matters as Art as Never Before* (New Haven and London: Yale University Press, 2008), p. 5.

2 The Moment of Colour: Colour, Modernism and Abstraction

THE MOMENT OF COLOUR: THE *FIN DE SIÈCLE*

Any mythology seeking a pre-eminent 'moment' of colour's liberation would have to take very seriously the candidacy of the *fin de siècle*. The preoccupation with colour may be most obvious in two arts, music – where Wagnerian chromaticism had shaken old harmonic regimes – and painting, which saw an efflorescence of colours unchained from their originally anchoring objects, but it strongly marks the other arts, as well as colonial society's concern with the exotic, description and the adjectival. (Other races have the secondariness of adjectives appended to the substantive 'universal' of 'white' humanity.) Whereas mid-nineteenth-century art history, as represented by the strangely appropriately named Charles de Blanc, coded line as male and colour as female (needing line, that Nietzschean whip, to bound and bind it), the moment of colour's liberation later in the century also echoes that of women's suffrage. A growing passion for colour may accompany modernism's general uprising of the subordinate: of colours once shackled to objects; of women hitherto subject to males; of the mirror or shadow-self; of the exotic staring into western art through the African masks of Picasso's *Demoiselles D'Avignon;* and of the adjective from the noun. Describing the ideological, mid-nineteenth-century view of colour, David Batchelor notes that '[o]ne thing that becomes clear from Blanc's thesis is that colour is both secondary *and* dangerous; in fact, it is dangerous because it is secondary'.[1] Indeed, its description as secondary and minor suggests a rationalisation intended to mute the major power's awareness of the possible precariousness of its pre-eminence. If I begin at the end of the above-mentioned chain of mutually reinforcing revolts by a series of 'secondary' entities, it is because it is the least fully investigated.

The *fin de siècle* sees a proliferation of adjectival styles. (Even a naturalistic novel as apparently opposed to decoration as Frank Norris's *McTeague* is crammed with adjectival formations.) Indeed, adjectivalism functions as the sign of proliferation, of an internal disintegration of world and self into a possibly ungraspable ('sublime') array of fragments: the 'heap of broken images' of T. S. Eliot's *Waste Land.* Previously subordinate to the noun, the adjective achieves equality through the necessity of its presence to delineate the growing number of objects discerned as mysterious, 'alienated' (if viewed negatively) or 'exotic' (if viewed positively) (a difference in point of view possibly isomorphic with the one between naturalism and symbolism). Indeed, the adjective may be the sign of alienation itself, of a breaking out of the object of dimensions once enfolded within it. Its counterpart, the human subject, also surrenders qualities, the residue being Musil's exemplary *Man Without Qualities.* The adjective's separation from its place of origin matches a homelessness of colour, its separation from the objects in which previously it had been lodged. One example of this is Kandinsky's ability to write in 1918 of the colours that made a strong impression on him in childhood: 'I saw these colors on various objects which are no longer as clear in my mind as are the colors themselves.'[2] If a painting from the Munich *Blaue Reiter* movement, of which he was part, displayed green skies, the colour transfer could be taken as a consequence of the accelerated motion of the modern metropolis, and as corresponding to Bergsonian theories of time – as if abbreviated processes of perception could not apprehend blue properly but registered it too late, after its smearing into the adjacent green on the colour circle. Should a painting display a blue orange, meanwhile, the mutual attraction of opposites (the sides of the colour circle, and also of a physical orange's life and decay) reveals the contradictions present within apparent unities, be they objects, persons or marriages. In other words, considered successively: adjectivalism reveals the splitting of the object, doubling shows the disunity of the person and female liberation displays the rifts within the 'one flesh' of a traditional marriage descending into conventionality. The green sky embodies a hidden mirroring, partaking dialectically of the unification of opposites, and breathing nostalgia for the place from which it has been removed: earth. That inward colonialism known as the peasant's attraction to the city participates in this moment also. As everything shifts, it recalls its origin, glancing backwards, dragging it along like a shadow in consciousness. At the same time, the mirage of a green sky may be visionary, using past phenomena to undergird prognosis: *Under a Green Sky*, after all, is the title of Peter Ward's book describing catastrophic climate change as an explanation for past extinctions of life on earth.[3] Meanwhile, the colour transfers evoked in *fin de siècle* art bear the mark of the episteme that informs the Saussurean theorisation of the sign's differential constitution, as a sky that is not inherently sky-like can become its opposite, indeed may even depend upon that opposite – upon earth's green, for instance – for separate being.

The epitome of this continual internal differentiation, however, may be the red of a fire that continually curls over into other colours, particularly yellow: Gaston Bachelard's flame that is the continual mutual transformation of red, yellow, blue and green, an endless shuffling of colours along a Möbius strip. For Bachelard, fire is the primary object of philosophical meditation.[4] Its motility is particularly revelatory of the philosophical difficulties of naming that afflict the *fin de siècle*, and then the movement itself problematically designated 'modernism' – as in Hofmannsthal's 'Chandos Letter' – red being widely recognised as endlessly shifting register into at least one other colour, yellow. Moreover, a description of flame by Georges Sand – as quoted by Bachelard – links it also to blue and white (a linkage of interest to any analyst of Krzysztof Kieślowski's *Trois couleurs* (*Three Colours*) Trilogy (1993–4) – of which more below); and this susceptibility of flame to transformation lends authority to Goethe's description of red, fire's central hue, as 'totalising'. The difficulty of naming becomes glaring when words encounter colour, whose sheer multiplicity far outstrips language's capacity to fix all its intermediate points, which are lost rather as another key phenomenon of the period, the cinema, 'loses' its isolated photographic frames: incinerating them in the Bergsonian flame of motion-picture life, drowning them in the image's flow through the projector's lock-gate. The 'loss' of separate frames and colours is like that of time in the infinitely divisible line of Zeno's paradox: 10 million variations of colour are distinguishable within visible light.[5] The awkwardness of linguistic attempts to distinguish some of the more proximate neighbours may be discerned in such a lame and barely comprehensible isolation as that of 'Cadmium red' and 'Cadmium red hue'.[6] Clyde Taylor reports that the absence of blue from the list of primary colours in Greek painting manuals caused one study to conclude 'that Greek painters considered blue an admixture and lightening of black',[7] while Alexander Theroux argues that because the Greeks knew only four colours, 'green then includes what we think of as blue'.[8] This sense of the fluidity of demarcation within the colour spectrum – of its possibly dizzying mutability – surely feeds the emergence of stream-of-consciousness writing (modernism's verbal afterimage of a water-obsessed Impressionism). As words dissolve into one another, they simulate – among other things – the ungraspable successions of colour translated into global visibility as they are lifted out of chemical vats and colonised countries. The *locus classicus* for this effect may well be the work of Virginia Woolf (as in the paint- and colour-obsessed *To the Lighthouse*). Only a music of endless flow can reflect them, which is why the *fin-de-siècle* credo runs *de la musique avant toute chose*. The difficulty of naming reflects the plethora of 'new' colours.

Scepticism regarding the feasibility of the sort of synaesthetic transfer between media envisaged by this Symbolist credo may be found in the early work of Walter Benjamin. In his dialogue on the rainbow, dating from 1915, a character named Georg explains to Margarethe that the colours of which she had dreamt are those of fantasy. 'Pure colour is itself infinite, but only its reflection (*Abglanz*) appears in painting.'[9] This painterly reflection inscription of colour upon surfaces subordinates its actual infinity to a mode later thinkers would call binarist, that of black and white. For Benjamin, painting's transcription of colour reduces it to servitude. In other words: it digitises the analogue.

Equally significant, however, is the degree to which the continual approximations of a Symbolist aesthetic of indirectness secularise and sublate taboo, lending a quasi-sacred *frisson* to the movement's 'religion of art'. For the ease with which one colour shades into another can feed naming mechanisms resembling the unnamings of taboo, as in the Outer Hebridean folk practice that said 'blue' instead of 'green', to utter the latter being deemed unlucky.[10] Seeking both to tap its power and yet defuse it, the dialectic of Symbolist enlightenment mimics this magic in the name of a paradoxical 'religion of art'. The doubleness of the enterprise acknowledges the ambiguity that charges colours themselves. Could it be that primary colours, as the only ones easily available to premodern periods, became polysemous through an inevitable multiplication of uses: concrete, visual forms of Freud's ambiguous 'primal words'?

Similarly, the emergence of an originally monochromatic photography within the nineteenth century visibly generates, and matches, a cleft within notions of 'reality'. The photograph seems to demonstrate that the coloured world of habitual perception has a perennial, 'dis-coloured' shadow. Perhaps in response to the environment's blackening by coal-dust, the underworld appears above ground. The mid-nineteenth-century fashion for spiritism follows naturally. As reality becomes susceptible of conceptualisation as the 'colouring-in' of pre-existent, non-coloured matter, its draining of colour, its whiting out or declension towards abysmal darkness, becomes foreseeable also. The relationship between colour and monochrome becomes analogous, and assimilable, to that between such binaries as surface and depth, body and soul; and the disparity suggests a dissonance at the heart of being. One consequence is that reality is seen to require 'reading'. Thus, for Freud everyday life has a psychopathology, mirroring the latent/manifest splits of the dream-work. The widespread *fin-de-siècle* preoccupation with depth/surface relations suggests a 'hermeneutics of suspicion' for which reality's duality is duplicity. Even where mirror and reality correspond, they remain separate, like Dorian Gray and his picture. The disjunction renders surfaces mask-like. If colours can migrate between objects, sky becoming green and oranges blue, these shifts intimate a sense of the modern world's openness to transformation. Utterly transfigured already by industrialism and new technologies, it might alter more radically still, bend into utopia or dystopia. The colours may assume a Huxleyan, psychedelic brilliance, or be charred and chastened to Orwellian black and white. Faced with such alternatives, no wonder Musil's Man Without Qualities – a noun without adjectives, albeit possessing a name (Ulrich) – is unable to act.

Thus the liberation of colour is an ambiguous utopia: both pre-revolutionary and alienated. If, for most of us, a colour is less a thing (only the painter in front of his paintbox lends colour this status) than a thing's property, the separation of the two can be seen as a splitting of its source. That splitting may be in the form of the civil war known as revolution, but it also precedes it as capitalist countries split and colonise themselves – in England, for instance, setting South as subject against an objectified North, the domain of colour against that of monochrome (as in Mrs Gaskell's *North and South*) – forcibly denuding their own territories of the raw materials their industries require. The process is then replicated in the extra-national ones of empire-building. This 'liberation' of resource from its point of origin entails its deracinating categorisation as a 'mere adjective' unevenly developed with the noun, and hence eminently alien-able from one noun (its country of origin) to serve another. If the *Doppelgänger* can be linked to majority/minority relations, as Taylor argues,[11] the encounter of self and other may be a Mexican stand-off with no happy ending. And, in this context, the liberation of colour that was perhaps most obvious in German Expressionism may be shadowed by fear of the occurrence within Germany of the dis-colouring industrial effects already known elsewhere, but which English artists of the late eighteenth century had not foreseen – except in the distorting, metaphorical mirror of a Sublime mistakenly identified with a geographic and historically less-developed elsewhere (Rome, and antiquity), rather than native green hills about to extrude 'Satanic mills'.

The moment of colour's cinematic liberation is harder to pinpoint, for all the frequency with which *The Wizard of Oz* (1939) provides a point of mythological origin (one definition of 'true beginning' might be that it sees proper use of something begun earlier …). Colour is already present in silent film's tints and tones, then does ambiguous duty by furthering the claims of both realism and fantasy in the 1930s. However, if colour's liberation means separation from the objects that first house it – a striking off of leg-irons – it may require a general loosening of the ('mainstream') 'classical' cinema's injunction to keep everything in focus, which softens focus for idealising purposes at most. After all, only objects placed out of focus register first and foremost as colours, having shucked off their defining shapes. (Since industry practice habitually applies soft focus to women, the identification of colour and femininity is reinforced.) This being so, another moment may figure as defining, albeit also mythologically, the liberation of cinematic colour. If widespread discolouration of the landscape follows industrialisation, as in its English prototype, it is hardly surprising that Michelangelo Antonioni should use such subject matter in his first colour film, *Deserto rosso* (*Red Desert*) (1964). One moment assumes particular importance: as three violet flowers appear in the foreground, out of focus, one's primary sense of them is of three bursts of violet, not three flowers. Colour's liberation involves an abstraction culminating in Derek Jarman's *Blue* (1993). (Total abstraction as the self-conscious, heroic sign of ending, in a film Jarman knew would be his last?) Furthermore, *Red Desert* linked colour's emancipation to a loss of focus in another respect also: the imperative to pursue a single character subsides, as Giuliana fur-nishes both the main focalising point of identification and its impossible object, being both sane and disturbed. The camera's recurrent slides away from the characters, for example, along a pipe at the workers' meeting, or direction towards things resistant to focus (the sublime and monstrous cloud of fac-tory discharge dwarfing the men beside it), move away from Giuliana but *under the aegis of her personality* (a two-edged phenomenon noted in Pier Paolo Pasolini's use of this film as his prime exam-ple of a 'Cinema of Poetry'[12] of 'free indirect subjectivity' modelled upon, but also transforming, the shifting viewpoint of literary 'free indirect discourse'). Since liberated colour is squeezed out of the tube of the object, which becomes a secondary leftover, the film's preoccupation with the sooty remainder of indus-trialisation is fitting. 'Focus' may be lost in another sense, meanwhile, in the possible symbiosis of

Red Desert: foregrounded yet out of focus, flowers become abstractions

colour and widescreen both in American cinema of the 1950s, and in 1960s European film: privileging widescreen rather as Bazin had depth of field, Charles Barr would argue that the expanded aspect ratio enhanced the freedom of the spectatorial look.[13] However, any symbiosis of widescreen and colour may well be dialectical, as the visual patterns and echoes achievable through colour bind together an image in danger of centrifugal disintegration.

An even more thoroughgoing emancipation of colour may pervade Antonioni's later *Il mistero di Oberwald* (*The Oberwald Mystery*) (1981) – at its time, highly experimental – whose computerised colour palette spilled hues unpredictably across the screen. Both films' colour movements enact a dialectic of liberation and entrapment that matches that of their female protagonists, as if developing traditional identifications of 'femininity' and the 'subjective' on the one hand, and, on the other, between 'femininity' and 'colour' (the displayed 'to-be-looked-at-ness' of a Mulveyan film theory), to the point at which they corrode mainstream cinema. In so doing they unfold a dialectic of the 'unpleasure' Laura Mulvey proposed as the remedy for patriarchal pathologies: 'unpleasure' does not merely negate pleasure, as she contends, but simultaneously refines and augments it, in line with Bergson's theory of the nature of negation. It might be said to enter the paintbox alliteratively as 'Baudelairean black', the modernist black of Adorno's *Aesthetic Theory*. Two of its strongest manifestations mark films made later than Antonioni's, and which will reappear in this book. In each black plays a key function corresponding to their director's deepening, increasingly multifarious relationship with the aesthetics of the *fin de siècle*: Krzysztof Kieślowski's *La Double Vie de Véronique* (*The Double Life of Véronique*) (1991) and *Trois couleurs: bleu* (*Three Colours: Blue*) (1993).

Whether the secondariness customarily ascribed to colour is simply a matter of ideology may be a moot point, however. Placing colour second need not manifest a prejudice in favour of line, or – in the case of cinema – the accident of the late acceptance of uniform colour processes, but may display an innate feature of humanity's processing of the world. Thus Temple Grandin remarks that,

> abstract categories like colour are hard for young children to learn. At first, a child will learn that grass and broccoli are green, and apples and roses are red, without figuring out that there is such a thing as *redness* or *greenness* as a separate category for itself. *Greenness* and *redness* are just part of the apple.[14]

It may be only modernity that extracts them and then bestows concrete form on an abstraction.

UT PICTURA KINESIS? *FRENCH CANCAN* COLOURED BY BAZIN

Although colour's liberation in painting antedates that in cinema (for a variety of reasons connected mostly with the latter's mortgaging to technology and commerce, both of which develop the habit whereby films seek to pay their way immediately and handsomely), question marks hang over any such purely linear historiography. Thus, in a strange temporal doubling, Jean Renoir's *French CanCan* (1954) can be seen both to gloss and to replicate the Impressionism of his father. Such a statement might be one way of summarising the view of this film offered by André Bazin, Truffaut's 'best critic, on the best director'.

An early move in Bazin's assessment of Renoir's film compares it with John Huston's *Moulin Rouge* (1952), a film often invoked to exemplify thoughtful cinematic use of colour. For Bazin, however, Huston's film, with its indebtedness to the iconography of Toulouse-Lautrec and Degas, 'fell into [the] trap' created by filmic colour, which 'carries the risk of a literal copying from paintings'. The result: 'little more than a decorative and dramatic rehash of the paintings which provided its source'.[15] Given *French CanCan*'s apparent vulnerability to a similar accusation, this initial judgment may prompt readers to wonder how Renoir might escape a skewering. Meanwhile, although 'decorative' may be obviously deprecating, the use of 'dramatic' as a term of criticism, rather than neutral definition, may be surprising. Any doubts about Bazin's intention of making 'dramatic' a term of disparagement are dispelled on the next page, which argues that '[i]f true painting is not anecdotal (and Auguste Renoir's certainly is not), then any temporal development of that painting cannot be dramatic'.[16] Does 'dramatic' here translate into 'theatrical' (or 'literary', in the manner of so much nineteenth-century painting?), consequently 'non-filmic'? Because this would be more Kracauerian than in the spirit of the Bazin who defended impure cinema, something else surely must be meant. What is at stake is the paradoxical status of time in Renoir's work.

For Bazin, Renoir's achievement in *French CanCan* is to have released 'the dimension of time … inherent in the painting'.[17] That temporality inheres in the need to engage in contemplation before the work, and can have the following consequence:

> The painting is only temporally static in an objective sense. In fact, for the person who looks at it, it represents a universe to discover and explore. This sort of study takes time; so, practically speaking, the dimension of time is indeed inherent in the painting. But if this painting came to life, began to *last*, and to undergo changes affecting its plastic equilibrium as well as its subject, it is clear that this sort of objective time would not take the place of the subjective time experienced by the viewer, but would on the contrary reinforce it. And this is precisely the impression one has after seeing *French CanCan:* that the movie exists in two modes of duration at once, the objective mode of events and the subjective mode of contemplating these events.[18]

In the sentence beginning 'But if this painting …', Bazin transforms his initial, realist account of the phenomenology of contemplation into a movement of reverie in which the image assumes 'a life of its own'. The underlying, unnamed myth is that of Pygmalion contemplating, and thereby fantastically animating, Galatea. The artwork's deliquescence into process does not fuse the objective and the subjective, as Bazin claims, but subordinates the former to the latter. Had he known the work of Benjamin, he might have invoked the *flâneur* as prototypical of the kind of viewer of Impressionist pictures represented by Renoir *fils*. Both theorist and director would take Paris as the capital not only of the nineteenth century, but of private reveries. (It would be worth considering whether such a phantasmagoric animation of the past correlates with the greater investment in a resurrection of the dead possessed by a son, rather than an historian, of the Impressionists, with the special status *this* past has for Renoir enabling him to animate it with a conviction Bazin fails to find in Huston. Such reanimation would mean refusing to admit that the loved one was indeed dead.)

Bazin follows this general statement with an example he hopes will clarify his point:

A certain shot in the film, taken from the outside through a gable window, shows a young woman going about her housework. The décor, the colors, the subject, the actress, everything suggests a rather free evocation of Auguste Renoir, or perhaps even more of Degas. The woman bustles about in the half shadow of the room, then turning around, leans out of the window to shake out her dustcloth. The cloth is bright yellow. It flutters an instant and disappears. Clearly this shot, which is essentially pictorial, was conceived and composed around the brief appearance of this splash of yellow. It is equally clear that the event is of neither dramatic nor anecdotal significance. The flash of yellow remains purely pictorial, like Corot's spot of red, but in eclipse.[19]

If the effect Bazin describes here is neither 'anecdotal nor dramatic', the reason may be because its *incidental* nature renders it 'pre-dramatic'. Too small to unfold in time, and hence to achieve the status even of that miniature form of drama known as the anecdote (that enemy of vanguard late-nineteenth-century painting), it nevertheless also unfolds in time, and so 'goes beyond' a painting. Releasing it into time, though not so far as to untether it completely from painting, it could be seen as 'taking it for a walk'. Such momentariness is, of course, the signature of Impressionism. It is also that of the musical, a genre with which *French CanCan* entertains intimate relations, whose skeletal form is less that of a drama than a series of numbers or events.

Bazin's account of *French CanCan* suggests that it constitutes a series of *respirations* of paintings, each allowed to breathe a *petite phrase* with an independent, non-dramatic logic. A viewer might counter-argue, however, that Renoir's film is not so much free of the dramatic (with its suspenseful, climactic worry over whether or not Nini will agree to dance at the Moulin Rouge's opening night) as prone to downplay all shrieks into background noise, local colour. It may matter to the public whether or not Nini performs, and the logic of a drama centred upon her cries out for her presence, as do her fellow-dancers. But the pattern of the dance, which is not a Kracauerian and Taylorised, industrialised 'mass ornament' but rather an explosion of vegetation in a flower bed, almost makes her disappear. Given the customary prevalence of the collectivity in Renoir, she has the ephemerality of *one colour* amid a crowd of 'jeunes filles en fleur'. It is not she but the particular hue she represents that the show requires, to ensure a totality of pleasure. The many flowers flow, tossed as undulating skirts on one of Renoir's rivers.

For Bazin, the imposition of a drama upon a painting would violate the fundamental stasis of a mood, within and over which contemplation can dwell, hover. The aesthetic sin is less a film's cross-referencing of a painting, than drama's traduction of the meaning of that point of departure. Moreover, for Bazin Renoir sets the seal on his escape from a false relation with painting by making it an endpoint, not a starting one: 'Jacques Rivette pointed out to me that, unlike those who think that to be inspired by painting means to compose a shot imitating a painting and then bring it to life, Renoir starts from a nonpictorial arrangement and cuts when the framing of a scene has evoked a painting.'[20] No longer dependent on painting (if anything, the composition does not resemble a painting but points backwards to the tableau in which melodrama dialectically reverses its tumultuous flow itself by halting, as opposing forces deadlock, and forwards to the freeze frame Renoir's pupil Truffaut would use definitively at the end of *Les Quatre Cent Coups* (1959)), cinema cannot be seen, as in Kracauer, as originating in an immobile image. Nor can colour film become decorative or kitsch, in the sense of Umberto Eco's definition: 'a quotation unable to generate a new context'.[21] If anything, it is painting that becomes a quotation from film, a still.

In the end, though, Bazin seems to deem colour secondary, almost distracting:

> I saw an early copy of *French CanCan* which had not been perfectly graded and several of the reels had a greenish hue to them. But the internal balance of the shots was such that this imperfection did not at all destroy their harmony. The same phenomenon holds true for certain Impressionist paintings which retain their beauty in spite of the fact that their colours have turned with time. The pink tones of 'Bal du Moulin de la Galette,' for example, have turned bluish with age, but the painting's grace and harmony remain intact. The reason is that any great painting is first of all a creation of the spirit which is sustained by the spirit. It has an existence beyond its material elements, which are only mediators. The disappearance or alteration of a single one of those elements simply engenders a spontaneous compensation, much as the human body tends to compensate for loss or injury of an organ in an attempt to maintain its vital equilibrium.[22]

If art can indeed survive without truth to its intended colours, the classicist verdict partakes dialectically of Romanticism: the invisible spirit prevails, and in any case works have lives beyond their makers' wishes. The idea that loss in one area strengthens another recalls such legends of sensory interdependence as the one whereby the poet is necessarily blind. Putting it less mythically and mystically, the fading of one strong element renders visible a sturdy understudy, revealing its possession of a dense sheaf of virtues resistant to grasping all at once. This effect of overspill is a definition of the Renoiresque (the breaching of the frame, the overwhelming richness of *La Règle du jeu* (*The Rules of the Game*) (1939)). And so, of course, is the concern for balance, even (perhaps because it was most needed there?) in the vertiginous *Règle du jeu*. Any fading in the (Romantic? certainly Impressionist) dimension of colour permits a foregrounding of the balanced volumes, plane, lines and structures of the Renoir who was also inspired by neo-classicism and the eighteenth century. The compensation occurs not in the work but in the viewer suddenly able to do justice to something overshadowed previously. It had to be there, and to be strong, to carry the extra, unexpected weight when the necessity arose. In other words, perhaps: it is as if the colour films of Renoir's post-war period (what Christopher Faulkner would describe as his aesthetic period[23]), contain within their shadows, and have as shadows, the monochrome ones of his pre-war self. Might the later ones even *be* the early ones, but colourised?

COLOUR, MODERNISM, POSTMODERNISM AND ABSTRACTION

If the *fin de siècle* initially liberates colour by allowing artists to apply it 'inappropriately', the logical conclusion is the complete separation of colour from object: abstraction. This may involve the arrangement
of a series of colours. It concludes in a dedication of the canvas to nothing but the manifestation of a single
colour.

The idea of an image comprising a single block of colour arrived in parodic form long before it
raised any claims to be taken seriously. In a deliberate *reductio ad absurdum* of modernist art *avant la
lettre*, Paul Bilhaud's *Combat des nègres dans une cave pendant la nuit* appeared in 1882 at the Exposition
des Arts Incohérents, thirty-seven years before Kasimir Malevich exhibited his *Black Square* in 1915.
Virtually identical though the two images may appear to be, the framing exercise of their titling makes
vastly different claims. For Bilhaud, the notion of an all-black image, stripped of figurative content, is ludi-
crous: a sane painter could have produced it only as an accidental consequence of the accumulation
of black elements of visible reality – 'darkness visible' with a vengeance. No one could possibly take the
painting of a black canvas as a goal, for it would have ended the activity of painting 'before it had
begun'. Bilhaud is critiqued in *Les Statues meurent aussi* (*Statues Also Die*) (1953) by Chris Marker and
Alain Resnais, whose sombre, acid wit shows a black screen briefly when describing the colonial
destruction of black history: 'black on black, a struggle of blacks ['combat des nègres', echoes Bilhaud's
title] in the night of time'.

In the case of Malevich, the critique comes from a different direction, as he questions what constitutes an end, and what a beginning. Could the black square even possibly be a painting of a rectangular,
dark object painted close-up, so all its context disappears? Could the figurative re-enter via the back (black?)
door? Or is it ruled out by a prior commitment to abstraction?

Cinema began with a view similar to Bilhaud's: abstraction is absurd, as only an extremely improb-
able conjunction of objects of a single colour could precipitate a 'natural realism' ascribed to art in
general, and apparently marking the new cinematic medium in particular, in its direction. Emil Cohl's
1910 Gaumont short, *Le peintre néo-impressioniste*, takes its cue from Alphonse Allais's 1887 album of
monochromes, including an all-red *Tomato Harvest by Apoplectic Cardinals on the Shore of the Red Sea*.
A painter and his female partner present a prospective buyer with a series of monochromes, including
the above-mentioned red one and a yellow one showing *Chinaman Transporting Maize on the Yellow River*.
Line drawings of these combinations of people and objects are animated, as if to build for the buyer plausible scenarios of how they might indeed be figurative – hence legitimate – art. In the end the enthusiastic
buyer takes them all.

The animations in Cohl's film involve those two key elements of most cinema: narrative and the figurative. Generally speaking, abstract single-colour screens have represented only moments in the
progress of a narrative, interrupting it either legibly (the colour flashes besetting Hitchcock's *Marnie*
(1964), the black screen representing the blacks ejected from the courtroom in Godard's *Vladimir et
Rosa* (1970)) or enigmatically (Kieślowski's *Three Colours* trilogy). Not until Jarman's *Blue* did any film
display a monochrome screen from start to finish: a move almost guaranteed to end a film-maker's
career, and perhaps for that reason reserved by Jarman for the very end of his life.

In his intriguing essay 'Color, the Formless, and Cinematic Eros', Brian Price has postulated a growing tendency in recent cinema to privilege colour patterns which either overlay moments in a narrative
– as in Hou Hsiao-Hsien's *Qian xi man po* (*Millenium Mambo*) (2001) – or interrupt it, in the manner of

the abstract Jeremy Blake compositions interpolated into Paul Thomas Anderson's *Punch Drunk Love* (2002). For Price, this privileging of colour amounts to 'an undoing of form that begins at the level of eros, but extends outwards into the aesthetics of global consumption'.[24] 'Eros' in this context may be read as invoking not just the sensuous appeal of colour but also the mingling of forms that confounds line. However, Price's contention that 'the subjective expansion of color abstraction counters the increasingly conventionalized narrative form of global cinema'[25] arguably considers only one side of the dialectic of abstraction and globalisation. One might add that colour's ability to appeal at a greater distance than line combines with its *fin-de-siècle*-inspired liberation from context to enhance its accessibility to consumption beyond the limits of its originating culture, while the appeal of the erotic is not necessarily simply liberating, chiming as it does with the increasing sexualisation of modern consumer culture. Moreover, one might wish to ask whether the developments whose probing Price usefully begins derive from an intra-aesthetic dialectic of modernism and postmodernism, or whether 'authentic' modernist stylistic strategies are compromised only at the point of insertion into globalised postmodern culture and consciousness industries. One might also wonder whether certain devices function 'modernistically' in relation to cultures of origin which are less permeated by modern techno-science and late capitalism, and so possibly inherently less 'alienated', while functioning 'postmodernistically' within a global sphere of circulation whose main arena of exhibition and advertisement is the film festival archipelago. Should the latter be the case, the text's modernist abstraction would be the unmoving arm of a compass whose other arm described increasingly wide – global – circles round it.

As noted, Price discerns this development in relatively recent films. As usual, and as my remarks on modernism and postmodernism should indicate, periodisation is controversial (as is terminology – which is why I will return later to the question of the meaning of 'modernism'), for such a development might be discerned – say – in Kieślowski's *Double Life of Véronique* or, earlier still, in Bo Widerberg's heavily romanticised late-1960s lingering over doomed love, *Elvira Madigan* (1967). In that film, after army deserter Lieutenant Sixten has helped Elvira, the ex-circus performer, descend from the clothes-line that has been her makeshift tight-rope, the two lie down in the grass and roll away from the camera, becoming an abstract blur of colour. (The globalisation connection, deemed recent by Price, may be present in Widerberg's film too: when Sixten's friend says he has betrayed his country, Elvira repudiates the notion of nation, her mother being German, her father Danish, her stepfather American, while she has friends in France and Italy. She concludes; 'Look. My hand is like a map. Here are the lines like borders. What does it matter where the lines are? I care about the hand, the whole hand.') The apparently chimerical nature of attempts to fix an origin for the linkage of eros and abstraction may simply reflect the long-standing affinity of romance and soft-focus, which can also function as a multiform tact. The softness may even be a synaesthetic form of the haptic, imitating the hand's caress, smoothing those wrinkles away. Interestingly enough, a vision characterised by swimming contours is thematised in the dialogue of *Elvira Madigan*, when Sixten's friend links his exclusive focus on Elvira to that on a single grass-blade located close to the eye, with everything beyond blurred. The equation of eros and the abstract has considerable longevity, as eros abstracts lovers from the world.

ABSTRACTION PLUS OR MINUS EROS

'Abstraction' being a term with a long history, whose most influential art-historical use may be the one by Wilhelm Worringer, opposing it to empathy,[26] the previous section could treat its relevance to colour only glancingly. If the obvious points of departure include Kandinsky and Mondrian, replayed in the 1960s' psychedelia and Mary Quant dresses respectively, more relevant to this book is the symbiosis of cinema and the avant-garde in the late 1920s, beginning with such European figures as Fernand Léger (whose *Ballet mécanique* (*Mechanical Ballet*) (1924) seems once to have circulated in a colour print[27]) and Walter Ruttmann, re-emerging in North America in the shape-changing whimsies and symmetries of Norman McLaren's nature-haunted abstractions, then the visceral ontologies of Stan Brakhage or the colour alternations of Paul Sharits, to name just a few key figures. This avant-garde version of the general liberation of colour in early-twentieth-century art is not the dialectic of narrative and *mise en scène* that structures feature films. And this non-representational avant-garde was, of course, not the only one, as it had a shadow, or itself shadowed, one that was directly socially engaged.[28] In the abstract avant-gardism of Ruttmann events occur, but non-figurative experiment occludes them. An enigmatic ontology unfolds beyond representation, its opaque occurrences answering and corresponding only to themselves. It could be argued that this opacity becomes open to interpretation nevertheless through the unlabelled quality of metaphors owning and disowning a range of possible referents. One could imagine a viewer taking the two colour blobs in Ruttmann's *Opus 1* (1921), for instance, as allegorising a primal human dance of love and aggression. However, nothing in the brief work itself hints that the abstraction

Opus 1: polysemic shapes orbit one another

intends a generalisation, or warrants any decipherment. A red spot and a blue spot are not 'a warm person and a cold one', and the legitimacy of such readings is dubious: after all, abstraction sought to cauterise the abounding literariness of late-nineteenth-century art. An allegorical reading of Ruttmann's *pas de deux* would be a literary, anthropomorphic domestication of a disconcerting Pongean *parti pris des choses*. *Opus 1* does not liberate colour into ambivalence or into a dialectic of simultaneous reference and non-reference; rather, the colours assume a self-sufficiency of exclusively sensory being that provocatively invites accusations of hermeticism and defines 'realism' as a localised nineteenth-century phenomenon with no genuine claims to normative status. Consider, for instance, Siegfried Kracauer's excoriation of the effects upon the documentary footage of *Berlin: Die Symphonie der Großstadt* (*Berlin, Symphony of a Great City*) (1927) of Ruttmann's abstract disposition.[29] Yet what was often decried at the time, in terms such as Kracauer's, as 'formalism', can also ascend and descend simultaneously to levels of being where particles or bacteria invisible to the naked eye mimic the movements of the spheres. (Compare the vegetable-like forms in the paintings and drawings of Wols.) Such levels can even be shuffled in like jokers amid the cards drawn by a narrative film, as in the close-up of the 'cosmic coffee cup' in Godard's *Deux ou trois choses que je sais d'elle* (*Two or Three Things I Know About Her*) (1967). If this sequence pursues a dialectic it is one of '*l'inhumaine*', grown proximate to the human by virtue of humanity's self-abstraction by the self-reifications of capitalism and prostitution. (In other words, Godard is not avant-garde in Ruttmann's sense – no proponent of 'pure cinema'[30] – but rather in that of the other, socially engaged avant-garde, or – if one prefers – suspended between 'modernism' and 'political modernism'.)

MODERNISM AND POLITICAL MODERNISM

As the inverted commas placed around the word in the last sentence of the previous section may have indicated, it is possible, even appropriate, to be highly sceptical of the usefulness of the term 'modernism'. Apart from a small group of *fin-de-siècle* Austro-Hungarians terming themselves 'die Moderne', the artists currently designated (and often denigrated) as 'modernists' did not identify themselves thus. The clubbable among them called themselves such things as 'Futurists', 'Imagists', 'Purists', 'Expressionists' and so on, while the more significant ones intersected with such groups only briefly, if at all (such as Kafka, Eliot, Joyce, Musil, Stravinsky, Picasso). The term has been applied retrospectively to an entire generation, with a glaring lack of discrimination. However, insofar as it is possible to use it meaningfully in the current context, it may be described as giving free rein to colour polysemy. Political modernism, by way of contrast, seeks to define and critique the functioning of colour within a socio-political system it claims to be able to stand outside completely. The difference between the two resembles that between the Godard of *Le Mépris* (*Contempt*) (1963) and the one of *Le Gai Savoir* (*The Joyful Science*) (1969). (Poised fascinatingly inbetween, and hence of particular interest, is *Two or Three Things I Know About Her*.) Alternatively, the difference may be illustrated by that between Antonioni's first incursions into colour and those of Godard. Where Godardian colour is flat, cartoon-like, infusing the feature with the primary colour aesthetic first associated with the Disney of the 1930s (no wonder Eisenstein met Mickey Mouse when he visited Walt's studios), Antonioni liberates colour by the opposite means: through the above-mentioned focus shifts that steam apart the separate layers of the image, melting objects into abstract instanciations of colours floating away from their original moorings. The world of connotation is an opening up; that of denotation, a Flatworld. In the former, the world separates like filo pastry; in the latter, it is flatbread.

If the artists usually grouped together as modernists are indeed linked by their assumption of an openness of signification, and the primary element in its grammar is the connotative sign, political modernism conceives signs only as denotative (pursuing a semiotic reduction), with any ambiguities besetting them being merely mystifications or the contradictions of an ideological system. The critique of 'modernism' formulated by political modernists, be they Brecht or his cinematic children of the 1960s (Godard, Straub and others), is arguably self-serving in its assumption that modernism either has no politics, or only an elitist or fascist one: an argument to which the most subtle rejoinder is Adorno's *Aesthetic Theory,* for which the disruption of the automatism of exchange by the autonomous artwork mounts the most genuinely intransigent attack on dehumanisation.

One's scepticism concerning the usefulness of 'modernism' as a term grows as one charts the variety of its uses in Film Studies. Thus, in an influential article, David Bordwell[31] distinguishes between the modernism of the late 1920s and the 'art cinema' that came into being three decades later, even though for many that art cinema represented a form of modernism,[32] albeit penetrating belatedly an artform whose chronic heavy dependence on finance often inoculates it against innovation. The most complex use of the term is that of John Orr, who discerns three categories within what many would term 'art cinema': a 'neo-modernity' of the 1960s and 1970s; a late-twentieth-century 'hyper-modernity' in Western Europe; and a 'meta-modernity' to its East during the same period.[33] Others, using as their template for modernism such works as those of Proust or Kafka, would restrict the term 'modernist' to the more radical, defamiliarising, surrealist and/or self-referential wing of art cinema, which requires spectatorial work but forbids arrival at the clear-cut conclusions Brecht (and, in his Brechtian phase, Benjamin) believed such work would yield. Although Bordwell rightly notes the adversarial relationship between art cinema and political modernism, for which he offers the useful alternative name of 'historical-materialist order of cinema', the possibility of its emergence within a single, Protean career, and therefore of a sort of compatibility between them, needs to be mentioned, particularly since one such career was surely the most significant cinematic one of the 1960s: that of Godard.

For this reason, the binaries suggested above work only in the broadest terms. The view favoured by this author would conceive modernism and political modernism not as opposites, but see the latter as a (partly punitive) straitening of a richer modernism. For whereas political modernism simply spurns identification, modernism both employs and critiques it. Such would also be the view of Gabriel Josipovici, for whom modernism pursues an identification it then undermines.[34] Two key filmic examples are Bergman's *Persona* (1966) and Andrzej Wajda's *Wszystko na sprzedaż* (*Everything for Sale*) (1969). Within the framework of such a definition, the true opposition, therefore, would be the one Bordwell sketched in the final sentences of his article: that of art cinema and political modernism. The former leaves identification formally unproblematised (any problematisation being only implicit in the usually unheroic, even unsympathetic, nature of the protagonist); the latter attacks it directly with Brechtian alienation devices. In terms of these distinctions, *Two or Three Things I Know About Her* marks the beginning of the politically modernistic Godard, albeit leavened by elements of modernism (the defamiliarising transformation into images of transcendence of the coffee cup and the lit cigarette; the hesitant, non-didactic voiceover; the worries about the naming of colours).

Similarly suspended between the constructed alternatives of 'modernism' and 'political modernism' is the entirety of the cinema of Eisenstein. The main consequence for colour-use is a privileging isolation of one hue – red – at the cost of an impoverishment of its meaning, which becomes singular and exclusively positive. The meanings of other colours remain more open and negotiable by context. Red might therefore be said to function only as a collective sign in a breathtaking political cartoon, while other colours are more individualised, potentially polysemous, or prone to indicate character and mood. Of course, this split may simply be an historical one within his work, marking the distinction between the thematisation of revolution in the works of the 1920s, which therefore privilege red, and the more conventionally narrated *Ivan Groznyy II: Boyarsky zagovor* (*Ivan the Terrible Part Two*) (1958), parts of which use Agfa stock captured from German factories, and whose pre-revolutionary subject matter permits a more even-handed interest in various colours. Although, Eisenstein's work of the 1920s may be termed both 'modernist' and 'politically modernist', using montage to generate spectators who were both active decoders ('modernist') and discerners of only one meaning ('the correct analysis'), there is no transitional work in which two streams meet, as in *Two or Three Things I Know About Her* – though *¡Que viva Mexico!* (1932) might have assumed such a status had it been completed.

Where European cinema was concerned at least, 'the moment of colour' occurred during the 1960s. Godard himself was drawn towards it early in the decade, repeatedly taking one step towards it and two steps back, as if fearful of a possibly inexorable suction and wishing to preserve independence and existentialist freedom. Its justification in *Une femme est une femme* (*A Woman is a Woman*) (1961) lay in the musical genre; in *Le Mépris*, it was the price exacted by moneyed backers. Each time Godard deployed colour with fascinating inventiveness; yet each use precipitated a retreat into black and white. Only in the mid-1960s, as colour became normative for the kind of films later to be called 'art cinema', and also – perhaps crucially – characterised a consumerism co-opting the intense colour-experiences counter-cultures sought simultaneously to mobilise against it, did he pitch his tent permanently in colour. Thereafter, neither he, nor cinema as a whole, would be allowed more than fleeting glances back. The possibilities of colour might be foregrounded periodically – as in the remarkable digital versions of sea and sky in *Éloge de l'amour* (*In Praise of Love*) (2001) – but they would no longer be the dominant form of Godardian experimentation, as in those strange bed-fellows (shot back-to-back), *Two or Three Things I Know About Her* or *Made in USA* (1966).

TWO OR THREE THINGS I KNOW ABOUT HER: MODERNITY AND MODERNISM

Whether or not this interpretive possibility was intended by Godard, the title of *Two or Three Things I Know About Her* may be correlated with its relentless tracking of the colours of the French flag in the modernising environment of a new housing estate on the outskirts of Paris. In the context of the film's general hesitation the reference to 'two or three things' seems to ask whether the white separating the red and the blue on the flag should be accounted a colour or not. The question becomes: in speaking of that flag, is one considering two things (two colours), or three? Whatever Godard's intentions, this possible correlation between the work's title and its most frequent colour scheme fits his punning pursuit of the word 'ensemble', which designates a housing complex such as the one we see, but wonders just what belongs together, what constitutes a group, and whether or not it is possible for people meaningfully to unite (or couple) in the atomised, consumerist society under scrutiny. His main protagonist, Juliette Janson – a housewife prostituting herself matter-of-factly to pay the bills – describes 'ensemble' as a favourite word, but there is little evidence of true interpersonal togetherness: at most, perhaps, the fact that the colours she wears are completely different from those of her friend Marianne (when Juliette sports a blue top and yellow skirt, Marianne wears a red top and green skirt), suggesting a friendly agreement to divide the colour field between them. Such combinations do not show the dominance of a single colour that would constitute an 'outfit' (an 'ensemble' in another sense, that of, say, an 'ensemble de trois pièces ('a three-piece suit')). Is it significant, given the work's interest in prostitution and in language as a Heideggerian 'house man lives in' that 'poser pour l'ensemble' means 'to pose for the nude'? Does the above-mentioned colour division of the female, between upper and lower, cement a self-division that feeds the persistence, at the heart of demythologised, increasingly unisex modernity, of age-old divisions of woman into top and bottom?[35] In her dreams Juliette fragments, waking with a sense that a piece may be missing. It is as if she has become one of the assemblages of colour that appear on several occasions in the film and represent the logical conclusion of a process of splitting. Could the white at the heart of the French flag be a marker or placeholder for that missing piece? Could whiteness, for all its association with absence, itself be the piece she needs? (In which case she would need to realise that absence can become presence, just as elements of the alienated quotidian – that coffee cup, that lit tip of a cigarette – become transcendent as the camera closes in on them, mystically enlarging them into images of the universe: for if 'everything is cinema' is the Godardian credo, it is because film can turn every thing into everything. This, of course, achieves the Godardian dream of making even the object seen in close-up appear distant.) Or could the missing part be one of the colours she wears, as the solid blocks of brilliant colour do not sustain one another but stand separately, lego blocks in a bright, blank consumer world that can easily be pulled apart? Is the very possibility of the 'ensemble' – of true matches, *mots justes*, *images justes* – mocked by the inevitable arbitrariness of the film's own collage juxtapositions, or of the linguistic signifier that obsesses it?

The ease with which colours can come apart is one cause of the recurrent appearances of colours in striped patterns noted in Ed Branigan's excellent dissection of the film.[36] Other causes include: an interest in mid-1960s female fashion; a concern with national identities and flags (and that irreverent other mid-1960s development, flags as fashion); and the preoccupation with naming and indifference (juxtaposition with another colour changes colour perception, and hence naming; but under certain conditions – a sufficient degree of social fragmentation? – colours may be adjacent without changing one another).

The opening titles use both the colours of the French flag and the colour green. Does the juxtaposition of green with the tricolour imply an incompatibility between French identity and the natural? If things go together and yet do not, is this another form of the prostitution that is not just a metaphor for discordant marriage but captures that apparent union's reality? The issue of the relation between the tricolour hues and others, raised succinctly in the titles, returns almost immediately, in less abstract form, as Marina Vlady (Juliette Janson) is shown in a sweater containing one colour found in the flag (blue) and one that is not (yellow). Framing her in a medium close-up that cuts off much of the sweater, Godard makes it hard for spectators to see it well, allowing them to wonder about the accuracy of the voiceover and the degree of fit between words and images, and hence also about the extent to which world and representation form an 'ensemble'. One can discern the blue the speaker mentions, but not the yellow stripes. (The fact that Juliette is not front-lit also hinders colour recognition, while the two shots of her seem even to have been taken at different times of day, reducing the perception of colour consistency.) If, according to the Heidegger dictum quoted later by Juliette, language is the house man lives in, how important are images? And, conversely, how much of an image can or should words encompass? (How skeletal is that linguistic house?) Describing Juliette, the speaking voice hesitates significantly over the right name for the colour of her hair.

Utilised in a film that thematises colour, the word 'ensemble' inevitably raises the issue of colour harmony: the question 'which colours go together?' Is there such a thing as an 'ensemble de couleurs' (a harmonious group of colours)? For instance, it seems as if the traditionally 'cool' blue and the 'warm' red can go together only when separated by a white inserted like cotton wool to mute the sharp contradictions of French society. Just after the car-wash sequence the commentary explicitly mentions the quest for harmony: 'My aim, for the simplest things to come into being in the world of humans, for man's spirit to possess them, a new world where men and things would interrelate harmoniously.'[37]

Just after this a brief epiphany appears to prefigure that harmony as Marianne in her red sweater is framed in the window of the red mini: for a moment, human and object display a unity, and yet it may be nothing more than the shared reification noted by a commentary that usually defines people and things as equally dead, thus echoing Juliette's description of her own condition as one of 'indifference' (in other words: non-differentiation?). (An alternative title for this film: 'Le confort et l'indifference'.) At the same time – in other words, considered in terms of the film's dialectical propensities – the colour echo may simply illustrate society's identification of woman as (pleasure) machine, in line with Branigan's observation that 'a woman's body is like a car's body'.[38] The duality of epiphany and reification would participate in the duality that allows a coffee cup and a lit cigarette to conjugate into images with cosmic connotations. On top of this, of course, an 'ensemble' can also be a musical group. Given Godard's preoccupation with dissonance and word–image relations, it is fitting that cacophonous industrial noise accompanies many shots, or that he wonders out loud which words should be attached ('married'?) to particular images. If using colour ensures that disharmony is visible, Godard makes sure it also echoes on the soundtrack and in the gap between soundtrack and image.

The split within the individual, the subject, matches one within the object, which takes the form of the arbitrariness of its relationship with its colour, which devolves into colouring. Colour clearly does not arise from it but is imposed from without, usually as a marketing tool, though Godard may deem the imposition homologous with the imperialism preoccupying him also. Such surface arbitrariness

Two or Three Things I Know About Her: colour's solicitation has a prostitute's as a rival

renders colour like a mask, or the advertisements dotting the work. Colouring the object gives it the function it performs in advertising: one of attracting attention and/or pleasing. As various individuals wear striped clothing and stripes also figure on the French flag, flags become forms of advertisement, and individuals are both advertisements and flags. If the function of colour is primarily an advertising one, its association with females aligns the mechanics of female attraction with those of the prostitute, reinforcing Godard's thesis concerning the all-pervasiveness of prostitution in French society. Colour display does not assert personality but becomes a form of the masking, self-dissociation and 'bad faith' found not only in the prostitute, but also in her spouse, who does not know, or wish to know, how she pays the bills.

On top of this, the arbitrariness of word–thing relationships makes language little better than an advertisement for the object: Juliette wonders what would have happened had blue been called green, as if this were a distinct possibility. The Saussurean premise combines with the dominance of the cultural to squeeze out that sign of the natural, the colour green, which appears at the work's beginning and end, but hardly at all in between, and with nothing like the frequency of blue and red. Characteristically, a close-up of leaves rustling in the wind – that image so often privileged as the first word of a 'natural language' of moving pictures upon cinema's first emergence – quickly pulls back to reveal a petrol station sign in the bottom left-hand corner. It is as if, obeying the inveterate Godardian dialectic of mystery and cynicism, the film needs to steady itself before the vertigo of unnamable nature by finding a cultural form to which to cling. Having done so, it can slow-zoom back in to the leaves alone.

When Juliette wonders whether blue might have been called green, she may be said to posit the existence of a blank between these colours, like that between blue and red on the French flag. This space, however, is not necessarily white; it may be 'green-that-is-also-blue' or, to name it with absurd exactitude (and a Heideggerian passion for neologism Godard himself would surely find piquant), 'grue'. This word was devised in 1954 by Nelson Goodman to describe, as Mark Kingswell puts it, 'an imaginary colour that is now green but at some unknown future point will be blue. Two things at that time T are both apparently green, but one is actually grue, meaning that at time $T + n$ it will be blue.'[39] Goodman's word can also function as a signal of the inherently dialectical mutability of colour. One may even wonder whether it prompted Godard's meditations on blue and green. '$T + n$' might represent a temporal version of the spatial formula for the transformative effect of one colour's juxtaposition with another, and 'grue' names a green that, in the new context, no longer resembles itself but has been tuned off-key (like Goodman's 'complementary' 'bleen', whose trajectory is towards green[40]). Cast in the terms of Godard's language-games, each word may be classed as mystifyingly suppressing the central hyphen that would betray its duality.

Godard's use of colour resembles that of his protagonist. Its animating principle approximates one enunciated by Julia Kristeva: 'it is through color – colors – that the subject escapes its alienation within a code … that it, as conscious subject, accepts'.[41] Insofar as Kristeva posits a conscious acceptance of this code, Godard diverges from Juliette in his conscious rejection of the society of which she is part. Nevertheless, in a film that repeatedly reworks Baudelaire's hailing of the reader of *Les Fleurs du Mal* as 'mon semblable – mon frère', it is quite possible that this difference makes little difference: that Godard sees himself doubled in Juliette, whose discomfort in her world is merely more instinctive, and sisterly. After all, while he quotes Wittgenstein ('the limits of my language are the limits of my world'), she references Heidegger ('language is the house man lives in'). Godard's self-doubt regarding which tree to show us, or the right moment for showing an image (so he gives it twice, enabling its arrival in different times), matches the hesitations of an important half-monologue, half-dialogue, spoken by Juliette:

It's because my impressions aren't always precise. Take desire for instance. I know sometimes what it is I desire. At other times, I don't know. For example, I know there's something missing in my life, but I don't really know what. Or I feel scared though there's nothing particular to be frightened about. [Pause] Which expressions are not related to any specific objects? Ah yes! Order. Logic. Yes, for example, something can make me cry, but … but the reason for those tears is not directly connected with the actual tears that trickle down my cheeks. In other words, everything I do can be described but not necessarily the reasons for which I do it.[42]

The dislocation of affect from any visible cause corresponds to the hesitations generated by the arbitrary relationship of colour and object – and possibly by the one-time black-and-white director's experience of colour as a 'colouring in' of objects that pre-existed differently in earlier and neighbouring films. This separation divides desire against itself, causing the subject to wonder whether what attracts it is the object itself, or the colour it bears, possibly mendaciously. Kristeva might well connect the two, at least with regards to the female: inasmuch as the realm she terms the semiotic, one of undifferentiated colours and sounds, marks infantile experience, it is also that of the infant–mother dyad, and of the identification of the mother, because female, with colour. Such a linkage, however, would paper over the structuring fissure of Godard's work (which also involves a separability of self from itself, from the double who is the sister). It replicates the division between love and sensual pleasure otherwise known as prostitution – the 'prostitute with the heart of gold' being a wish-fulfilling or nightmarish substitute for the mother, rediscovering her after leaving home, on the street. The indifference Juliette feels towards the world flows from her status as 'mon semblable – ma soeur'. Unlike the mother, the sister represents a sphere from which desire has been erased. It is almost as if the projection of a sister figure constitutes a defensive response to the disintegration of the mother's image by the tarnishing realisation that, for all her warmth, she obeys the beck and call of another man. The fact that the primal 'elle' of Godard's title is an alienated Paris shows the city's capacity to push the child away even while professing affection for it. (Given the film's setting, could it be said to push it away into the suburbs?) The resultant condition is what Gregory Bateson terms a 'double-bind', the result of simultaneous, opposed injunctions: a mother stiffens as her son embraces her, then asks him, 'Don't you love me any more?'[43] It is as if Godard posits the generation of a similar effect by the co-existence of red and blue in the flags of imperialist nations constituting an 'axis of disharmony', which seems to attract as well as repel him: France, the USA and the UK. Whereas blue coolly recedes, being – as Branigan notes[44] – focused before the retina, red is focused within it, and so is perceived as 'warm' and 'interior'. Pulling in opposite directions, the two colours divide the perceiver like Bateson's aetiology of schizophrenia, of which both Juliette's dreams and Godard's fragmented film are analogues. Only at this level is there any harmony: one of artistic modernism and an equally dissonant social modernity.

POLITICAL PRIMARIES: *LA CHINOISE* (*THE CHINESE GIRL*) (1967)

Where *Two or Three Things I Know About Her* uses the word 'ensemble' to kick-start meditations on the odds against meaningful unity within a large-scale Parisian suburban housing complex, in the subsequent

La Chinoise 'the central question is perhaps how to do something *together* to remedy whatever is not past recall'.[45] The previous film having shown one cell of togetherness – the couple – as mutual separation and indifference, Marcuse-like, Godard seeks an effective collective subject in the young. After all, unity of purpose ought to be possible in a Maoist revolutionary cell, cells being singular, basic 'living atoms', but since this cell includes the 'revisionist' Henri, unity proves illusive. The primary colours forge similarly illusory connections. A colour-generated unity seems seductively possible when the armed Yvonne (Juliet Berto) crouches, bloody-faced, against a red wall behind a barricade of 'little red books'. However, a statement by Kirilov bears more weight, being backed up by Godard's montage and by his determined use not only of all primary colours but also of black (the blackboard) and white (the walls, the bookcase filling up wittily only with the 'little red book' – as if Mao's thought really did embody all earthly knowledge). Kirilov remarks: 'You sometimes hear statements like "use only the three colours, the three primary colours, blue, yellow and red, in their perfect purity and perfect balance" under the pretext that other colours are there already.' His derision of such 'pretexts', with their artificial exclusion of difference, is seconded immediately by Godard's insertion of a colour chart including such non-primaries as Egyptian violet and Prussian blue. The meaning of Kirilov's painting of a rainbow across the apartment's walls and furniture just before committing suicide is enigmatic, as he has not been excluded from the group, and the film intertwines anti-tsarist Russian anarchist/nihilist slogans with its Maoist ones. Whether Kirilov's cell membership indicates the confusion of his more Maoist comrades, Godard's own hope for a coalition of these movements, or an extension of the self-doubt pervading *Two or Three Things I Know About Her* remains moot. After all, suicide and murder are mutually translatable both for Freud and for many terrorists. Godard may quote Sartre, but his juxtaposition of suicide and terror recalls Camus, and it may be significant that his thoughts on political terrorism, *The Rebel,* followed the meditation on suicide of *The Myth of Sisyphus*.

One thing is certain, however: colour was the logical point of arrival of Godard's 1960s project. Pauline Kael astutely noted: '[t]he frames in a Godard film are perfectly suited to fast comprehension – one can see everything in them at a glance – and to quick cutting. They can move with the speed of a comic strip.'[46] Whence the attraction for Godard of the strong primaries of the comic strip to which he likened contemporary society. Their adoption airbrushed the grey that had haunted his black-and-white films, strengthening and simplifying the compositions still further, making figures and things pop out sharply against a recurrent whiteness. Moreover, the move to colour lends substance to his self-criticism, by placing his own images on the same plane as the seductive advertisements they quote, as well as ushering in a serious confrontation with the political sphere to which colour is central. Like all fundamental aesthetic changes, Godard's had multiple motivations. That array of reasons for change yielded increasingly complex images, as he became the colour montagist Eisenstein never had the chance to be.

NOTES

1. David Batchelor, *Chromophobia* (London: Reaktion, 2007 (2000)), p. 31 (emphasis in original).
2. Wassily Kandinsky, 'Reminiscences', in Robert L. Herbert (ed.), *Modern Artists on Art: Ten Unabridged Essays* (Englewood Cliffs, NJ: Prentice-Hall, 1964), p. 20.
3. Peter D. Ward, *Under a Green Sky: Global Warming, the Mass Extinctions of the Past, and What They Mean for Our Future* (New York: Smithsonian/HarperCollins, 2007).
4. Gaston Bachelard, *The Psychoanalysis of Fire*, trans. Alan C. M. Ross (Boston: Beacon Press, 1964), p. 95.

5. Victoria Finlay, *Colour: Travels through the Paintbox* (London: Sceptre, 2002), p. 4.

6. Ibid., p. 15.

7. Clyde Taylor, *The Mask of Art: Breaking the Aesthetic Contract – Film and Literature* (Bloomington and Indianapolis: Indiana University Press, 1998), p. 46.

8. Alexander Theroux, *The Primary Colors: Three Essays* (New York: Henry Holt, 1994). p. 58.

9. Quoted in Howard Caygill, *Walter Benjamin: The Colour of Experience* (London and New York: Routledge, 1998), p. 10.

10. John Hutchings, 'Folklore and the Symbolism of Green', *Folklore* 108 (1997), pp. 55–64.

11. Taylor, *The Mask of Art*, pp. 167–8.

12. Pier Paolo Pasolini, 'The Cinema of Poetry', in Bill Nichols (ed.), *Movies and Methods* (Berkeley, Los Angeles and London: University of California Press, 1976), pp. 552–3.

13. Charles Barr, 'CinemaScope: Before and After', from Richard Dyer MacCann (ed.), *Film: A Montage of Theories* (New York: E. P. Dutton, 1966), pp. 318–28.

14. Temple Grandin and Catherine Johnson, *Animals in Translation: Using the Mysteries of Autism to Decode Animal Behaviour* (New York: Scribner, 2005), p. 243 (emphasis in original).

15. André Bazin, *Jean Renoir*, trans. W. W. Halsey II and William H. Simon (New York: Delta, 1974), p. 130.

16. Ibid., p. 131.

17. Ibid.

18. Ibid. (emphasis in original).

19. Ibid., p. 132.

20. Ibid., p. 135.

21. Umberto Eco, 'The Structure of Bad Taste', *Italian Writing Today* (Harmondsworth: Penguin, 1967), p. 119.

22. Bazin, *Jean Renoir*, p. 130.

23. Christopher Faulkner, *The Social Cinema of Jean Renoir* (Princeton, NJ: Princeton University Press, 1986).

24. Brian Price, 'Color, the Formless, and Cinematic Eros', in *Color: The* Film *Reader*, ed. Angela Dalle Vacche and Brian Price (New York and London: Routledge, 2006), p. 85.

25. Ibid., p. 86.

26. Wilhelm Worringer, *Abstraction and Empathy: A Contribution to the Psychology of Style* (New York: International Universities Press; London: Routledge and Kegan Paul, 1953).

27. Ryszard Koszarski, '*Foolish Wives*: The Colour Restoration that Never Happened', *Film History* vol. 12 no. 4 (2000), pp. 341–3.

28. András Bálint Kovács begins his thoughtful discussion of the relationship between the notions of 'modernism' and 'avant-garde' by noting that '[i]n general, "avant-garde" is used to designate politically conscious, antibourgeois, activist art movements', Bálint Kovács, *Screening Modernism: European Art Cinema, 1950–1980* (Chicago and London: University of Chicago Press, 2007, p. 14). His conclusion, however, is that in cinema '[t]he avant-garde practice opposes fictional narrative, and this opposition seldom translates into political terms' (Ibid., p. 28). I too would qualify the generalisation he quotes at the outset, but slightly differently. First, all modernists might be deemed 'anti-bourgeois', albeit differing from an avant-garde conceived in the terms Bálint Kovács summarises, for their non-activism and frequent apparent depoliticisation gave a different meaning to (and inserted into different social contexts) a stylistic defamiliarisation otherwise coeval with that of the avant-garde. (This partial kinship was what enabled Benjamin to laud both Brecht and Kafka and to forge his unstable personal synthesis of surrealism and Marxism.) It should be added also that the activism mentioned here is of the left; modernists were unlikely to

join parties, not even the right-wing ones with which some clearly sympathised. Second, the notion of avant-garde itself could be considered internally polarised, encompassing both activist artists and completely non-figurative and apparently apolitical ones. This polarisation manifested itself primarily in the visual arts, where movements proliferated to an extent unseen in the other artforms, generating a plethora of those quasi-political entities known as manifestoes. Thus the visual arts contain more figures describable as avant-gardists, while the other arts number more designable as 'modernists'. The film-maker's position as almost invariably part of a collectivity complicates nomenclature considerably where cinema is concerned. Membership of a collectivity, for instance, pushes him or her towards the visual artists who also tend to form movements; however, the use of successive images usually sparks a dialogue with an idea of narration rejected by most visual art avant-gardists.

29. Siegfried Kracauer, *From Caligari to Hitler: A Psychological History of the German Film* (Princeton, NJ: Princeton University Press, 1974 (1947)), pp. 182–8.

30. Pauline Kael, *Going Steady* (Boston and Toronto: Little, Brown and Co., 1970), p. 83.

31. David Bordwell, 'The Art Cinema as a Mode of Film Practice', *Film Criticism* vol. 4 no. 1 (1979), pp. 56–64.

32. Cf., for instance, Bálint Kovács, *Screening Modernism*, pp. 7–32.

33. John Orr, *Contemporary Cinema* (Edinburgh: University of Edinburgh Press, 1998), pp. 1–19.

34. Gabriel Josipovici, *The World and the Book* (St Albans: Paladin, 1973), pp. 293–317.

35. For insightful discussion of this division, see Anne Hollander, *Sex and Suits* (New York: Knopf, 1994), pp. 61–2 in particular.

36. Edward Branigan, 'The Articulation of Colour in a Filmic System: *Deux ou trois choses que je sais d'elle*', in Dalle Vacche and Price, *Color*, pp. 171–2.

37. Jean-Luc Godard, *Godard: Three Films* (New York, Evanston, San Francisco, London: Harper and Row, 1975), p. 146.

38. Branigan, 'The Articulation of Colour in a Filmic System', p. 178.

39. Mark Kingwell, *Concrete Reveries: Consciousness and the City* (Viking Canada: Toronto and New York, 2008), p. 12.

40. Ibid., pp. 12–13.

41. Julia Kristeva, 'Giotto's Joy', in Kristeva, *Desire in Language: A Semiotic Approach to Literature and Art* (New York: Columbia University Press, 1980), p. 221.

42. Godard, *Godard*, pp. 135–6.

43. Gregory Bateson, *Steps to an Ecology of Mind* (New York; Ballantine Books, 1972), p. 217.

44. Branigan, 'The Articulation of Colour in a Filmic System', pp. 174–5.

45. Jacques Bontemps, '*La Chinoise*', in Charles Barr, Stig Björkman, Barry Boys *et al.*, *The Cinema of Jean-Luc Godard* (New York: Praeger, 1969), p. 158.

46. Kael, *Going Steady*, p. 83.

B : MONOCHROME AND THE PRIMARIES

3 Colour and/as Monochrome

THE DIALECTIC OF COLOUR AND BLACK AND WHITE

The terms 'colour' and 'black and white' enact a dialectic of simultaneous opposition and prickly supplementation, as white and black may also be seen as 'colours' and their supposed 'opposition' to colour be a trick of language, ideology or history. In the cinema, of course, monochrome was for many decades the norm against which colour film defined itself, be it as the luxurious sign of technological wonder and/or fantasy, or as an adjunct of the realistic reproduction of a world we assume is coloured. Disparities between often crudely supersaturated screen colours and the actual subtlety of real ones could either be pilloried as kitsch or – less frequently – excused as art's inevitable tribute to convention. Whether white and black should be seen as colours or as the prelude and epilogue to colour is a moot point, despite their absence from the spectrum, or the fact that the colours of objects become visible only when their illumination rises above the basic level that reveals only their shapes. After all, Brent Berlin and Paul Kay have argued that the first 'colour' names to manifest themselves in any language are those for black and white, with that for red coming next.[1] When Eisenstein speaks of black and white as 'colours', he may seem to be guilty of special pleading.[2] And yet a long tradition exists of seeing black and white not as extra-territorial to colour, but as each containing potentially one half of the range of the spectrum. Thus Margaret Visser notes, summarising recent scholarship, 'red used to be really the only colour. Before the discovery of the spectrum in the seventeenth century, all other colours tended to be considered variations of either black (brown, blue, green, violet) or white (yellow, beige, cream and other very pale tints). Our colour range was therefore black–red–white.'[3] Michel Pastoreau argues that the present moment is one at which '[b]lack has reclaimed the status it possessed for centuries, even for millennia – that of a color in its own right'.[4] For him, the effects upon the definition of 'colour' of the Newtonian discovery of the spectrum are now past. The 'new' language games now playable with the word are, for him, really recrudescent ones. Setting black and white against colour may also be a late-nineteenth-century reflex, for which black and white represent unnecessary limitations on the wealth of colour rendered available by colonialism and industrial chemistry. If the revolt against black and white often charges them with oppressiveness, repressiveness or blandness, such libertarian rhetoric is also a capitalist protest against restrictions on trade, that is, limits on the process of alienation. The revolt is surely related also to the perception of black and white as absolutes, and hence as pillars of a religious ethos becoming subject to questioning. The rapid expansion of Nietzsche's influence suggests he was not the only *fin-de-siècle* intellectual to wish to go beyond the Good and Evil they had symbolised, but rather watered a seed dormant elsewhere.

The dialectic of colour and monochrome assumes various forms, some of which will be considered later in this book. Libertarian in mode, the *fin-de-siècle* resurgence of colour is one of expressivity: in particular, the blocked expressivity of the feminine in a society of monotonous, monochrome repetition, the nineteenth century run by tribes of 'men in black'. Ironically, of course, those men themselves made such expressivity possible through the new industrial dyeing techniques they developed. Insofar as colour stands out, it signifies any individualistic self-assertion. Thus Hawthorne probably need not have used red, let alone the hyper-visible red stigmatised as scarlet, as the key colour of his best-known work: any strong colour might have done. Strong colours further the modernist dispute with realism, casting the latter as a repression conceived as monochromatic, and either advocate its supplementation with a liberating colour – the optimistic early phase of modernism known as impressionism – or demonstrate the effects of that repression, as in the later, more pessimistic expressionism, whose scream is the loudness of a colour unable to find a proper place in the world. Is this one reason why Munch's famous *Scream* exists in so many versions, the multiplicity indicating the essential homelessness of colour, whose plurality of possible contexts can add up to a lack of context?

If filmic colour is defined in part through a dialectical relationship with monochrome, it is high time to sketch some of the key forms of this dialectic.

First comes the above-mentioned relationship with realism, and the contradictoriness of its signifiers. In *Der Stand der Dinge* (*The State of Things*) (1982) Wim Wenders identifies realism with black and white, though without mounting any protest against this form, as it is in fact the (at the time) anomalous one of his own film. If realism is as 'gritty' as stereotype dictates, it will indeed gravitate towards monochromaticism, though a Lukács might deem this indicative of a degeneration into naturalism. Ironically, though, at a certain stage in film history monochrome assumes a nostalgic glamour whose use in rock videos can compromise songs defined as committed to institutionalised protest. Monochrome is thus contradictory, its sharp contrasts paradoxically breathing both the melodrama of realist protest against social oppositions and the sharp outlines of a fashion whose bearers cut through the world with the smoothness of the commercial, the couturier's scissors.

Inasmuch as realism vaunts both its sobriety and its (concomitant) commitment, the probability rises that film-makers who have reflected upon the connotations of colour use and seek the impact of political protest would utilise monochrome, in part or in whole, to indicate identification with deprivation and the virtue stereotypically attached to a 'poor cinema'. Thus motivated, a once-frequent founding parti pris for black and white may override one element of the political that would favour colour film: after all, the political sphere is one of the primary areas in which colour is continually present, both verbally and visually, designating allegiances in ways that are often felt not to be arbitrary. The red usually taken as denoting passion appears logically to signify revolutionary anger, the belief that making history necessarily involves the bloodshed sometimes euphemistically yellowed into a 'making of omelettes'. Meanwhile, for the conservative, calm blue designates the untroubled naturalness of the social order, a valued restraint. Simultaneously, bluebloods demonstrate how far cultivation has raised them above a nature where blood is normally red. Owning such blood, they think it bound never to flow, but always to be preserved as a set of blue canals coursing the surface of the skin, while their opponents may become all the more determined to shed it precisely to show it as red as any commoner's. Where colour is made to signify politically, even colour harmonies become dissonant through their subordination to the hidden melodramatic logic usually described as one of 'black and white'. It is thus appropriate that Lars Von Trier's most explicitly political work, *Europa* (1991) – which is also 'melodramatic' in almost all of the senses of that often-elastic word, and whose subject is contestation at the heart of the body politic – should take black and white as its main tonality, while also allowing colour to bleed into it at points (at one, quite literally, as blood oozes from slit wrists).

Von Trier's film (of which more below) is particularly interesting in its overlaps with another form of film that activates the colour/monochrome dialectic at the levels structuralist film theory calls *histoire* and *discours*, in story and in its formal enunciation, to demonstrate the reality of realms usually deemed fantastic. Since the most significant examples of this mode lie in the films of Andrei Tarkovsky (particularly *Solyaris* (*Solaris*) (1972) and *Offret Sacrificate* (*The Sacrifice*) (1986)), Von Trier's indebtedness to the Russian is hardly surprising. If Tarkovsky's first colour film is both cast in the science-fiction genre and yet tolerates the apparent ancientness of passages in black and white, Stanley Cavell, who deems colour indicative of futurity, might well have seen the director's misgivings about the morality of humanity's cosmic probings as an unsurprising rider of the inserted monochrome moments. It is worth noting that the colours pervading the earth whose natural forms and rhythms Tarkovsky reveres are shown as already withdrawn from it in the city traversed, pre-launch, by the former cosmonaut Berton.

Where colour film is the norm, and a combination of realism and spectacle the default position of mainstream narrative, the norm for representation of a past defined as different becomes not monochrome but a *muted* colour. Such muting is overdetermined, capable also of signifying such forms of Otherness as the rural (the past of so many modern city-dwellers) or another country (in its fully overdetermined form, 'the country as another country'). It functions thus in *Capote* (2005) and *Das Leben der Anderen* (*The Lives of Others*) (2006). In the former, it represents both the rural and the past; in the latter, the past and another country. Thus, the design team for *Capote* eliminated blues and reds from the film's palette. Similarly, Von Donnersmarck created a sense of 'East Germanness' by removing these two colours from the locales where *The Lives of Others* was shot. Spectatorial comments lauding the unusual realism of the resultant image of East Germany surely illustrate the intersection of this muted colour scheme, perceived as realistic, with the projected stereotype of Eastern-bloc greyness. The film also fused this idea of uniformity with one of the pervasiveness of the typical muted (camouflaged) hues of uniforms. It is as if the audience believed – not without reason – that a society under heavy surveillance could only be a militarised environment. The German Democratic Republic itself becomes a fusion of colour and monochrome whose 'seeping sepiasation' of reality may have sought to anaesthetise the populace, neutering the oppositions that could have engendered change.

The Lives of Others: predominantly grey GDR

Finally, it is worth mentioning a category of possible particular interest to the above-mentioned Tarkovsky, with his fascination by the transcendent and the invisible: what might be called 'invisible colour', as its application to the image *behind the scene and behind the seen* materially yet invisibly alters its impact. Thus Tonino Delli Colli, the cinematographer on Pier Paolo Pasolini's *Mamma Roma* (1962), described the effect of shooting it through an orange filter: the whites popped out and the blacks became more intense.

THEORISING COLOUR, BLACK AND WHITE AND THE REAL

Some of the most useful theoretical reflections on the relationship between colour and monochrome may be found in the writings of Stanley Cavell, Anne Hollander and Aldous Huxley. Inasmuch as the theories of Cavell and Hollander overlap in several respects, I will consider their work first. Huxley's, although earlier, may then be taken as in part a corrective, or alternative, to theirs.

The ruminations on colour and its relationship to monochrome found in Cavell's *The World Viewed* are often penetrating, if unsystematic. Although he does not number them, Cavell distinguishes three colour strategies, all involving fantasy: 1) the 'children's tale' fantasy of *The Wizard of Oz* (1939) or the Errol Flynn *The Adventures of Robin Hood* (1938); 2) the film that uses colour to declare that its present is in fact impregnated with futurity (*Deserto rosso* (*Red Desert*) (1964), *Petulia* (1968), *Bullitt* (1968)); and 3) the film whose colouration signals a private fantasy (*Vertigo* (1958), *Rosemary's Baby* (1968)). With each successive category, unfortunately, the argument explicitly relating the relevant films to colour becomes more and more exiguous. The reader can only guess how the presence of colour in the film, or even the narrative it unfolds, renders, say, *Petulia* or *Bullitt* futuristic, though references to abstraction offer a hint (the full-screen blood-slide of *Petulia* is 'a frame-filling abstraction',[5] and *Bullitt* offers 'a complete and abstract world'[6]). The implication is that abstraction loosens the grip on the present, an effect augmented by the foregrounding of technology and possibly more apparent to non-Americans, given the widespread view of the American present as the probable (often desirable) future of much of the globe's remainder. Although one man's private fantasy is obviously central to *Vertigo*, its relationship to the fact of colour is addressed only through the somewhat vague notion of 'colour space': 'the film establishes the moment of moving from one color space into another as moving from one world into another'[7] – an idea of different worlds one might assimilate into the film's play with symbols of the supernatural. If '[f]antasy is precisely what reality can be confused with',[8] the reader can only assume that adding colour to the arsenal of filmic reproduction renders it more overwhelmingly prone to the fantastic, anticipating the lurch towards fantasy in mainstream American film-making as of the late 1970s, and the subsequent ascendancy of Lucas and Spielberg. More to the point is a later definition of 'the work of colour in serious films as a de-psychologizing or un-theatricalizing of their subjects',[9] which implicitly underpins the correlation of colour with futurity (in category 2) and with fantasy (categories 1 and 3). It is in its linkage of the perception of drama to that of monochrome, and the advent of colour to a de-personalisation of characters, that Cavell's essay is most suggestive.

That linkage inaugurates the work's more tightly integrated comparison of the effects of monochrome and colour. The intense visual contrasts of black and white persuade viewers to take reality 'dramatically', and so accept as reality a world of similarly sharp contrasts. This 'clarifies what it is about film that invited the outline clarity of types and justified those decades of melodrama, comedies, machines and scenes of exploration, motions of adventure and chase'.[10] It is significant that melodrama, whose moral black and white draws the clearest outlines of all, should appear first in this list of forms of mono-chrome film. Its paradigmatic relationship to the subsequent list passes unmentioned, however, while Cavell alternates confusingly between fusing melodrama and drama[11] and deeming melodrama drama's historical successor.[12] And yet the thesis that, in the late nineteenth century, '[s]ociety and the percep-tion of society move past drama into melodrama',[13] requires a fuller definition of 'melodrama'. Bearing in mind the theories of Peter Brooks, one might characterise it as a drama of faith and salvation dis-placed from the church in which it had first been promulgated.[14] In the context of the compressed intellectual history Cavell provides, this development could be described as unconsciously reattach-ing to the Hegelian and Marxist dramatistic view of history the religion they had pared away from it. Thus cinema, born in the late-Victorian heyday of melodrama, might be seen not so much as persuading viewers to cease to take reality 'dramatically'[15] as affording a fusion of the surfaces of the real with a melo-drama animated by a fantasy of legible reality, in a period whose doubts concerning such legibility are registered in modernism.

Meanwhile, the theorisations of 1950s melodrama by Thomas Elsaesser and Geoffrey Nowell-Smith[16] link its development then to colouristic 'excess'. All these theories could be correlated with Cavell's gnomic remarks. Thus (Brooks), in the work of Griffith in particular, with its sacralisation of female beauty and evocations of Good and Evil in the conflicts of groups, religious categories are cinema-tised. Similarly (Elsaesser and Nowell-Smith), the excess of colour in later melodrama can blunt the thrust of drama by luxuriating in the detail of its depiction, the Sirkian levelling of the distinction between characters and objects in particular suggesting the overwhelming reification of their world. However, not only are these two incarnations of melodrama not fully compatible; neither takes into account the 'women's picture' that overlaps partially with both. Thus Cavell needs – and fails – to define some of his key terms. Had he defined more closely the relationship between drama and melodrama, for instance, he might have joined Anne Hollander in deeming the thriving media tendency to link the graphic, the truthful and the sensational a defining feature of modernity.

Hollander's elegant, eloquent aphoristic formulations trace the lineage of the identification of mono-chrome with truth to the post-Renaissance tradition of graphic reproduction of paintings in popular printed art. 'The language of monochrome vision has been the great *lingua franca* of Western art,' she concludes.[17] If 'graphic' means both 'the written' and 'also means "like truth"',[18] the implication is that filtering out colour, while diminishing the verisimilitude of the image, clarifies an original of which it constitutes a reading. Increased clarity is the direct result of the elimination of colours defined as dis-tracting, dazzling, deceptive. In an equation whose Protestant and Puritanical underpinnings Hollander might have emphasised, black and white radiates 'unadorned truthfulness'.[19] In an arresting, disturbing dichotomy, she opposes the truth of monochrome to the reality of colour, and, possibly echoing Cavell, argues that '[b]y extension, photographs and movies in black and white are considered good because they are so true, not because they are so real'.[20] Indeed, the quotient of lifelikeness available to colour is inversely proportional to that of truthfulness. If colour can be deemed 'entrancing and misleading',[21] its suitability for fantasy becomes patent. Such fantasy lacks the near-synonymity with 'the subjective' often attributed to it; however, as the centrality of lighting to monochrome enhances its capacity 'to suggest … the subjective truth of feeling, which is signified by the image of presently falling light that must always illuminate one particular point of view'.[22] Narrative can manage without colour, as '[i]n colored popular art, the color serves the interests of pleasure, not of meaning'.[23]

For all their suggestivity, Hollander's remarks are limited by their primary derivation from a graphic tradition whose centrality to North European (Dutch and Germanic) art correlates with a Protestantism for which the graphic – as text and reading – mattered as much as the image, and with the muting of colour's insistence in North European climates. Moreover, the focus on graphic art and its popular cinematic legacy downplays the significance of modernist practices. This is regrettable, as Hollander displays keen insight into some of the qualities of colour that motivated its privileging by the modernists. For instance, her remark that '[a]mbiguous feelings, uncomfortable facts, or uncertain circumstances may be apprehended only through the sensory veil of color, which then gives the subject an extrinsic measure of stress or delight'[24] illuminates the modernist privileging of both undecidability and form. The comment that in a Matisse painting '[t]he web of color holds the woman on the sofa and inside the room forever'[25] suggests the Antonioni of *Red Desert*. Modernist colour means more than beautification and distraction. Even its luxury is more than that: as Eric Rohmer subtly notes, in films such as *Jigokumon* (*Gate of Hell*) (1953) or *Lola Montès* (1955) '[c]olour is an additional refinement, a luxury, which, for these luxurious subjects, is almost a necessity'.[26] Hollander's bias – derived in all probability from her overriding commitment to the narrative forms modernism critiqued – causes her to conclude that 'disjointed' works can be 'irritating and easy to forget'.[27] Despite her awareness of the pervasive randomness of film,[28] her sophisticated denial of realism to colour does not extend into an appreciation for modernist anti-realism. After all, only of mainstream movies can it be stated that 'even movies in colour are graphic – that is, essentially black-and-white'.[29] The modernist colours of Antonioni, Godard, or Kieślowski refuse the melodrama of the graphic.

Although the identification of colour with fantasy is common, and theorised pregnantly by both Cavell and Hollander, an opposed identification also exists: it ascribes colour both to quotidian solid reality, and to domains claiming to trump it. In a passage interweaving mysticism and science, Huxley adduces dreams as primary exhibits in his theorisation of two varieties of symbolisation and the distance they create from the reality of 'the given': the transfer from colour to monochrome often thought to prevail in most dreams; and the abstraction from reality effected by language.

> Colour turns out to be a kind of touchstone of reality. That which is given is coloured; that which our symbol-creating intellect and fancy put together is uncoloured. Thus the external world is perceived as coloured. Dreams, which are not given but fabricated by the personal subconscious, are generally in black-and-white.[30]

> The images of the archetypal world are symbolic; but since we, as individuals, do not fabricate them, but find them 'out there' in the collective unconscious, they exhibit some at least of the characteristics of given reality and are coloured. The non-symbolic inhabitants of the mind's antipodes exist in their own right, and like the given facts of the external world are coloured. Indeed, they are far more intensely coloured than external data. This may be explained, at least in part, by the fact that our perceptions of the external world are habitually clouded by the verbal notions in terms of which we do our thinking. We are forever attempting to convert things into signs for the more intelligible abstractions of our own invention. But in doing so, we rob these things of a great deal of their native thinghood.[31]

'Symbol' here does not mean the Romantic synonym for plenitude but rather the sign. If, in the domain of visionary experience Huxley terms 'the mind's antipodes' 'objects do not stand for anything but themselves',[32] this self-sufficiency matches a fullness of colouration indicating that *nothing is missing from them*, unlike the absence constitutive of the sign. What Cavell, Hollander and all materialists would decry as fantasy is for Huxley a self-sufficient, transcendent reality comparable to that of the Platonic forms of which human symbols – be they dreams or words – are abstractions and veiled reflections. If colour features prominently in mystical texts, its widespread association with filmic fantasy may be a dim, secularised afterimage of a disposition expelled from the public sphere under modernity, but possibly living on, as memory and shadow, in the unconsciousness represented by the cinema's darkness.[33]

BLACK AND WHITE, COLOUR AND SIEGFRIED KRACAUER

Siegfried Kracauer's theory of colour, sketched in a brief 1937 article for *Das Werk* entitled 'On the Aesthetic of the Colour Film', begins with paradox declaring monochrome more colourful than colour. The colour of a film like *The Garden of Allah* (1936),

> can express nothing of what the black-and-white film … is able to express without its help. It [black and white] has conjured up the blue distance more tenderly than occurs now through the mixing in of blue; it has caught the harsh light, the heat and the powerful contrasts of the desert landscape in images whose colourfulness far outstrips that of *The Garden of Allah*.[34]

Lest anyone think the desert an excessively convenient example for such an argument, relentless sun having stripped it of the variegated colours of living entities, one should note how Kracauer underpins it in terms derived from Vsevolod Pudovkin's advocacy of montage as a constructor of meaning opposed to the 'confused accumulation of accidents'[35] found in faithful reproductions of the appearances of nature. Montage 'destroys insignificant resemblances' in order to bring out the truly significant, imbuing images with 'the power of language', dismissing the conventional 'postcard perspective'.[36] For Kracauer, an 'independence of the object' resembling that forged by montage was achieved in black-and-white film by the absence of colour.[37] Like the film-maker employing montage, the painter in colour 'masters the task of compelling meaning from the colour material, and his images are eloquent to the extent that they are not "reproductions"'.[38] In this respect, as in several others,[39] Kracauer seems to anticipate the Antonioni who would literally paint natural objects in *Red Desert*. However, inasmuch as Kracauer attributes a 'childish joy' in the technically feasible to the colour film, he may be seen as implicitly echoing the (compensatory?) European ascription of childishness to an America conceived as the well-spring of such technical innovations. Colour film yields 'a diffuse multiplicity' that has not been 'penetrated'[40] – in other words, shaped, organised and understood. Its banal modality of vision reduces the world to picture postcards. Nevertheless, because montage has become habitual in film-making (it is unclear whether the term here means ordinary editing, or a Soviet-style contrast-oriented one), it appears even in colour films.

Positing the principles of montage and colour as opposed, Kracauer might well have deemed colour films aesthetically incoherent. And yet, his last three paragraphs critique not colour film per se but its yoking to clichés. Colour film needs to proceed from a basis in montage. Given Kracauer's pointed earlier contrasting of these two elements of film-making, readers might think this unlikely, but his move away from considerations of possible representation shows how it might happen: through the constitutive abstraction of animation. (The appreciation of animation and montage suggests a move from a Pudovkinian model to an Eisensteinian one.) The tired dog on the glacier who receives brandy from a St Bernard goes from green to red as he is rejuvenated.[41] In other words, colour functions here not as an object's property but as a sign, and the image has the linguistic quality ascribed to montage earlier. Even the otherwise deplorable *Garden of Allah* achieves a non-banal use of colour in its dance sequence. It is surely significant that Kracauer terms this dance 'kaleidoscopic',[42] the implication being that, as in a kaleidoscope, the dance's rapid succession of colours undermines the trite realism of pairing one colour immutably with one object. Kracauer's intention, both here and in his cartoon example, is to separate colours from objects to stress objects' openness to metamorphosis. One might even see this as transforming the temporal forward movement of images by montage into a 'montage within the image', the firework-like unfolding of a series of possibilities on a single spot. By emphasising the brevity of such passages,[43] he provides further grounds for reading colour as best keyed to transition and transformation. One might link this to a central characteristic of fantasy: the visibility of metamorphosis. Colour would thus be an ephemeral, temporarily highlighted element of cinema, like the fantasy Kracauer's later *Theory of Film*[44] subordinates resolutely to realism. The Kracauer of this essay might well have found in his theory an approved place for the dance sequence in Eisenstein's *Ivan Groznyy II: Boyarsky zagovor* (*Ivan the Terrible Part II*) (1958). His final statement that, when used in this way, 'colour becomes a necessary component of the overall montage',[45] represents somewhat less of a concession when one realises how it marginalises colour into a momentary mythology.

COLOUR AND STARDOM

Writing of how 'the rule of five' furnishes 'an approximate formula for the number of stimuli that the eye can perceive and integrate simultaneously',[46] Gerald Mast argues that the simplification of the visual effected by black-and-white film 'frees our concentration for such stimuli as the evocations of the faces of the stars, the richness of verbal dialogue, and the complexity of narrative structure'.[47] Writing in the late 1970s, he sees all three declining in tandem with monochrome.

Asserting a decline of stardom may appear unusual amid a pervasive cultural obsession with celebrity, and Mast notes the possible influence of other factors: the way 'the repetitive exposure of audiences to a star in the studio era not only fixed the archetype in the culture, but also produced expectations in an audience about what each archetype would do'.[48] (Following a different tack, one might distinguish between stardom and celebrity: the former involving an unassailable, studio-maintained elevation; the latter, 'wheel of fortune' revolutions of rise and inevitable fall.) Although Mast does not put it thus, the studio reinforcement of a type could indeed propel it towards the archetypical. What frees 'type' to become 'archetype' is the absence of the 'noise' of such aspirations as actors' desires to demonstrate range by going against type, to become directors themselves and of an uncontrolled celebrity magazine gossip seeking not the fanzine's strengthening of a single image but rather its prurient subversion. Equally important factors, however, may be the possibility of describing the monochromatic processes Mast rightly deems simplifying as ones of abstraction and etherealisation. It may indeed matter little that Don Lockwood, the silent star of *Singin' in the Rain* (1952), cannot act, as he is essentially elevated into an image whose simultaneous difference, mobility and mortality tantalisingly suggest the possibility that his form, albeit refined by monochrome, might intersect at some level with the fan's everyday reality. Contrastingly, colour reassigns him to the flesh from which monochrome had extracted him. (The converse of this is, of course, the possibility of a different monochrome, that of Von Stroheim, whose naturalistic glee drains away human anima to leave only a residue of the animal, yielding not gods but beasts.) Colour seems to replace stars with figures who alternate between celebrities and actors. The stars tumble to earth, limp away from the site of their fall.

THE GRAPHIC, THE TRUTHFUL AND THE REVOLUTIONARY

Commenting on the long European tradition of reproducing famous paintings and sculptures in graphic art, Anne Hollander notes two sedimented associations of the word 'graphic': ' "Graphic" means "like writing"; it now also means "like truth".'[49] She overlooks a third one, revealed as primary by a straw poll among my undergraduate students: 'the sensational'. Hollander's decision to mention it only later, and only incidentally,[50] may be motivated by the frequency with which sensation and truth are seen as opposed. Nevertheless, the words often intertwine: for instance, the perception that a truth is being uttered, puncturing regimes of falsehood, can unleash a sensation. Truth is often described as 'naked', its unvarnished charge blowing away the de-fusing, filtered sophistication of 'the nude'. If pursuits of 'the sensational' are often identified with ones of popularity, it is because truth creates a sensation by over-throwing established orders. If its populism has political ambitions, they are those of English Puritans whose 'world upside down' was kingless, or of Orson Welles' Citizen Kane employing the yellow press as a plat-form towards high office. This meaning of 'graphic' joins the others inasmuch as the truth in question is that of a new word, or language itself dispelling images and idolatry. For the Puritans, of course, this new word was the biblical text in the vernacular. Its 'black and white' is both 'black on white' and the vir-tuous poverty of its consumers, who lack the wealth to commission and possess coloured paintings, or – later – to take the Grand Tour and view the originals. Black and white thus becomes the sensa-tional sign of revolutions of image and word. Its abstracting distance from the world fosters viewers' unworldliness. Later, for the Russian revolutionaries, the text would be the revolutionary tract, the per-nicious image the falsely icon-like tsar. Because of the prevalence of the assumption that, as Hollander puts it, 'if a picture is in black and white, it can be apprehended more clearly, though it may be enjoyed less',[51] its graphic appearance facilitates popular understanding, dispelling the hedonism, distractions and mystifications of the ruling class at one thrust.

Thus a context emerges for the consideration of two texts: Sergei Eisenstein's 'On Colour',[52] and Vsevolod Pudovkin's Mat (Mother) (1926). On one level, their juxtaposition is an obvious one, as Eisenstein himself cites Mother as his main Soviet example of black and white functioning as 'colours'. His employment of the word 'colour' suggests a sophisticated recognition that any discussion of filmic colour should not only discuss, but probably begin with, black and white. It may also constitute a com-pensatory assertion that a colourless Soviet cinema can match its foremost ideological rivals, whose film industries were beginning to apply colour to features in the late 1930s. In maintaining that Soviet cinema has colour too, Eisenstein effects a revolutionary inversion of the apparent significance of the tech-nological superiority of American capitalism and German militarism. At the same time, such declarations are tempered by a recognition of realities. The first is that the schema of an advance from black, to grey, to white is not applied in a thoroughgoing fashion in Mother. Thus Eisenstein states that 'all three thematic colour tones might have merged into a final "coda" in the last scene; the black crowd of work-ers, the grey tones of the police and the victorious onrush of the white ice'. Not only did this not occur but '[u]nfortunately the third schematic colour – white – was not utilized in the overall colour compo-sition and was never brought out photographically'.[53] This particular reality may not be hard for Eisenstein to acknowledge, disputes with Pudovkin pervading his theory. More difficult, even traumatic, to accept are personal failings. Eisenstein's self-criticism may be fuelled by a mixture of admirable honesty and a hope that this exercise might avert the more vicious self-flagellations sought by Stalin's regime. He concludes by proposing to make a film in black and white that would invert their conventional moral valences, as it would concern a black revolt against slavery, with Paul Robeson in the lead.[54] Somewhat surprisingly, given his ongoing dialogue with Griffith, this prospective work's overturning of the racist symbolism of *The Birth of a Nation* (1915) goes unmentioned.

More can be said about the graphic in *Mother*, however. One might note that many of its images tap a reservoir of western artworks Pudovkin would probably have viewed in the monochrome reproductions Hollander describes. Jay Leyda gives chapter and verse, though his argument that the film makes its sources seem 'ornamental' may well be the effect of a comparison of black-and-white film with coloured originals, and of acceptance of a stereotypical identification of colour and ornamentation:

> Throughout *Mother*, unusually unified in graphic style as it is, the image often seems to have been scientifically stripped of every distraction. … By comparison with these stripped images, their many sources appear almost cluttered or ornamental – Velásquez' 'Bollo' that brought the famous camera angle of the monumental policeman into being; Van Gogh's 'Prison Courtyard' (after Doré), inspiration for the scene of the prison exercise hour; the carefully composed realism of Degas, the haggard blue-period paintings of Picasso and the prints of Käthe Kollwitz, that all contributed to the graphic representation of the mother; Rouault's three 'Judges' that helped to characterize Pudovkin's three judges.[55]

Moreover, graphic intentions inform the frequent low and high angles: the former silhouetting figures against sky; the latter, approximating them to shadows cast on ground whitened by sunlight, snow, or both. The graphic angles reinforce the work's analysis of brute power, as authorities loom with oppressive inhumanity, and managers look down upon prisoners. The 'graphic truth' here involves society's polarisation in class struggle: a reality the mother does not grasp until her son Pavel's imprisonment. The popular overthrow of the high and mighty may not yet be possible, as the film's demonstrations are the defeated ones of 1905, but its future occurrence is blazoned forth by the red flag whose fluttering is graphic and allegorical in the sense of implicitly spelling out a word, 'revolution', at the work's end.

On the other hand, in the course of time very different Soviet films would emerge, using colour and monochrome very differently. Among the most striking is Andrei Tarkovsky's *Solaris* …

SOLARIS, COLOUR AND MONOCHROME

On various occasions in Tarkovsky's *Solaris,* the camera will slide past a character's head – usually cosmonaut Kris Kelvin's – into a blankness or blackness, often that of a porthole, though sometimes a doorway (as occurs near the end of Kris's dream-visit to his mother). Timothy Hyman links this camera movement to the cosmonauts' experience of the ocean-planet Solaris: '[I]n the earlier sequences, where the camera will frequently pass out through windows into the blankness beyond, the ocean is experienced as a void, a threat the greater for being unspecific.'[56] Apt and evocative though this remark is, the blankness is surely multifunctional, being multicoloured, varying between black, white and yellow-gold. These colours may mark the time of planetary day, but they also represent tonalities of the transcendent, which resists representation: their variability embodies an oscillation between positive

Solaris: Hari materialises in the white, icon-like porthole-cum-portal

and negative poles that itself defines a transcendence of everything in between (in a sense, of the variegation of the earthly; tellingly, Tarkovsky avoids the blue–red alternation of Stanisław Lem's novel). The linkage is most obvious in the case of the gold-lit porthole, which echoes, and moves from a level of unconsciousness to one of consciousness, the smaller golden circles surrounding the heads of the Trinity placed unobtrusively in the Andrei Roublov reproduction in the background of Kris's room.

Within the work's dream-logic, this magnification is a de-condensation, while repetition on various scales embodies the endlessly re-embodying reproductiveness of the dream-work of the planet itself. (One recalls how Berton's report had described its reproduction of an infant in monstrously large dimensions.) Although the white porthole might seem simply positive, the description of Hari's demise as 'white light and wind' gives it the ambiguity of a partial conjugation of her suicide. Most thoroughly ambiguous, however, is the black porthole, reminiscent of the 'Black Circle' of Kasimir Malevich's 'modernist icon' series of black geometric shapes. This series had begun with his *Black Square* of 1915, the signature image of his Suprematist movement, which he hung in the top corner of a room, the place traditionally reserved for an icon. Some of Malevich's remarks resonate particularly strongly across the notions of science fiction Tarkovsky both activates and revises. 'My new painting', Malevich stated, 'does not belong to the earth exclusively. The earth has been abandoned like a house eaten up with worms. And in fact in man and his consciousness there lies the aspiration toward space, the inclination to "reject the earthly globe".'[57] Tarkovsky thus becomes an anti-Malevich, both recalling and revoking his project by simultaneously retaining the black icon and filling it with images of earth, and of the house, dissolving Malevich's earth–space opposition.

This dissolution is fullest during the camera's exploration of the work's key image, Pieter Brueghel's *Hunters in the Snow*. Given the film's shifts between monochrome and colour, it is hardly surprising that this privileged image balances between them, its reconciliation of different regimes of perception adumbrating one of separate orders of being. The key role played by Brueghel's painting allows one to speculate that the shortage of Kodak colour stock in the Soviet Union, noted by Richard Misek, may even have been the director's alibi for utilising both stocks, in line with intentions outlined in a 1966 interview, rather than the pragmatic cause of this approach, a suggestion Misek favours at first but then complicates.[58] Hari's contemplation of this image sparks her realisation of what it means to be on earth, which she is able to enter via the visually simplified, stripped-down forms of a winter landscape. (This is also, symbolically, an entry into emotion from what for her is the most accessible point, the one on its continuum marked 'cold', and signifying proximity to non-existence, as she edges into humanity at its degree zero – which is also close to where Kris himself is set emotionally.) The scene also foreshadows the ambiguous ending, when Kris may or may not really be upon the planet, may or may not really be at home, as the planet's imperfect recreation of the earthly images uncovered in Kris's mind also reconciles film and painting by restaging Rembrandt's *Return of the Prodigal Son* as the reunification of Kris and his father. Furthermore, its dark trees echo the ones that frame Tarkovsky's career, beginning *Ivanovo Detstvo* (*Ivan's Childhood*) (1962) and ending *The Sacrifice*, while the Brueghel view of the hunters from behind suggests his preoccupation with heads averted in spiritual resistance, obdurate self-absorption and mystery. As Hari dwells upon this picture, scanning it in a manner that matches her body's floating through the library together with Kris in the period of weightlessness shortly thereafter, she starts connecting the snowy scenes of Kris's home movie with a larger life. The continual dissolves suggest co-existent differences, even a dialectic within a picture plane incubating the qualitative leap that links it to the home movie. Painting and film, image and narrative, stasis and flux, are reconciled also, as the sequence's dissolves generate story and succession from the painting's simultaneity. The image could be defined as a materialisation within a porthole – belying Snauth's statement that the library has no windows – its status as a filling out of blankness emphasised by its recurrence on the surface of the blank TV screen in Kris's dream, like a dream-within-a-dream projected on what psychoanalyst Bertram Lewin would have called a 'dream screen'. (The fact that such 'dream screens' 'are thought to relate to infantile sleep and to symbolize the mother or breast'[59] renders it virtually a *mise en abyme* image of the dream of the mother in which it appears.) Within that dream, meanwhile, it is a dream-image that has not yet expanded to full identity with the screen onto which it is projected. The placement of a margin between the edge of the TV and that of the painting matches the tendency of film-makers to begin to employ colour expressively, as Tarkovsky does here and Hitchcock did in *Vertigo*, when seeking to dramatise a separability of surface and depth, the possible duplicity or substitutability of a reality whose colour-coding could equally well have differed. These two films echo one another in other ways, of course, as each interweaves memory, mourning and the fetishisation of a woman in a quasi-Freudian version of time-travel: fetishisation as the fantastic recovery of the pre-traumatic moment, freezing the clock's second hand into juddering, obsessive repetition. (No wonder Cavell describes Hitchcock's film in terms of the futurity it shares with science fiction, or that it should be a key film for the philosophical science fiction of Chris Marker's *Sans soleil* (Sunless) (1982).)

Hari's contemplation of *The Hunters in the Snow* immediately precedes the period of weightlessness. As that begins, and her body rises, a multicoloured stained-glass window becomes visible just behind and to the left of her head, while the space to her right includes a patch of blue (Kris's shirt) and one of green (below the Brueghel reproduction). It is as if Hari's connecting of the blacks and whites that dominate the painting to Kris's childhood home movie then permits her to link its fire to that of the movie, her ontogenetic recapitulation of the phylogenetic sequence of the emergence of colour words leading her, and the film, into a wider range of colours, as well as into the eros signified by the weightlessness. This happens gently and discreetly, as patches of white intersperse and buffer the contrasting reds and

Solaris: double vision: portions of *The Hunters in the Snow* over each other like ice-floes

blues of the stained-glass window, and the patches of blue and green are lapped by a more generally brown-black, shadowed space. Hari's development into ecstasy charts an evolution, recalling Tarkovsky's deliberate abjuration of the Eisensteinian pairing of revolution and ecstasy.

If *The Hunters in the Snow* represents the thematic heart of *Solaris*, it is because its wintry subject matter commits it equally to colour and to monochrome, suspending the distinction between two filmic optics that need to fuse for Hari, the planet's emissary to Kris, to achieve humanity, and for Kris to do so also. Hari's contemplation of this painting adumbrates a possible fusion of colour and monochrome whose simultaneous 'reality' and 'non-reality' is marked by her floating together with Kris immediately afterwards, a dialectical moment of both ecstatic metaphor and matter-of-fact rendition of the loss of gravity on the space station. This possibility, dependent upon a suspension of opposites, collapses in Kris's subsequent fevered dream, whose first half is coloured, but whose remainder is black and white.

The first part of that dream presents multiple images of Hari vertiginously circulating in a brightly lit room around Kris's bed, taking turns with an image of his mother in her youth, while its second part shows Kris and his mother alone in the family home. If the first half of this dream is overwhelming, coloured and silent, its latter half, conversely, is monochrome and replete with sustained dialogue between Kris and his mother. Hari's absence from the second portion of the dream suggests a move away from the unspoken and unspeakable earlier contamination of the image of the mother with the libidinal, during which wife and mother became interchangeable. Just as the advent of language distances primary process, monochrome divests the image of its sensuality. Insofar as it constitutes a moment of denial, it reprises Kris's earlier rejection of Hari. However, on this occasion the negation of Hari also involves her sublation: when Kris says he cannot recognise his mother's face, he echoes an earlier remark by Hari concerning her viewing of her own face, making the seeing of the mother readable as a form of the misrecognition of Hari herself by herself. In addition to this, the possibility of the mother's hidden identity with Hari – and status as her continuation by other means – is betrayed by her standing in front of *The Hunters in the Snow*, as had Hari. The echo of Hari's words within those of Kris measures the strength of her continued presence within him: after all, the planet had distilled her from a scanning of his brain. It is as if he has identified with her deep down, enabling him to say 'now I love her', and the two to become 'one flesh'. At the same time, though, the dream seems to intuit the death of Hari, which occurs at some undiscerned point in its unfolding. The onset of monochrome, and the disappearance of her image, may register unconsciously the moment of her real destruction. If she persists, and is resurrected again, this time it is invisibly, within the bodies of the mother and of Kris himself.

If Hari's is a double vision, suspended between humanity and the non-human, the hue in *The Hunters in the Snow* with key status for her will not be black or white, mutually bound in a binary, but the colour Richard Rodriguez has described as inherently double, essentially impure: brown, which,

> bleeds through the straight line, unstaunchable – the line separating black from white, for example. Brown confuses. Brown forms at the border of contradiction (the ability of language to express two or several things at once, the ability of bodies to experience two or more things at once).[60]

The final clause matches Hari's experience particularly closely: Rodriguez's experience as a Hispanic (his preferred self-designation) can stand for that of another tolerated alien. Moreover, if, inasmuch as they are named first in most languages, black, white and red constitute the three primal colours – not primaries of course – brown mediates between the regimes seen or classified as monochrome and that of the colours fanning out peacock-like across the spectrum, which we suppose 'true colours' in the apparently (though only apparently) tautological sense of 'most colourful'. Brown, the colour of branches, leads naturally to the colour it, and they, feed: the red of the fire in Kris's childhood home movie, which she links with the one in *The Hunters in the Snow*. The red that emerges from brown makes a primal connection: the leaping spark whose role in Hari's evolution matches that of fire for human culture (as in Lévi-Strauss's maps of 'the raw and the cooked', or the myth of Prometheus).

Hari's double vision correlates both with Tarkovsky's bisexuality,[61] and his awareness of censorship (and its near-inevitable progeny, self-censorship). The link between the bisexuality and the awareness of censorship can be made through some other reflections on brown by Rodriguez:

> My advantage (my sympathy toward brown and the bifocal plane) was due to the fact that from an early age I needed to learn caution, to avert my eyes, to guard my speech, to separate myself from myself. Or to reconstruct myself in some eccentric way.[62]

Such reconstruction is needed by Kris Kelvin, with Hari – the planet's gift – the instrument thereof. Man and wife become one flesh indeed, seeing with at least two sets of eyes. Insofar as the bisexuality involves an identification with the mother, Kris is 'pregnant' with Hari. It is because that pregnancy is only metaphorical that her abortion occurs so easily.

Tarkovsky experienced coloured shots as 'unbelievably, monstrously false', speculating that '[t]he explanation must surely be that colour, reproduced mechanically, lacks the touch of the artist's hand'. He argued therefore that its effect 'should be neutralized by alternating colour and monochrome sequences, so that the impression made by the complete spectrum is spaced out, toned down'.[63] In their careful study of Tarkovsky, Vida Johnson and Graham Petrie describe him as working 'within a deliberately restricted range in each film, rarely moving beyond muted tones of brown, green, blue, yellow, and grey, while using black and white as colours in their own right'.[64] Observing that no clear system appears to govern the colour/monochrome alternations, they declare it random, going so far as to attribute it on occasions to 'a shortage of good-quality colour stock'.[65] Along with the rationale for these movements, however, the effect on the spectator, along with any possible relationship between that effect and the film's themes, requires consideration. A good test case is the first sequence in *Solaris* of which it is an ongoing, puzzling characteristic: Berton's car-ride through the city of the future. This sequence, accompanied by an electronic soundtrack suggesting both relentless traffic-drone and the noise of a rocket's lift-off, focuses primarily on the road ahead of Berton. Brief sets of shots of Berton – later, beside his son – intersperse the sequence and appear in black and white. The sequence begins in black and white, but eventually shifts to colour, before returning to black and white and ending in colour. Viewers may wonder whether the appearance of a red taxi on the right-hand side of the screen motivated the first shift, as red declares a presence of colour that otherwise is not obtrusive, road and light being drab and monochromatic, and the car repeatedly swishing through tunnels and below overpasses. Later, there is another shift to black and white, showing Berton and his son, before a final return to colour in a night-time crescendo of multiple cars, their red rear lights flowing between buildings sporting mostly blue neon signs. The eventual cut away from the cacophonous autoroute is followed by a silent shot of the rural setting that had preceded the sequence, though this time in black and white, not colour.

One effect of these unrelenting images of the autoroute is to emphasise that even its colour is monotonous, rebarbative. The continual aural suggestion of both traffic and lift-off combines ambiguous meaning and monotony, yielding a blank unreadability. We may well be surprised that the final cut-away does not intensify still further the growing sense of alienation from the earth by projecting us into outer space, but rather shows quiet countryside. Despite the relief of a rural setting, we view it in a changed light. On one level, its monochrome appearance corresponds to a draining of vibrancy by the world from which it had seemed an oasis: our assaulted senses are still ringing. On another level, meanwhile, the cut prepares viewers for the possibility of a superimposition of displaced, technologised vision upon the image of home, a possibility actualised by the work's ending. (A similar fusion of at-homeness and displacement characterises Hari's scanning of *The Hunters in the Snow*, whose dissolving images will be married to electronic dissonances.) The alternation of monochrome and colour on the autoroute may demonstrate the oppressiveness of technologised experience, but, more positively, it also participates in the work's destabilisation of distinctions between reality and dream, outer and inner. The sequencing of a hypnotic monotony across different film-stocks may cause viewers to wonder just what they are seeing, as the differences seem not to signify. In retrospect, they may doubt the reliability of their memories, wondering what was monochromatic, what coloured. The nature of memory is a key theme of *Solaris*, of course, as the cosmonauts' 'guests' materialise their memories. The work's sheer length underlines the difficulty of remembering, as few spectators can retain all its elements and register on a first viewing the multiple interconnections between them. (In this respect, Tarkovsky's religious art is also modernistic.) Most important, however, is the sequence's role in Tarkovsky's evocation of a depersonalised humanity on the friable, uninhabitable edge of its world.

'LIFE, LIKE A MANY-COLOURED DOME OF GLASS': *STELLET LICHT* (*SILENT LIGHT*) (2007)

If Carlos Reygadas's *Silent Light* may be termed mystical, it is not just because of its indebtedness to Carl Dreyer's *Ordet* (*The Word*) (1955), whose Presbyterian white interiors return here as those of a

Mexican Mennonite community, while Dreyer's resurrection-scene white dazzles again in quotation. Perhaps more important is that this event is one termed impossible by one of its characters (Marianne, the object of the adulterous love of Johan, the protagonist), although she too subscribes to a Christian belief system founded upon resurrection: the turning back of time (a project resembling Kris Kelvin's?). It is as if the resurrection occurring here represents a cosmic response both to Esther's wish, as she sat in the car with Johan shortly before her death, that all would prove a bad dream, and to Johan's own desire to recover an innocent past. Reygadas's characters may be Christian, but his own position is more spiritual than religious, and more individualistic than communitarian or aligned with any creed. It is hardly surprising, therefore, that his title foregrounds that mystical element central to many religions, Light. Reygadas's interest is in the sacred. On the sole occasion of the word's use, Johan's friend Zacarías states that his feelings for Marianne may be 'sacred' in origin. Later, when his father describes them as coming from the Enemy, Johan himself declares 'I think this is the work of God.' Reygadas's interest in shooting interiors through a glass that both reveals inside reality and reflects the one without suggests a ghostly double exposure, in which each material reality is simultaneously immaterial – and this, in turn, is like Tarkovsky. No wonder this *sacrum* is ambiguous, its mysticism not just aspiring to distant light but embracing its coloured emanations, its messy encounter with the materiality of perspiring bodies. It is not only the supra-sensual One but the sensual everyday too: not just Shelley's 'white radiance of eternity', but 'the many-coloured dome of glass' he terms life, and describes as staining that radiance.

Reygadas's concern therefore is not just with the light that dawns for an awe-inspiring six minutes, as if in the Book of Genesis, at the film's start, sinking away at its end, as if to de-create the stumblings of the day measured by its solar passage: it is also with the epiphenomena of light, the sparks it emits. The camera opens itself to these emanations whenever it shoots straight into the sun, which sends transparent coloured balls floating all across the lens, light breaking up against it, like a wave becoming foam (the particles that represent the other identity of light). These flare-effects are particularly obtrusive on two occasions of earthly mysticism, one sacred-profane, the other more obviously sacred: when Johan kisses Marianne, and the sun shines from beyond them into the lens; and just after the resurrection of Esther, Johan's wife, cut down in the rain by a cardiac arrest upon learning of Johan's continuing infidelity. In each case, the event seems to be caused by a kiss (Johan and Marianne kissing; Marianne kissing the lips of Esther's dead body). The red and orange balls of colour gliding across a wheat-field at these moments suggest benign versions of the maleficent fireball of Nikita Mikhalkov's *Utomlyonnye solntsem* (*Burnt by the Sun*) (1994). Reygadas's primary Russian debt is to Tarkovsky nevertheless: if the motif of the turning back, or even stopping, of time suggests *The Sacrifice* (early on, Johan halts the pendulum of the family's kitchen clock), more Tarkovskian still is the balancing of a transfigured mysticism of light-as-fire with one of water. What one sees through is both a camera lens and an eye blurred by the tears all three protagonists shed: this lens does not bounce light off it in the form of variously hued balls and streaks, but rather dissolves. Water also veils objects in a manner congruent with Reygadas's interest in showing people and things out of focus – in one case dwelling lengthily on a purple flower as Johan and Esther bathe off-screen, though later it does appear clearly. It is as if, in another manifestation of mysticism, objects are thereby abstracted, losing their shape, acquiring a Kandinskian identity as sheer colour. Even when the sun is not shining, mysterious forces are brewing, freeing colours from the site of their first location, in an infidelity that is primal.

The space dominated by white light towards the film's end, the white space of resurrection, may be described rather as Gilles Deleuze characterises the 'lyrical abstraction' of Dreyer, in words possibly inspired by *The Word*, though it is not mentioned explicitly:

> as soon as this light is reached it restores everything to us. It restores the white to us, but a white which no longer confines the light. It finally restores the black to us, the black which is no longer the cessation of light. It even restores to us the grey, which is no longer uncertainty or indifference.[66]

Deleuze's enigmatic reference to a white that 'no longer confines the light' may be clarified by Dreyer's use of overexposure in the resurrection scene to blur the edges of the windows through which the light enters. Reygadas himself comments: 'the beauty in my film is the sun itself. ... I also like the white light that she sees when she wakes up. Pure white. We worked with particular lenses to do it.'[67] The blurring of the window's edges in Dreyer's film (and, in Reygadas's, of the outside world spectrally visible through it) may be the sign of the mystical, in which objects no longer inhabit the realm of correspondence, of measurability. In other words (Deleuze's),

> [w]e have passed, on the spot, from one space to the other, from physical space to spiritual space which restores a physics (or a metaphysics) to us. The first space is cell-like and closed, but the second is not different, it is the same in so far as it has merely discovered the spiritual opening which overcomes all its formal obligations and material constraints.[68]

As the word 'opening' and the mention of light should make clear, the key, hinge role – that of something material granting access to the spiritual – belongs to the window. As Marianne leans over Esther to give her the kiss after which she wakes, the only thing visible through the window behind Marianne is an intense glow of white light.

Reygadas's allusion to *The Word* sublates colour film into a monochrome that tangibly embodies the contrasts within being grounding the necessity of existential choice. His own film is, as it were, X-rayed to reveal that of Dreyer beneath it. And, as Deleuze rightly puts it, here '*[s]pace is no longer determined, it has become the any-space-whatever which is identical to the power of the spirit*'.[69] For Deleuze, this power is synonymous with 'the perpetually renewed spiritual decision',[70] and although the impersonality of this phrasing renders this event hard to assimilate directly into the individualist Christian existentialist tradition, as Deleuze seeks to do, the impersonality matches the idea of a spirit which – to use the subtitle of another work in this tradition, Bresson's *Un condamné à mort s'est échappé* (*A Man Escaped*) (1956) – is indeed a wind regarding which humans 'do not know where it comes from and where it is going' (John 3. 8). (Just such a wind, or amplified breath – the Hebrew *ruach* means both – is heard as Esther returns to life.) Reygadas, however, takes a step beyond Dreyer, suggesting that the resurrection involves a turning back of time that logically requires the undoing of a day given over to adulterous uncertainty throughout. The restoration of which Deleuze writes does indeed demand that of the dark, which, read realistically, may be no more than dusk, but in the newly revealed spiritual realm in fact reverses the dawning that opened the film, restoring the time before its beginning. At the heart of the film's cyclical, ambiguous *sacrum*, regenerative white summons up a generative darkness.

CHROMOPHOBIA?: *BLACK NARCISSUS* (1947)

Associated with perfection and ice, white is seldom thought of as moving. Perfect, cold, it is more likely to be a goal towards which others move, a magnetic pole, like the white garments of the glorified saints in the Book of Revelations, or T. S. Eliot's 'still point of the turning world'. (As the previous two films under consideration have indicated, a preoccupation with monochrome and one with transcendence often accompany one another.) A movement of white is its breaking up, like that of the ice at the end of *Mother*. In Michael Powell and Emeric Pressburger's *Black Narcissus*, however, white is always mobile, tossed by a wind that may be the one continually blowing around the Himalayan heights or the effect of the passion of the running nun (its mobility suggesting that of *donna è mobile*). If, for St Peter, being tossed hither and thither indicates childhood in the faith, this quality renders the nuns seeking to establish the convent of St Faith ironically more childish than the indigenous people they themselves call children. The ever-blowing wind is the movement that, in the end, shifts the settled state of the nuns, with their white habits, towards colour, in aspiration or memory. It indicates the failure of things to stay in their place – ultimately, western culture's unwillingness to admit its limits, until compelled to do so and leave – and will culminate in the appearance of a once-forbidden colour on the face of one who had been a nun: the red applied to her lips by Sister Ruth underlines the implications of her non-renewal of vows. At the same time, she has uncovered the red hair that makes her like one of the ladies of the palace painted on its walls, one of whom is intercut into this sequence. The red lipstick suggests her red hair and scarlet dress concentrated in one essence. Applying the lipstick makes her the disavowed double of Sister Clodagh, who sits opposite her as she does so: each linked by another colour, green (Ruth by green's association with jealousy, Clodagh with its stereotypical Irishness and the Emerald Isle emeralds she was to have worn upon marriage). The strength of the difference between green and red indicates that of the disavowal. For Ruth is the fully formed version of the madness of grief welling up in Clodagh upon recollection of her lost love. As Ruth applies the lipstick, the force she wishes it to have is indicated by the larger round and equally red compact she uses to monitor its application. A colour opposition is reinforced and intensified by one of abstract shapes, Ruth holding red and a circle, Clodagh the black of a book whose rectangularity denies the sensual.

Red has marked Ruth from the outset, the blood of a sick woman staining her white habit as she bursts in on an early conference between Clodagh, the other nuns and Mr Dean, the Englishman they would doubtless describe as having 'gone native'. But although Dean rejects the advances of the red-lipped Ruth, and in the end is clearly, longingly drawn to Clodagh, the madness is not all on Ruth's side. As Ruth reproaches him with loving Clodagh, he cries out 'I don't love anyone'. The screen's red suffusion of his image at this moment combines with the unexpectedness of his outburst to suggest that the emotional extravagance is his as well as hers; that each is scarred by a disturbance for which in the end, in a sense, Ruth is scapegoated. All three main protagonists are damaged, and only the effort of the will known as the stiff upper lip preserves two of them from collapse. Clodagh herself approaches collapse when alone in the chapel, crumpling under the stress of Ruth's disappearance. If the wind blowing the white habit seemed to want to shake it out into a revelation of the colours white contains, that possibility becomes virtual reality when choral voices of crisis crescendo as Clodagh pulls herself to her feet, resisting the pressure of ambient lighting colouring her habit part-blue, then part-green. 'There's something in the atmosphere that makes everything seem exaggerated,' Dean had said, evoking the spirit of the place. That something is surely the heightening of experience also known as 'colour'. And yet the sign of life is the preservation of colour at one point at least, the face, however 'white' it may seem beside those of the Indians. When one's face becomes genuinely white, like Ruth's just before she seeks to kill Clodagh, one has joined the undead before death. It is a tragically ironic end to Ruth's pursuit of colour.

MONOCHROME AND 'STUNDE NULL': *EUROPA*

In Lars Von Trier's *Europa,* the intermittent use of colour – again part of the legacy of Tarkovsky – performs various functions. Von Trier himself points out the most conventional one: 'to highlight certain things'.[71] Several such things spring to mind immediately: the red emergency brake on the train where the protagonist, Leopold Kessler, is serving the apprenticeship that will show the concern that he, albeit American-born, feels for a devastated post-war Germany; the yellow de-Nazification questionnaire Max Hartmann, whose family founded the Zentropa system in 1912, will need to complete to regain administrative supremacy over it; the bullet rolling on the train compartment floor in the foreground after it has fallen from the gun two young 'Werewolves' will use to kill an American-appointed mayor. However, colour also serves to intensify, marking emotional highpoints, usually involving love or death: Leopold's first sight of Katarina in the train compartment, for instance, or the blood-soaked water flowing out under the bathroom door after the suicide of her father. Indeed, colour highlights people and events more frequently than it does objects; the highlighted objects are simply keys to an event or a character's action. Often the colour seems to radiate from one person in particular: Katarina Hartmann, Max's daughter, who works for the Werewolves – the Nazi guerilla opposition to the new order – and who has an affair with Leopold, then marries him. This usage may appear to be firmly and predictably in line with mainstream cinema's identification of colour with the female star (in this case, Barbara Sukowa);[72] however, it is more complex than that. The colour Katarina emanates in Leopold's eyes can be withdrawn from her and transferred to him: she may be coloured when Leo first sees her, but their

Europa: dialogue with the woman with a past from the 'archaic' past that is black and white

dialogue about his reasons for coming to Germany begins with him foregrounded and coloured, while shortly after her move to join him in the coloured foreground, he edges away into monochrome. The fact that these two characters are the first to appear in colour, and then to do so together, may simply signal their future romantic connection. Their spatial interplay in this early bed-making scene in particular is a formal dance of colour and monochrome. When Leo moves into black and white and the background to state his wish to show Germany some kindness, the sense of distance created by the monochrome reinforces Katarina's smiling comment that such a sentiment 'seems to come from a place far away' (and possibly also 'long ago').

The recurrent preoccupation with a distance at the heart of closeness reinforces Von Trier's simultaneous adoption and dropping of melodramatic codes, their Brechtian quotation and questioning. Long before the overtly distancing theatricality of *Dogville* (2003) or *Manderlay* (2005), he is in dialogue with Brecht. As if in anticipation of those extremely theatrical later films, the alternation of colour and monochrome here goes beyond melodrama and Brechtianism to encompass mutually interrogating theatrical and cinematic codes. Overlaying a melodramatic cinematic code identifying colour, femininity and excess is a theatrical one whereby characters step in and out of spotlights. As Leopold voices his desire to show Germany some kindness, Katarina's 'what you say seems to come from a place far away' applies both to his idealism and to the mechanisms of the staging, of which she and all the other characters are unconscious, and which not only places him at a distance at this moment but underlines the remoteness by draining his image of the immediacy of colour.

Von Trier's use of black and white and colour is related therefore to the way in which back-projections repeatedly split the apparently unitary space of a scene, usually along the lines of individual characters or characters grouped in couples (Katarina and Leopold foregrounded in colour under the table while kissing, as others sit behind and above them in monochrome). The disparities between individuals or groups are emphasised by the frequent spatial mismatches of background and foreground, in whose realistic dovetailing Von Trier has little interest. One could even say that the work foregrounds back-projection, with both the screens and the highlighting colours conspiring to underline a mood created by one of the work's first images, which picked out Leopold in colour against a monochrome background: one of isolation. Even when apparently present to one another, the characters occupy screens. In Leopold's case, Katarina is usually projected onto an idealising screen that is often coloured. At the same time, though, other characters can enter the colour spotlight – like the Werewolf leader as Leopold and Katarina pass him at their wedding. His ability to do so indicates his threat to Leopold's fantasy of exclusive possession of a Katarina whose identity as lover and wife is destabilised by prior allegiance to the Werewolves. The charmed circle of colour loses some of its charm as it widens.

From its opening voiceover, *Europa* investigates and dramatises processes of layering. That voiceover addresses a hypnotised subject, enjoining it to pass through 'still deeper layers' and finally awaken in Europa. The preoccupation with layering is most consistently evident in the frequency with which Von Trier's back-projections are misaligned with its foregrounds, scoring fault-lines across scenes. However, this layering is also one of monochrome and colour, which separate out. It is as if colour were seen as layered upon black and white, with the work's excavation of European history also entailing one of cinematic history that discovers monochrome as an archaic level. If colour is viewed as a foreground patina upon a deeper, monochrome background, this may strengthen Katarina Hartman's argument that Leo should have chosen: black and white may be the primitive, determining level of reality at which choice is required, and at which failure to choose is condemned as Laodicean. This view of colour as surface is also – of course – in line with Puritan traditions (interestingly, both Danish *and* American, as if at some level Von Trier himself were failing to choose, identified with his male protagonist) that decry it as sensual; traditions that dovetail with assertions of masculinity by identifying colour with femininity and seduction. This tradition is invoked in Katarina's *femme fatale* presentation in colour when Leo first sees her. However colour is not simply a late-coming layer superimposed upon an earlier monochrome, as secondary as 'appearance' or 'the second sex'. It also signals the presence of layering whenever it manifests itself as a single point breaching a surface, be it as the highlighted single object linked to spectacular imminent trauma – like the bullet on the carriage floor – or as the blood spurting from beneath the bland surface of the body. Be it as surface differing from depth, or depth subverting surface, this partial colouration asserts the existence of layers: of mystery, conspiracy, concealment.

The splitting of space in *Europa*, which corresponds to that between monochrome and colour, is also homologous with one within the characters. If Katarina is self-confessedly one person by day and another by night, when her Werewolf persona writes threatening letters to her father, the tonalities of day and night are aligned with colour and monochrome. The filmic world's alternation between these registers validates Katarina's belief in the existence of two orders, between which characters oscillate. In the end even the humble Leo displays a dark side, terrorising the train with a machine-gun. If all the train travellers have betrayed multiple times in order to survive, as she states, it is because their European condition causes continual switches of allegiance. The same is true of Von Trier's film; not for nothing does he himself play the turncoat Jew whose exoneration of Max permits the return of the old order. His film's recurrent twitches of colour may be deemed ostentatiously indicative of the failure of any nostalgia project, of the impossibility of seeing the moment of Stunde Null German *Trümmerfilm* clearly through the eddies of pastiche, as the colour that is normative for 1992 European cinema keeps breaking through the surface. (Whether or not this constitutes a critique of the Fassbinder of the monochrome *Die Sehnsucht der Veronika Voss* (*Veronika Voss*) (1982) might be worth discussing.) Consequently, the attempt to bridge the gap between now and then by incorporating the styles of multiple directors of the intervening period, as if tracing a continuity of (projecting backwards) Fassbinder, Tarkovsky, Bergman (*Tystnaden* (*The Silence*) (1963)), Sirk, Carol Reed and Orson Welles, sees the baton drop repeatedly between the hands of their film-historical relay. There is no stable point of rest in Von Trier's film, the repeated cracking of the veneer of monochrome indicating that anything and everything can slip away from one at any time, that self-identity is impossible. The film is, as it were, pre-digitised, open to alteration from any point within it. Similarly, in the river whose endless movement denotes the unconscious, endless undermining of the intended stability of European states, identity finally slips away from Leo himself, along with his life. His only development has been to lose the colour he had at the start.

NOTES

1. Brent Berlin and Paul Kay, *Basic Color Terms: Their Universality and Evolution* (Berkeley and Los Angeles: University of California Press, 1969). Since Berlin and Kay contest what they term 'extreme linguistic relativism', arguing that their research 'strongly indicates that semantic universals do exist' (p. 1), it is likely to encounter resistance from quarters of Film Studies seeing it as lending succour to Post-Theory. (As will be seen shortly, I do not believe this to be the case but see it as offering evidence both sides might utilise, perhaps thereby indicating the problematic nature of the Post-Theory wars.) More damagingly, their work 'readily suggested to some the now-taboo late-nineteenth-century picture

of an evolutionary culture chain, with Papua New Guineans at the bottom, scarcely a step above the beasts, and sophisticated Europeans situated comfortably and properly at the top' (C. L. Hardin and Luisa Muffi (eds), *Color Categories in Thought and Language* (Cambridge: Cambridge University Press, 1997), p. 5). Hardin and Muffi dismiss this as a misreading of the Berlin/Kay thesis, declaring it 'no part of the authors' perspective', and therefore giving it 'no further attention' in their volume (Ibid.). A further defence of Berlin and Kay might read the 'evolution' mentioned in their subtitle as a matter of the temporality of logical categorisation rather than of human groups. Thus, although their statistics could be interpreted as establishing a primary triumvirate of black, white and red extremely strongly, their subsequent colour-orderings include increasing numbers of equivalents (either green or yellow may follow red; either purple, pink, orange or grey may follow brown), arguably marking thereby the passage from the universal to the variable, and a point of opening to cultural difference. Indeed, that difference may even be present from the outset, as Berlin and Kay note that various languages accord primacy to *either* white *or* black, which therefore also figure as equivalents (Berlin and Kay, *Basic Color Terms*, p. 4).

2. Sergei Eisenstein, *Selected Works Vol. III Writings, 1934–47*, ed. Richard Taylor, trans. William Powell (London: BFI, 1996), p. 264. (For further comments on this statement by Eisenstein, see the introduction to Chapter 4.)

3. Margaret Visser, *The Way We Are* (Toronto: HarperCollins, 1994), p. 292. For a similar view of the encapsulation of all colours in black and white, see Sartre's account of his childhood experiences at the cinema: 'I loved the cinema even in plane geometry. To me, black and white were the super-colors that contained all the others and revealed them only to the initiate' (Jean-Paul Sartre, *The Words*, trans. Bernard Frechtman (New York: Vintage, 1981), p. 123).

4. Michel Pastoreau, *Black: The History of a Color* (Princeton, NJ, and Oxford: Princeton University Press, 2009), p. 11.

5. Stanley Cavell, *The World Viewed: Reflections on the Ontology of Film* (enlarged edn) (Cambridge, MA, and London: Harvard University Press, 1979), p. 82.

6. Ibid., p. 83.

7. Ibid., p. 84.

8. Ibid., p. 85.

9. Ibid., p. 89.

10. Ibid., p. 90.

11. Ibid., pp. 90, 92.

12. Ibid., p. 93.

13. Ibid.

14. Peter Brooks, *The Melodramatic Imagination: Balzac, Henry James, Melodrama, and the Mode of Excess* (New York: Columbia University Press, 1985).

15. Cavell, *The World Viewed*, p. 90.

16. See Thomas Elsaesser, 'Tales of Sound and Fury', in Bill Nichols (ed.) *Movies and Methods 2* (Berkeley and Los Angeles: University of California Press, 1985), pp. 165–89, and Geoffrey Nowell-Smith, 'Minnelli and Melodrama', in Nichols, *Movies and Methods 2*, pp. 190–4.

17. Anne Hollander, *Moving Pictures* (New York: Knopf, 1989), p. 33.

18. Ibid.

19. Ibid.

20. Ibid.

21. Ibid.

22. Ibid., p. 34.

23. Ibid.

24. Ibid., p. 37.

25. Ibid., p. 38.

26. Eric Eric Rohmer, 'Of Taste and Colors', in Angela Dalle Vacche and Brian Price (eds), *Color: The* Film *Reader* (New York and London: Routledge, 2006), p. 123.

27. Hollander, *Moving Pictures*, p. 49.

28. Ibid., p. 50.

29. Ibid., p. 46.

30. Huxley's contention that we dream in black and white was a widespread belief when he wrote. Eric Schwitzgebel links it to the prevalence of black and white in the visual media of the first half of the twentieth century (Eric Schwitzgebel, 'Why Did We Think We Dreamed in Black-and-White?', *Studies in History and Philosophy of Science* 33 (2002), pp. 649–60). If this is so, the dream factory would literally have produced our dreams, in the sense of depriving them of colour, or introducing colour into mental environments to which it is irrelevant. Of course, the possible presence or non-presence of colour in actual dreams does not alter the long-standing association of enhanced consciousness with the luxury of multifarious colouration, which may in this context simply connote richness of choice, while the divided consciousness so often thematised in Expressionism may have matched, and been aggrandised by, its films' sharply divided black and white.

31. Aldous Huxley, *The Doors of Perception and Heaven and Hell* (London: Flamingo, 1994), p. 67.

32. Ibid., p. 70.

33. Huxley's interest in movements between colour and black and white, and colour and line, was a long-standing one, as can be seen from a passage in his early novel *Crome Yellow* (London: Chatto and Windus, 1969 [1921]), pp. 22–3: 'That part of the garden that sloped down from the foot of the terrace to the pool had a beauty which did not depend on colour so much as upon forms. It was as beautiful by moonlight as in the sun. The silver of water, the dark shapes of yew and ilex remained, at all hours and seasons, the dominant features of the scene. It was a landscape in black and white. For colour there was the flower-garden; it lay to one side of the pool, separated from it by a huge Babylonian wall of yews. You passed through a tunnel in the hedge, you opened a wicket in a wall, and you found yourself, startlingly and suddenly, in the world of colour.'

34. Siegfried Kracauer, 'Zur Ästhetik des Farbenfilms', in Kracauer, *Kino: Essays, Studien, Glossen zum Film*, ed. Karsten Witte (Frankfurt: Suhrkamp, 1974), pp. 48–9.

35. Ibid., p. 49.

36. Ibid., p. 50.

37. Ibid.

38. Ibid.

39. Cf. My 'European Film Theory: From Crypto-nationalism to Transnationalism', in Temenuga Trifonova (ed.), *European Film Theory* (New York and London: Routledge, 2009), p. 12.

40. Kracauer, 'Zur Ästhetik des Farbenfilms', p. 51.

41. Ibid., p. 52.

42. Ibid., p. 53.

43. Ibid.

44. Siegfried Kracauer, *Theory of Film: the Redemption of Physical Reality* (Princeton, NJ:Princeton University Press, 1997 [1960]).

45. Kracauer, 'Zur Ästhetik des Farbenfilms', p. 53.

46. Gerald Mast, *Film/Cinema/Movie: A Theory of Experience* (New York, Hagestorn, San Francisco, London: Harper and Row, 1977), p. 91.

47. Ibid., pp. 91–2.

48. Ibid., p. 92.

49. Hollander, *Moving Pictures*, p. 33.

50. Ibid., p. 35.

51. Ibid., p. 33.

52. Sergei Eisenstein, 'On Colour', in Eisenstein, *Selected Works Vol. II: Towards a Theory of Montage*, ed. Michael Glenny and Richard Taylor, trans. Michael Glenny (London: BFI, 1991), pp. 254–67.

53. Ibid., p. 264.

54. Ibid., p. 267.

55. Jay Leyda, *Kino: A History of the Russian and Soviet Film* (3rd edn) (London, Boston and Sydney: G. Allen and Unwin, 1983), p. 210.

56. Timothy Hyman, '*Solaris*', *Film Quarterly* vol. 29 no. 3 (Spring 1976), pp. 55–6.

57. Arthur Danto, *Unnatural Wonders: Essays from the Gap Between Art and Life* (New York: Farrar, Straus and Giroux, 2005), p. 257.

58. Richard Misek, '"Last of the Kodak": Andrei Tarkovsky's Struggle with Colour', in Wendy Everett (ed.), *Questions of Colour in Cinema: From Paintbrush to Pixel* (Bern: Peter Lang, 2007), pp. 167–8.

59. Burness E. Moore and Bernard D. Fine (eds), *Psychoanalytic Terms and Concepts* (New Haven and London: American Psychoanalytic Association and Yale University Press, 1990), p. 58.

60. Richard Rodriguez, *Brown: The Last Discovery of America* (New York and London: Penguin, 2002), p. xi.

61. Vida T. Johnson and Graham Petrie, *The Films of Andrei Tarkovsky: A Visual Fugue* (Bloomington and Indiana: Indiana University Press, 1994), p. 17.

62. Rodriguez, *Brown*, p. 206.

63. Andrei Tarkovsky, *Sculpting in Time* (New York: Knopf, 1987), p. 138.

64. Johnson and Petrie, *Films of Andrei Tarkovsky*, p. 189.

65. Ibid., p. 190.

66. Gilles Deleuze, *Cinema 1: The Movement-Image*, trans. Hugh Tomlinson and Barbara Habberjam (Minneapolis: University of Minnesota Press, 1986), p. 117.

67. Karin Luisa Badt, '*Silent Light* or Absolute Miracle: An Interview with Carlos Reygadas at Cannes 2007', *Bright Lights Film Journal*, <www.brightlightsfilm.com/57/reygadasiv.html> (accessed 26 May 2009).

68. Deleuze, *Cinema 1*, 117.

69. Ibid. (emphasis in original).

70. Ibid.

71. Stig Björkman (ed.), *Trier on Von Trier* (London: Faber, 2003), p. 153.

72. Steve Neale, *Cinema and Technology: Image, Sound, Colour* (London: BFI/Macmillan, 1985), pp. 151–5.

4 On the Dialectics of Filmic Colours (in general) and Red (in particular)

INTRODUCTION: IN THE SHADOW OF EISENSTEIN

> I wanted there to be red drops of blood in the black-and-white part, after the murder of Vladimir Andreyevich; but Fira Tobak would not have it; saying that would be Formalism. (Eisenstein, of *Ivan the Terrible*)[1]

One of the most powerful theorisations of colour, as one might expect, stems from Sergei Eisenstein, and appears in his late-1930s drafts of *Towards a Theory of Montage*.[2] The theory antedates Eisenstein's actual acquisition of colour film, when the Red Army's capture of German Agfa stock permitted the filming of portions of *Ivan Groznyy II: Boyarsky zagovor* (*Ivan the Terrible Part II*) (1958) in colour. Rather than lamenting his lack of access to colour stock, however, Eisenstein surprises readers by classifying black and white as colours, though he later parenthetically admits their status as tones.[3] (Deleuze agrees with Eisenstein when he states '[i]n certain respects, Expressionist dark and lyrical white played the role of colours',[4] though the traditions he considers – one at either end of a German–Scandinavian axis – do not interest Eisenstein, doubtless because their dramas are spiritual ones.) Eisenstein's initial description of black and white as colours may reflect his undoubted impatience to incorporate reflections on colour into his montage-based theory, and may even indicate a desire to maintain – fearfully, belligerently, or both – that nothing any film-maker might need could be lacking in the Soviet Union. Moreover, black, white, and red all had figured in *Bronenosets Potyomkin* (*Battleship Potemkin*) (1925), the flag flying at its end being tinted a triumphant red. With those three colours at his disposal (the black and white of melodramatic political confrontation, and the red of the blood flowing from them uplifted – sublated? – into the sacredness of the flag), Eisenstein may have felt he had all he needed. Whatever its motivation, his theoretical move may also be salutary for contemporary readers, subverting our entrenched binary of monochrome and colour. If there is anything potentially significant at stake in its dissolution, it may well be the gendering of monochrome as male and 'colour' as female; after all, with few exceptions – such as the Roger Corman film mentioned below – it is always 'the woman in red'. This is one reason for my interest in films that blur this opposition by pairing a colour usually acknowledged as one of the primaries with colour schemes that privilege black, white, or both these hues.

The frequency of couplings of red with black or white probably reflects red's customary appearance as the first unequivocal colour word in languages, after black and white,[5] whose status as colours remains controversial. There are obvious reasons for this near-primacy[6] and these juxtapositions: as the Old Testament asserts, 'the blood is the life', its emergence often preceding either the symbolic blackness of death or the pallor of the blood-drained body – or staining sheet whiteness with the menstrual marker of virginity, fertility. In all these cases, red gains power from its status as a hidden principle. Moreover, it is concealed not just within the human body but within that of earth itself, from which emerged the 'Adam' whose name means 'red': as Theroux points out, '[t]here is in nature a hidden palate (sic) of reds. … It is found in soils everywhere.'[7] Because one may be startled to realise that so visually arresting a color should somehow have remained out of sight, the moment of its appearance has the *éclat* of a potentially dramatic turning point (as in Roger Corman's *The Masque of the Red Death* (1964)).

If it is customary to define colours relationally, this may well be partly because the process of naming them is so steeped in equivocation that adding one or more can help to stabilise the viewer's sense of the range within which any individual one falls. Thus I would argue that cinematic colours should be studied in terms of the periodic tables of the systems that surround, generate and stabilise them, however uncertain the chemistry of celluloid itself may have been at times; however often the films' titles themselves privilege only one colour; and however well the colour circle itself conceals the nameless transitions among its named hues. The frequency with which cinema foregrounds red – promising drama, danger, romance and possibly all three – makes it a particularly fruitful example of the dialectical relationships one colour may develop with others. The following meditations therefore aim to tease out some of the implications of the colour dialectics within four films, in three of which a particularly intense use of red is often noted, while its complex relationship with other hues is either ignored or underplayed (a fine exception to this rule being P. Adams Sitney's work on *Viskningar och rop* (*Cries and Whispers*) (1972)).[8] In each of the first three films, red is paired not with one or more of the other primaries (be they the painter's primaries or the physical or psychological ones, whose difference Ed Branigan has defined with admirable succinctness[9]), but rather with those hues that – as noted above – are in a sense dramatically even more 'primary', in the sense of 'fundamental': black (*Trois couleurs: rouge* (*Three Colours: Red*) (1994)), white (*Deserto rosso* (*Red Desert*) (1964)), and – in the final turn of this dialectic – both white and black (*Cries and Whispers*). Consequently, an insistence on the dialectical, polyvalent functioning of any cogent film's keynote colour is a central accent of this chapter. If it also includes *La Double Vie de Véronique* (*The Double Life of Véronique*) (1991) – a film usually associated with yellow – it is in the belief that its use of red provides a generally overlooked key to its meaning and aesthetic procedures.[10] Indeed, this film's placement beside *Three Colours: Red* is logical for reasons that go beyond theme and casting (the double use of Irène Jacob), as the appearance of a screen fully suffused with red in *The Double Life of Véronique* can be seen as a reason for the omission of the full-screen appearance of red that would have been expected by viewers of *Trois couleurs: bleu* (*Three Colours: Blue*) (1993) and *Trois couleurs: blanc* (*Three Colours: White*) (1994), both of which give this privilege to their key colour at one point.

THE RED AND THE BLACK: *THREE COLOURS: RED*

In *Three Colours: Red,* as already stated, red appears often in tandem with black. Valentine often wears combinations of red and black, the former colour indicating her vitality, the latter reining it in in a way whose connotations may include either modesty or masked depression at the state of her relationships. The black also underlines her placement at the opposite pole from the women who betrayed both Judge Joseph Kern, whom she befriends, and the judge's double, Auguste, with whom it appears at the end she will be linked romantically – not just coincidentally, as so often in the film. The whiteness of the apartment of Kern's lover, or the blondness of Auguste's girlfriend Karin, connotes a deceptiveness of surface. Other black–red combinations – to name only a few from the film's first few minutes – include the red cloth beneath Valentine's black phone, the black and red colouration of Auguste's car and the black shirt of the bartender against the red of the wall.

Three Colours: Red: Valentine's room, its central multicoloured fruit masking with realism its status as a two-tone, red–black abstract

In addition to this, the pairing of red and black formalises the work's interest in the moment of sunset, which parallels that of the judge's retirement: the moment at which the sun reddens before disappearing into darkness (that moment that persuaded the Egyptians that Osiris had been torn limb from limb, his blood flowing before his night-time death). The moment at which light passes into dark, as one of co-incidence, is linked to the work's thematics of chance. If black and red appear together frequently (for instance, the black beneath the seats of the fashion show where Valentine models), the most telling such pairing is probably that of the red cherries with a black background in the slot machine played by Valentine, whose winning means real bad luck in the things that matter, those concerning the heart suggested by her name. For the red–black combination is the signature one of so many games of chance, from cards to roulette. Red and black are thus not only Valentine's obvious colours but the cryptic ones of the judge himself, who shares the gambler's awareness of the potentially life-determining effect of a single moment: who tosses a coin at the same time as Auguste does, as if to predetermine his choice to go bowling; who denounces himself on the assumption that chance will lead Valentine to a newspaper report of the trial, and then bring her back to him; whose law-book fell open at the right question just before his exam, in the same way as does that of Auguste. And, of course, chance is a subject of long-standing interest to Kieślowski, furnishing the title of one of his finest films, *Przypadek* (*Blind Chance*) (1987).

As the colours of games of chance, red and black are also linked, of course, to money. A black such as that of Valentine's hair provides the background that offsets red and so allows it to stand out as an agent of commerce. The colour's imbrication with commerce is evident: Kieślowski clearly had little difficulty finding and purchasing over 400 red objects to strew across his set, particularly in the apartment of Valentine. The red of the billboard on which she figures is that of desire subordinated to commerce. The statement that in doing such work she is allowing herself to be exploited may issue from the most dubious of sources, the pathologically jealous boyfriend (Michel) who would probably prefer to incarcerate her, and who thus in a sense becomes a double of Karol Karol, whom he met in an omitted subplot, but it is also true. As that red puts Valentine forward, it threatens her privacy, prompting children to block her apartment keyhole with the 'Hollywood' bubblegum she is advertising. That blocked keyhole symbolises the ironic frustration of her private life and links it to her universal accessibility as an image. This frustration can be undone only by a combination of events that sees the image first being taken down and then magically replicated after her rescue (as if cleansed by the storm, or transformed into something 'rich and strange'): its rediscovery is redemptive, with the sorrow that first prompted it during the commercial photo-shoot no longer being taken in vain. Thus, Kieślowski's privileging of red interlocks with his preoccupation with the issues of privacy raised by this colour, whose come-hither goes out to beholders, sinking into them the grappling-hooks of a generalised solicitation. The red awning of the café Chez Joseph, located near Valentine's apartment, also participates in this confusion of public and intimate space.[11] For Kieślowski, the confusion of those two spaces had been the primary temptation of documentary cinema, from which he withdrew in order to preserve the privacy of prospective subjects. In *Red* even fictional cinema appears as a possible violation of privacy, perhaps because the scenario has the reputation of being the director's most personal. It is as if, like the judge denouncing himself, he too is violating his own privacy in order to bring something to an end, perhaps punishing himself belatedly for his actions as a documentarist by paralleling them with the judge's electronic surveillance. It may therefore be hardly surprising that he declared that *Red* would be his last film.

The linkage of red and black is not just that found in the games of chance whose issue is money, however; it also embodies less material forms of value, and so participates in the mystical dimension of Kieślowski's late work. Noting the connection between colour and the 'self-luminous objects' encountered in visionary experience,[12] Aldous Huxley goes on to speak of flame – whose primary colour is red – as 'a living jewel', concluding that its power to transport one into an Other World 'increases in proportion to the depth and extent of the surrounding darkness'.[13] The red–black combination of this film is thus thoroughly overdetermined. And since the significance of the inhabitants of the self-luminous realm involves being rather than doing,[14] the judge's statement that Valentine need only *be* identifies her as just such an instanciation of being: no wonder then that she appears finally as a photograph, an image removed from the continuousness of action.

Although *Red*, unlike its predecessors in Kieślowski's *Three Colours* trilogy, never floods the screen with its key colour, it comes close to doing so twice, in what may be called the work's repeating standout image: that of Valentine frozen in sorrow against a red background (first that of the billowing red sheet suspended behind her during the bubblegum ad shoot, then that of the red anorak of a passer-by held behind her in a freeze frame after her rescue from the ferry disaster). Given the first image's implication in processes of selling the film critiques, it is both fitting and ironic that it should most frequently have been used to 'sell' the work, on boxes containing videos and DVDs, or in articles about it. It is a 'standout' image in two senses: because of the prevalence of that attention-soliciting colour, red; and because, as a photograph, it juts out of, and negates, the continuousness of film. Since photographs are common *aides mémoire*, one may wonder whether this image might represent one the judge would take into an afterlife, following a process akin to the one envisaged by Koreeda Hirokazu in his film *Wandâfuru*

Three Colours: Red: the TV freeze frame resurrects Valentine's downed billboard image

raifu (*After Life*) (1998), about people recently deceased passing through a limbo where they are asked to choose one memorable moment from their past before moving on to the next stage. It is as if the film acts in accordance with Goethe's belief that red was the noblest of all colours, containing all other colours within itself:[15] an image dominated by red therefore becomes the most appropriate aid in the recollection and in-gathering of an entire life. A double freezing of the image could be said to occur, the possible result of the way the weight of experience distilled within it renders it hard to move through it: thus, after the initial freeze frame, the camera delves into it until it yields up Valentine's face in profile against a red background (the abstracted form of what was seen earlier as a rescue-worker's anorak), a moment that recalls the work's title and her own earlier framing thus across a billboard. On excavating the TV image and discovering this one, the film locks, locking it in a second time. This freezing immobilises us with its inscrutability. Is it only chance that has generated this imagistic rhyme between the two moments, or could it be something else? Or is the quasi-magical force of red, which includes the power to sum up a life? (In other words, which of the two codes operating throughout the film should be deemed finally to prevail: the realistic or the fantastic?) Initially, the TV image contained somebody else – Auguste, whom we have been led to expect will be Valentine's love in the future, though they stand close to one another in this picture for the first time – but the process of homing in on Valentine and red has excluded him. This insertion of a male (Auguste) into a picture initially containing only a female (the billboard) itself echoes the insertion of Karol Karol into the final version of the white wedding flashback in the previous film in the trilogy, *White*. The subsequent exclusion of the sight of the male figure shows the capacity of 'the same' image to see-saw back and forth in time. Thus, what seems like a freeze frame may, in fact, be something else, a folding together of past and future. It may be both memory and prophecy. Is the judge excluding Auguste from the image to preserve a fantasy in which time has been abrogated so that the place of Auguste – in so many respects the judge's double – can be occupied by him alone? Does the rhyme not also encompass the film's very first image, which showed Valentine's photograph on the desk of her jealous, absent boyfriend, Michel, so that the freeze frame becomes that by which the judge remembers the girl of whom he has no photograph? And might the occasional, apparently unmotivated, precipitous backward movements of the camera, which then come to rest upon an object or still life (in a sense, upon a photograph yet to be printed), mirror with estranging literalism the movement of memory itself within a space in which past and present exist simultaneously – the time of the recollection of death, the symbolic moment before sunset (as we have seen, the moment of the meeting of red and black) that preoccupies this film?

RED AND WHITE: *RED DESERT*

Red Desert, Michelangelo Antonioni's first colour film, has been critiqued on occasions as ostensibly allowing itself to be seduced from thematic concerns by the director's fascination with the possibilities of colour experimentation. Here, for instance, are the words of Andrei Tarkovsky, who was usually highly respectful of Antonioni:

> *The Red Desert* is the worst of his films after *The Cry* [*Il Grido*]. The color is pretentious, quite unlike Antonioni usually, and the editing is subservient to the idea of color. It could have been a superb film, if only it had been in black-and-white. If *The Red Desert* had been in black-and-white, Antonioni wouldn't have got high on pictorial aesthetics, he wouldn't have been so concerned with the pictorial side of the film, he wouldn't have shot those beautiful landscapes, or Monica Vitti's red hair against the mists. He would have been concentrating on the action instead of making pretty pictures. In my view the color has killed the feeling of truth. If you compare *The Red Desert* to *The Night* [*La Notte*, 1961] or *The Eclipse* [*L'Eclisse*, 1962] it's obvious how much less good it is.[16]

Unlike Tarkovsky, I will argue that the work's themes mesh with its aesthetic in a manner that is fascinating, subtle and profoundly innovative. In it a central concern with contamination conjugates into a multi-levelled examination of pollution, displacement, homelessness and uncertainty over boundaries, all of which are probed formally through a fine-grained use of colour and focus shifts.

For Angela Dalle Vacche, a key opposition of the work runs between an architecture she describes as 'masculine' and a painting she deems 'feminine': 'In *Red desert* if architecture applies to masculinity, painting leads towards femininity.'[17] However, the film's destabilisation of boundaries shakes this distinction also. The industrial factory where we first see Ugo, the husband of the protagonist (Giuliana (Monica Vitti)), and Corrado (Richard Harris), who will have an affair with her, is the most prominent architectural feature in the landscape, and is indeed run by men. Nevertheless, even here we note that the painting that apparently belongs to a separate, 'feminine' regime has occurred. Antonioni himself may comment in an interview that this painting is motivated by contemporary industrial practicalities ('if a pipe is painted green or yellow it is because it is necessary to know what it contains and to identify it in any part of the factory'[18]), but the viewer's ignorance of any such motive and the way the work's title has primed him or her to note all colours as significant makes these ones appear to represent a visual regime for which function is secondary. Moreover, these painted objects' divergence from the general spectatorial imaginary template of a functional, grey–black–brown factory colour scheme makes their brightness seem primarily decorative, even superfluous. It is as if the 'feminine' regime of painting has entered the factory, as if brought there by Giuliana herself passing through it and passing, among other things, a red metal railing and a blue cylinder from which a yellow pipe issues. Since form and function are not obviously matched, the orders Dalle Vacche identifies as 'masculine' and 'feminine' contaminate one another. It is no surprise then to see that Giuliana's domestic space has clinical white walls and a prominent blue metal railing round the stairwell, suggesting the partial presence here of a visual regime the film so far has led one to associate with the industrial. Although bright colour is traditionally identified with the feminine in the modern western imaginary, and grey, brown or black with the masculine, this film places them on a single plane. In other words, and in the terms of my opening remarks on red, white and black, the collapse of traditional gender markers entails that of the distinction between 'monochrome' and 'colour' also.

The erosion of borders between the industrial and the domestic, and masculinity and femininity, is reinforced by the breakdown of the distinction between 'objective' and 'subjective' point of view. Antonioni achieves this through his use of colour and focus. One pertinent example is the much-discussed scene featuring fruit painted grey on a street barrow. On one level, it is possible to view the fruit's colouration as motivated by Giuliana's condition, in the sense both of her general neurosis and the particular tiredness she voices at this moment: as she sits down beside the barrow, the film shows her point of view of the seller and his barrow. Its momentary loss of focus could be taken as an expressionistic manifestation of either her neurosis, her weariness, or both. However, shots not linked to her point of view – from in front of the barrow – also display grey fruit. The fruit is grey all the time, not just when seen by Giuliana. The film oscillates in and out of an expressionistic motivation of its shifts of focus. Another focus shift occurs a few minutes later, as Giuliana and Corrado visit the home of a worker Corrado is seeking to recruit to travel to Patagonia, but without any hint of a subjective anchoring. Three flowers they have left behind appear out of focus, as three blobs of pink: the shift separates colour from object in a manner that can seem simply reflective of Antonioni's fascination by formal methods for highlighting colour, but which also reiterates the concern with the blurring of boundaries, as the flowers, shot thus, lose their clarity of outline. (The film's interest in mist and smoke, and interest in boundary-blurring, may suggest one in the form of painting known as *sfumato*.) In the terms of a time-honoured art-historical opposition, line succumbs to colour. Antonioni's own acquaintance with, and long-standing interest in, this distinction is apparent from its appearance in his prose piece 'Suggerimenti di Hegel' of 1942, in which he had compared the relationship of black and white to colour in cinema to that between design and painting.[19] Both, of course, are central to *Red Desert*.

The contamination of masculine 'objectivity' and a 'subjectivity' identified primarily with Giuliana pervades both the street scene mentioned above and the sequence preceding it. Before emerging onto the grey street with the grey fruit, Giuliana and Corrado converse in the empty basement where she is considering opening a shop, albeit with no clear notion of what she wishes to sell. The shot-reverse-shot mechanism structuring their dialogue reinforces its identification of Giuliana with the issue of colour, which she is discussing: as she suggests that cool colours will be best for the walls, as they will not divert attention from the objects to be sold, she appears against those white walls and the colour samples painted in squares upon them. This background strikingly validates Lucja Demby's comment that Giuliana 'sees the world as coloured blotches that do not add up to a whole'.[20] The dialogue ends when Corrado moves into a position against the white wall previously occupied by Giuliana herself. Her cutting off of the conversation at this point implies an unconscious realisation that although the sense of homeless-ness mentioned by Corrado indicates his ability to empathise with her, the extent of his resemblance to her will preclude him from helping her. Indeed, his indecision over where he belongs mirrors her own over the choice of colour and objects to sell. Her uncertain relationship with the commercial is then echoed uncannily and ironically by that of the fruit-seller: each has only 'nothing' to sell (grey fruit is not attractive, and certainly does not stand out against the grey background of a street that in any case con-tains no prospective buyers other than Corrado and Giuliana). The would-be feminine seller (Giuliana) is remarkably akin to the (masculine) fruit-vendor. The resemblance may prompt speculations whether the man's appearance itself is motivated partly expressionistically (for all the cues suggesting his reality) as an image of hallucination and denial: it could be read as the means whereby Giuliana simultaneously asserts similarity ('we both are depressed would-be sellers with nothing to sell') and denies it ('we differ in every respect: age, class and gender').

Throughout the film, colours not only appear in combinations but are largely defined by their inter-relationship. The demonstrable preoccupation with a dynamic of colour interaction gives the lie to Tarkovsky's accusations of mere pictorialism. In an interpretation of the film's colour scheme that tends to read them allegorically, Ned Rifkin usefully notes one of these moments of dynamisation, when the black hull of the ship enters the frame to dominate the green of some trees (a moment possibly comparable to Bazin's interpretation of the spectral entry of a ship into the frame in Murnau's *Nosferatu, eine Symphonie des Grauens (Nosferatu)* (1922)).[21] Within the work's system of colour relations, however, the key one is not the green–black (for all its ecological significance and privileging through place-ment at the work's beginning and end, where Giuliana appears as a small speck of green in a largely darkened landscape) but the one privileged by its title: that involving red. Red appears repeatedly in com-bination, and alternation, with white. This red–white combination may be viewed as a deliberate inversion and conjugation of the green–black one noted by Rifkin. It is nautical, of course, and so related to the work's imagery of possible escape, figuring both on the ship where Giuliana and Corrado converse and at the end of the pier where her car stops just short of the brink. Its most important and exten-sive appearance is in the shack beside the water, where the wooden slats painted red on one side are white on the other. The combination of these two colours seems to frustrate an impulse to action it displaces into substitute action. If red aims at passion, white dampens it. Thus, although the couples crawling into the red-slatted area of the shack grow erotically excited as they do so, and Giuliana mentions how the quail's eggs she has eaten make her want to make love, nothing happens. The mood of incipient orgy veers away into titillation, and Ugo informs Giuliana with embarrassment that there is no way love can be made in company. Because the social context constrains the impulse promoted by the intimacy of the shack and the colour red, it manifests itself only in displaced form: the inner wall of slats, which looks white from the side from which it is attacked, is broken up – primarily by Corrado, whose desire for Giuliana can only be displaced – and used to feed a fire that translates impulse into the disappointingly metaphorical.

The final form of this colour interaction sees Giuliana pass through white hotel spaces – tellingly described by Rifkin as reminiscent of the hospital space she inhabited after her suicide attempt[22] – towards Corrado's room. Prominent in that room is a red bar across the end of the bed. The dialectic of red and white concludes in the room's appearance as pink after her unsatisfactory love-making with Corrado. Although the difference of their masculinity and femininity might be mapped onto that between

Red Desert: rearranging the proportions of red and white in the hut

red and white, the final dominance of pink wittily and ironically shows their intercourse as not a triumph of the male who has longed to possess her physically, but one of the most stereotypically 'feminine' of colours. It is as if Corrado has not so much succeeded in seducing Giuliana as seen his space flooded by her femininity, been unmanned. The earlier echoes of her mode of perception in the scene showing his recruiting of workers for his Patagonia project – the freezing of faces before him, the distracted following of the blue painted line – becomes in the end an absorption by it, as prefigured by the fusion of two drops of blue dye demonstrated by Valerio.[23] As the scene re-emphasises his inability to support her, as established earlier in the prospective shop, it is no surprise that she flees to fantasy's symbol of endless displacement – the ship, whose reality bars her entry. Even there, in the natural home of the homeless, there is no place for her, and the end finds her where she began, watching a poisonous yellow smoke rise from a factory chimney. Now, however, its flame has become a metaphor for the quarantine flag that precludes her from sailing away to the lonely utopia of the fantasy island, free of visual distortions, she had described in a story for her son.

RED, BLACK, WHITE: *CRIES AND WHISPERS*

An early, inescapable move in most discussions of Ingmar Bergman's *Cries and Whispers* is to quote the director's own statements identifying the red that dominates the film as the colour of the soul:

all our interiors are red, of various shades. Don't ask me *why it must be so*, because I don't know. I have puzzled over this myself and each explanation has seemed more comical than the last. The bluntest but also the most valid is probably that the whole thing is something internal and that ever since my childhood I have pictured the inside of the soul as a moist membrane in shades of red.[24]

If, in triads of black, white and red, red indicates undifferentiation, as Malcolm Bull suggests,[25] then it could also be aligned with the form of undifferentiation known as transgendering, a feature of the film discussed below, making it all the more appropriate a dominant colour for Bergman's work. Somewhat startlingly, it also arguably displays some of the qualities found in the coding of black, white and red employed by the tribes of the lower Congo, as described by Anita Jacobson-Widding: 'moral neutrality, lack of rules, chaos, non-structure, magic, power, emotionality etc.'.[26] In the societies described by Jacobson-Widding, red's neutrality requires its qualification by one of the other two colours (the white worn by the sacred chief indicates his positive direction of a red magical power whose direction would otherwise be indeterminate).[27] Whether or not any clear cross-cultural correlation exists here, within *Cries and Whispers* red might also connote a Girardian 'founding sacrifice', as Bull suggests red does in general.[28] As in Hitchcock's *Marnie* (1964), the non-availability to consciousness of the events of that sacrifice provokes a generalised fear response to red, upon which the narrative floats unstably, much as *Persona* (1966) does on its pre-credit sequence.

Pauline Kael, who skewers the work as a nineteenth-century masterpiece in a twentieth-century form, aligns its use of black, white and red with that in Edvard Munch's allegorical *Dance of Life*, where a woman in red is identified with life while a black-dressed one represents death and decay, and one in white, innocence.[29] Particularly fruitful is Bruce Kawin's interpretation of the film's red in the context of his analysis of the projection of first-person consciousness onto the screen, a process he terms 'mind-screen':

> Although there are numerous ways to interpret Bergman's use of red (and its counterpart, white) in this film, the one that seems most interesting in this context is the possibility that the image field is retinal; that of all the blood in this film, the most inescapable is that which circulates through the retina and which, analogously, gives color to the eyelids closed against intense light. Such an interpretation is consistent with the device's intent here – which is to introduce a sequence of private 'vision' – as well as useful in suggesting that the screen is itself retina.[30]

The implications of Kawin's description are various: the brightness is that of the summer's day, now inconceivable, when the sisters all walked together, and when Agnes followed her mother; but it is also that of an internal experience of the female Other as an overpowering light shone in the eyes of an unseen viewer, who thus has to keep them closed (and so open to a dream world) so as not to be blinded. 'Retinal red' is the colour seen whenever the characters close their eyes, be it in physical pain or in recollection, or to mark the painfulness of a recollection. It is the colour of a seeing that does not 'see' but rather analyses an abstract undifferentiation of colour into the screening fantasy it then projects as separate, concrete figures. This projection may be a defence against the intense anxiety decontextualised red can provoke, with the film's narrative apparently seeking to overcome a fear that is as free-floating as the colour itself, and therefore essentially Expressionist. Nicholas Humphrey's experiments with primates' reactions to red may be relevant:

> When red occurs in an unfamiliar context it becomes … a highly risky colour. The viewer is thrown into conflict as to what to do. All his instincts tell him to do *something*, but he has no means of knowing what that something ought to be. No wonder that my monkeys, confronted by a bright red screen, became

tense and panicky: the screen shouts at them 'this is important', but without a framework for interpretation they are unable to assess what the import is. And no wonder that human subjects in the artificial, contextless situation of a psychological laboratory may react in a similar way.[31]

The drawing off of red into a narrative, of course, has a frame, the white and black mentioned by Kael. In Bergman's film, however, these extremities of colour are more polyvalent than in Munch's painting. They connote not only innocence (white) and deathly corruption (black), but also the times before and after life, the pre-story and that story's epilogue. The white and the black might even be conceived of as possibly one, the absence of images being either a uterine *tabula rasa* or sepulchral darkness. This potential polyvalence, along with the tendency of one colour to slide over into the others, is hinted at very early on in the film, as Maria, whose sensuality is associated primarily with red, views a portrait of her mother, whose hair is black but whose dress is white, and who resembles Maria. Since Liv Ullman plays both parts, the image can seem like a self-portrait. If red can decline into white or black, it can also become the white-red of the flesh so tellingly exposed in the film. In the case of Karin, the white–red–black spectrum is assigned between a black dress, white flesh and – smeared upon that flesh, including the face – the blood of her self-mutilation. The red that is come-hither in Maria's deep décolletage has a warning tone in Karin's case, where it can also be described as brandished deliberately before her husband, possibly to simulate a menstruation that would forbid his sexual approaches. If, of the three sisters, only the dying Agnes is linked consistently with one colour – white – this may indicate her proximity to death, the fading of the dialectical oscillation of life and opposed colours. Bergman's colour palette is thus far more complex than Kael recognises, though her juxtaposition of the three key accents points in the right direction.

Cries and Whispers may appear to differ profoundly from *Red Desert* – its luxurious late-nineteenth-century mansion surrounded by a park radically unlike the polluted twentieth-century wasteland near Ravenna – but it is as much of its time as Antonioni's film. Indeed, it is possible to see the two works as linked quite closely: one might analyse each with reference to a female figure's aural hallucination of the cry of a child. (Perhaps not surprisingly, in each case also an interest in hallucination generates an engagement with Expressionism.) Thus *Cries and Whispers* is not the 'nineteenth-century European masterwork in a twentieth-century art-form' Kael deems it to be,[32] but is equally preoccupied with the nature of modernity, albeit taking a long view of it, discerning its origins in the late nineteenth century and in the post-religious moment of Nietzsche. The key element linking the two works is the destabilisation of gender borders. Again, despite appearances, Bergman's work is not obsessed with a female Other but presents the signifiers of masculinity and femininity as in free-flow between the sexes. Frank Gado comments: 'at about the time of *Cries and Whispers*, Bergman began to acknowledge a feminine component within himself that he had previously suppressed; as a result, he said, he had rejected his former practice of conceiving his characters as solely male or female'.[33] Moreover, P. Adams Sitney notes, 'here as elsewhere Bergman has defended against autobiographical reference by transposing genders'.[34] The rationale for such transpositions goes beyond autobiographical self-defence, however, to underpin Bergman's analysis of modern gender relations. The transposition is, in fact, systematic, motivating the interlocking within the work of repetition, inversion and Expressionism.

To begin with the most frequently invoked, almost notorious aspect of Bergman's work: Expressionism. For Bergman, Expressionism is more than an early-twentieth-century style preoccupied with anguish, shock effects and startling colouration. It also models the self's creation through projection and mirroring. In understanding Expressionism thus, *Cries and Whispers* extends the practices of *Persona*, albeit in a less overtly modernistic fashion. The process of projection includes a back-and-forth movement of signifiers associated with masculinity and femininity, placing on a single plane the black commonly associated with the former and the white and red stereotypically linked with the latter in the nineteenth century. The very boldness of the colours is correlated with the thematics of isolation, which becomes most ironic within a family grouping. As if aware of this irony, however semi- or unconsciously, the characters repeat and multiply themselves in an effort to escape isolation: Maria is repeated in the painting of her mother; Karin, in her mirror (the glass in which she will seek liberation by using another of its forms – the shattered wine-glass – to mutilate her labia); and Agnes in her diary. The irony enters a vicious circle as this doubling deepens the isolation. The central implicit viewer of the dream-work may be Bergman himself, whose own soul it is that appears coloured red, but it contains multiple images, both male and female, in introjected form. Moreover, like all modernists he builds into his work a scene that functions as a *mise en abyme* image of the process of his work's generation. Since that principle involves revealing the beholder within the beheld, the scene is that of David's analysis of the face of Maria. If, while analysing that face before the mirror, David makes comments whose relationship to the visible evidence, and hence whose accuracy, is not always apparent, the reason why can be stated by Maria: he sees these qualities in her because he sees them in himself. In other words, the focus may be upon the women, but it rebounds upon the male, implicating him too.

In acting thus, Maria demonstrates her power also, which is that of what Adorno terms the 'she-man':

> One need only have perceived, as a jealous male, how such feminine women have their femininity at their finger-tips – deploying it just where needed, flashing their eyes, using their impulsiveness – to know how things stand with the sheltered unconscious, unmarred by intellect.[35]

Maria brandishes the signs of culturally coded femininity – seductive red, soft pink – as weapons: if power is 'masculine', she is far more powerful than her castrated husband Joakim, or her sister Karin, whose eyes flicker nervously before her, and who fears her touch. The signs of 'femininity' are thus always deceptive. To put it modernistically: they need to be interpreted. The greater extent of Maria's power becomes apparent through one of the work's many (transgendering) repetitions: Karin's self-mutilation transposes into another key the apparent suicide attempt of Joakim in reaction to Maria's obvious preference for David. And, of course, Karin herself is a variation upon Maria. After all, even though Adorno's words on the 'she-man' appear obviously to apply to Maria, does not Karin's pursed image imply a self-masculinisation, with the following words in turn blatantly applicable to her?

> If the psychoanalytical theory is correct that women experience their physical constitution as a consequence of castration, their neurosis gives them an inkling of the truth. The woman who feels herself a wound when she bleeds knows more about herself than the one who imagines herself a flower because that suits her husband.[36]

Moreover, the very naming of the two characters renders each of them a mother figure: 'one bears the name of Bergman's mother; the other, the script explicitly states, of the Virgin Mother'.[37]

Throughout the film, inversions and repetitions invite one to compare the characters, blur the boundaries between them. This blurring goes even further than the fusion of Karin, Maria and Anna as 'aspects of the mother'.[38] It encompasses Agnes also. Thus both Agnes, who is dying of cancer, and Maria clutch David's hand to their upper bodies. If there is difference between them, how deep does it go? The similarity in the gesture prompts one to ask whether there is a similarity beneath the profound disparity between the two women's conditions. The dolls' house viewed by Maria has cooler colours than the red rooms in which most of the drama plays itself out. For all the difference, though, one may wonder whether the house too is a dolls' house, with Bergman himself playing with the larger-than-life figures in a dolls' house of the soul.

One of the key elements of repetition and inversion, therefore – inevitably – involves the relationship between red and blood. If Godard, in a Brechtian mood, famously described *Pierrot le fou* (1965) as displaying not blood but 'red', Bergman's work may be taken as a response to – an inversion of – that statement. Here red is not just a sign, but also a reality: the most deadly reality. And yet even though, by realist conventions, red is most viscerally 'real' when Karin mutilates her labia and smears the blood on her face, one may wonder whether this too is simply a sign. Should one think that Ingrid Thulin really smeared her own blood on her face, or that the red on her upper thighs was not just a red stain? The ultimate blurring of boundaries involves red, as this sign of interiority – be it of the body or, as Bergman himself would have it, of the (bleeding?) soul – is smeared all over a set of walls.

Cries and Whispers: black dominates the three key colours in an early image of the dying Karin

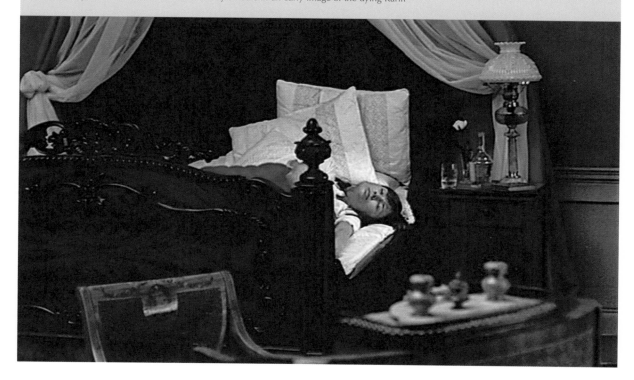

Cries and Whispers: an inversion: predominant red in Maria's countershot shifts the accent to characterise her very different world (one of delectable sleep, not death)

RED AND *THE DOUBLE LIFE OF VÉRONIQUE*

Framing devices often define the cinema of the fantastic – the category to which *The Double Life of Véronique* may be said to belong – establishing a reality from which the work departs, and to which it returns. One form of framing device involves the use of colour – most famously, in *The Wizard of Oz* (1939), which begins in monochrome and then establishes Technicolor as appropriate to fairy-tale wonder. Yellow filters may laminate Kieślowski's film with a single colour, but there is no differently coloured or monochrome domain that might represent a reality from which it stands apart, by which it is framed. The only other colour to achieve any dominance – the red that suffuses the frame after the guttering of the anamorphic image of Weronika inside a candle flame – is itself classifiable as a derivative of yellow, and hence merely as its transformation, not as an alternative to it. The move from yellow to red simply echoes the work's theme of transformation. And since the only other colour to occupy the entire frame is the black that follows Weronika's death, the linkage between a whole-frame colouring and death suggests that not only is red not its opposite (not the 'life' red so often connotes), but that it is linked to it. Meanwhile, if colour is traditionally linked to Romanticism, this association leads logically to the doubling that so preoccupied the Romantics: separated from the object in which it originates, perhaps echoing it in a composition, a colour becomes an object released into a new form of being, a doubling of the original object by a phantom one that is as vague and shapeless as ectoplasm. Squeezed out of the object like a juice that becomes a separate entity, the colour indicates a possible doubleness of being.

The Double Life of Véronique is not usually associated with the colour red: Kieślowski himself described its dominant colour as 'golden-yellow', and argued that '[m]ost people think that the world in *Véronique* is portrayed with warmth; this warmth comes from the actress, of course, and the staging, but also from the dominant colour, namely, this shade of gold'.[39] Its cinematographer, Sławomir Idziak, named its colour shift as yellow–green. However, its featuring of a full-screen red at one point links it to *Three Colours: Red* by providing a possible explanation for that film's lack of the momentary flooding of the screen with its titular colour that had characterised *Three Colours: Blue* and *Three Colours: White*. Moreover, following that moment of screen-engulfing red, red not only begins to appear more frequently in *The Double Life of Véronique*, but arguably assumes a key role, with redness seeming to represent the growing point of the unconscious gravitation of Véronique, the work's French protagonist, towards her dead Polish soul-sister, Weronika. It is as if, like the many painters who have inserted a mobilising dash of red into their canvases, Kieślowski and Idziak felt that neither yellow nor yellow–green possessed sufficient dynamism to push the narrative forward, to prevent it coagulating in the lyrical.

The full-screen red in question appears as if in illustration of Goethe's statement, in his *Theory of Colours*, that 'one can very easily elevate and lift yellow into red, through thickening and darkening'.[40] It is preceded immediately by an anamorphic image of Weronika, singing and collapsing, within a flame-like yellow that can be taken as representing her life. The camera then swings left into a redness, until red suffuses the screen entirely. Since this occurs as Alexandre's anonymous phone call is relaying Weronika's final concert, a connection is made between red and Weronika, whose image appears to form unconsciously within the psyche of Véronique. Subsequently, red enters the wardrobe of Véronique herself. The importance of red's addition to the work's dominant colours is underlined when, at her father's house, the image splits among three colours: as she leans on her side, in a red sweater, strips of green and yellow light fill the middle and upper layers of the window opposite her. Shortly afterwards, she agrees to lie on behalf of a friend dressed in a red skirt. This decision suggests her continuing unconscious attraction to the red now associated with Weronika. When she falls asleep, only to be woken abruptly by a yellow light playing on her face, while approaching the window, seeking the source of that light, she passes a mirror whose upper half is lit red. Her lack of attention to an object that bears a double quotient of elements associated with Weronika – through its redness, and Weronika's status as 'the mirror image' of Véronique – shows an intensification of the Polish girl's presence in her unconscious and ironically prolongs the unconsciousness of the other's presence she had evinced when in Kraków. One may wonder therefore whether the red glass vase that recurs in several adjacent scenes also represents an oneiric reconjugation of this image, 'la glace rouge' (the red mirror) becoming 'red glass'. Is the French 'glace' reflected here in its English homonym, 'glass'?

When declaring to her father her love for someone she does not know, Véronique wears her red sweater. Since Weronika both stood out through her talent and died by maximising it, Véronique's decision to begin wearing red could be interpreted as simultaneously identifying with the trait of putting herself forward, by adopting the most assertive of colours, and toning herself down by translating it into a clothing choice: something that will not threaten her heart, as continued singing would have done. As Véronique draws nearer and nearer to the St Lazare station location of Alexandre, who has bombarded her with clues to his whereabouts, the 'warmer, warmer' game involves surrounding her with red: the red bar on the swing glass doors of the brasserie, the red walls behind her as she pushes them open. The red is triply determined as a sign of love, of Weronika, and of proximity to a goal. This overdetermination means that when, in the hotel room, Véronique tells Alexandre how long she had felt his call, the remark suggests a possible intertwining of his summons with the call of the absence created in her

The Double Life of Véronique: Véronique in the Orphic mirror, the red nimbus of her reflection suggesting an unseen Weronika-Eurydice behind her

by the demise of Weronika, which aches to be filled. Although Alexandre is a puppeteer and the manipulator of Véronique, that manipulation may have been avenged already by her soul sister, as he too may have been used. Invisibly, the stubbornly persisting, absent presence of Weronika may have employed him to bring to Véronique's attention the photograph of her Polish double on the Kraków market square: to force her to return the gaze with which she herself had viewed her shortly before her death.

SPECULATIVE CONCLUSION

A juxtaposition of these four films suggests that the various triangles of colours deserving of being called 'primaries' may include black, white and red (though, of course, unlike the others, they are not 'primary' in the technical sense of mixing to form all other colours). Each triangle would have its own separate dialectic. Red would be the triangles' point of interference. The juxtaposition also suggests that any film foregrounding the red that is the 'strongest', in the sense of the most dramatic, in each of the sets of three may need to link it with one or more of the only two colours able to 'live with it', black and white, whose status is even more fundamental. Should red form part of a system involving any other colours, the need to prevent it overwhelming them by assigning it a subsidiary position runs the risk of making it seem no more than an accent, a marker of a particularly dramatic moment, or causing it to be overlooked. This would seem to be borne out by the general lack of attention paid to the key role of red in *The Double Life of Véronique*.

NOTES

1. Sergei Eisenstein, 'From Lectures on Music and Colour in *Ivan the Terrible*', in Eisenstein, *Selected Works Vol. III: Writings, 1934–47*, ed. Richard Taylor, trans. William Powell (London: BFI, 1996), p. 326.

2. Sergei Eisenstein, 'On Colour', in Eisenstein, *Selected Works Vol. II: Towards a Theory of Montage*, ed. Michael Glenny and Richard Taylor, trans. Michael Glenny (London: BFI, 1991), pp. 254–67.

3. Ibid., p. 264.

4. Gilles Deleuze, *Cinema 1: The Movement-Image*, trans. Hugh Tomlinson and Barbara Habberjam (Minneapolis: University of Minnesota Press, 1986), p. 118.

5. See Brent Berlin and Paul Kay, *Basic Color Terms: Their Universality and Evolution* (Berkeley and Los Angeles: University of California Press, 1969). For more comment on Berlin and Kay, and on critiques of their work, see Chapter 3, note 1.

6. They may also be experienced as the originary colours of a social order. Thus, when speaking of 'elementary considerations' concerning American experience, Richard Rodriguez adds: 'I mean the meeting of the Indian, the African, and the European in colonial America. Red. Black. White. The founding palette' (Richard Rodriguez, *Brown: The Last Discovery of America* (New York and London: Penguin, 2002), p. xii).

7. Ibid., p. 162.

8. P. Adams Sitney, 'Color and Myth in *Cries and Whispers*', *Film Criticism* vol. 13 no. 3 (Spring 1989), pp. 37–41.

9. Edward Branigan, 'The Articulation of Colour in a Filmic System: *Deux ou trois choses que je sais d'elle*', in Angela Dalle Vacche and Brian Price (eds), *Color: The* Film *Reader* (New York and London: Routledge, 2006). Branigan distinguishes between the three sets of primaries as follows: 'The physical or light primaries (which mix toward white light) are red, blue, and green. The pigment or painter's primaries (which mix down toward black) are red, blue, and yellow. The psychological primaries (which mix in vision toward gray) are red, blue, yellow, and green' (p. 173).

10. Of the critical texts known to me, only Lisa Di Bartolomeo's meticulous PhD thesis recognises that red plays a noteworthy role in *The Double Life of Véronique*, helping link Weronika and Véronique. See Lisa Di Bartolomeo, *Other Visions: Krzysztof Kieślowski's Trzy kolory Trilogy* (PhD dissertation presented to the Department of Slavic Languages and Literatures, University of North Carolina, Chapel Hill, 2001), pp. 151–3. The fact that two researchers noted this link independently speaks for the likelihood of its significance.

11. See my 'Kieślowski and the Anti-Politics of Colour: A Reading of the *Three Colours* Trilogy', *Cinema Journal* vol. 41 no. 1 (2002), p. 60, for more on this issue.

12. Aldous Huxley, *The Doors of Perception and Heaven and Hell* (London: Flamingo, 1994), p. 71.

13. Ibid., p. 79.

14. Ibid., pp. 88–9.

15. Johann Wolfgang von Goethe, *Sämtliche Werke* Vol. 10: *Zur Farbenlehre*, ed. Peter Schmidt (Munich: Carl Hanser Verlag, 1989), p. 236.

16. Andrey Tarkovsky, *Time Within Time: The Diaries 1970–1986* (London and New York: Verso/Seagull, 1993), p. 357.

17. Angela Dalle Vacche, 'Michelangelo Antonioni's *Red Desert*: Painting as Ventriloquism and Color as Movement (Architecture and Painting)', in Dalle Vacche and Price, *Color*, pp. 185–6.

18. Michelangelo Antonioni, *The Architecture of Vision: Writings and Interviews on Cinema*, ed. Carlo di Carlo and Giorgio Tinazzi (New York: Marsilio, 1996), p. 203.

19. Roberto Campari, '"Il deserto rosso" et la couleur', in Carlo di Carlo (ed.), *Michelangelo Antonioni 1: 1942/1965* (Rome: Ente autonomo di gestione per il cinema, 1988), p. 309.

20. Lucja Demby, 'Rzeczywistość bez słońca. O symbolice CZERWONEJ PUSTYNI', in Bogusław Zmudziński (ed.) *Michelangelo Antonioni* (Cracow: Rabid, 2004), p. 118.

21. Ned Rifkin, *Antonioni's Visual Language* (Ann Arbor, MI: UMI Press, 1982), p. 97.

22. Ibid., p. 101.

23. The idea that one plus one can equal one recurs, perhaps ironically, in the Tarkovsky film many deem *his* least successful, *Nostalghia* (1983) – indicating that for all his disparagement of *Red Desert*, he had paid close attention to it. (Whether this connection to a film he found unsatisfying betrays his own possible unconscious dissatisfaction with *Nostalghia* might well be worth discussing.)

24. Ingmar Bergman, *Four Stories by Ingmar Bergman*, trans. Alan Blair (London: Marion Boyars, 1977), p. 60 (emphasis in orginal).

25. Malcolm Bull, *Seeing Things Hidden: Apocalypse, Vision and Totality* (London: Verso, 1999), p. 89.

26. Anita Jacobson-Widding, *Red–White–Black as a Mode of Thought: a Study of Triadic Classification by Colours in the Ritual Symbolism and Cognitive Thought of the Peoples of the Lower Congo* (Uppsala studies in cultural anthropology; Uppsala: Almqvist and Wiksell, 1979), p. 366.

27. Ibid., pp. 359–60.

28. Bull, *Seeing Things Hidden*, p. 89. The most thoroughgoing attempt to correlate Bergman's *oeuvre* with the thought of Girard is to be found in Paisley Livingston's rigorous and suggestive *Ingmar Bergman and the Rituals of Art* (Ithaca and London: Cornell University Press, 1982).

29. Pauline Kael, 'Flesh', in Kael, *Reeling* (Boston and Toronto: Little, Brown and Co., 1976), p. 91.

30. Bruce Kawin, *Mindscreen: Bergman, Godard, and First-Person Film* (Princeton, NJ: Princeton University Press, 1978), p. 17.

31. Dr Nicholas Humphrey, 'The Colour Currency of Nature', in Tom Porter and Byron Mikellides, *Color for Architecture* (New York: Van Nostrand Reinhold Company, 1976), p. 98 (emphasis in original). Meanwhile, since various experiments with child colour preferences, including those of Tom Porter, suggest one for red in the under-seven age group (Porter and Mikkelides, *Color for Architecture*, p. 93), Bergman's red screen might be primal (and possibly even pre-linguistic, anxiety-evoking because unnameable?) among humans as well as primates.

32. Kael, 'Flesh', p. 92.

33. Frank Gado, *The Passion of Ingmar Bergman* (Durham, NC: Duke University Press, 1986), p. 408.

34. Adams Sitney, 'Color and Myth in *Cries and Whispers*', p. 41.

35. T. W. Adorno, *Minima Moralia: Reflections from Damaged Life*, trans. E. F. N. Jephcott (London: New Left Books, 1974), p. 96.

36. Ibid., p. 95.

37. Gado, *The Passion of Ingmar Bergman*, p. 409.

38. Ibid.

39. Danuta Stok (ed. and trans.), *Kieślowski on Kieślowski* (London and Boston: Faber and Faber, 1993), pp. 186–7

40. Goethe, *Sämtliche Werke*, p. 235. Bearing in mind the remarks on the anxiety-provoking qualities of decontextualised red mentioned above (note 31), the insertion of a full-screen red into this film might correlate with the degree to which its ambiguities display an uncanniness that is alien to the later, more mellow *Three Colours: Red*, which might eschew spreading red across the entire screen in order not to disturb.

5 Declensions Along One Side of the Colour Circle: from Yellow to Green to Blue

If yellow and blue, which we consider as the most fundamental and simple colours, are united as they first appear, in the first state of their action, the colour which we call green is their result. (Goethe, *Theory of Colours*, 801)[1]

All this long eve, so balmy and serene,/ Have I been gazing on the western sky,/ And its peculiar tint of yellow green. (Coleridge, 'Dejection: An Ode')

With their vacant blue eyes, they were gazing intently at the yellow star, as though at a field to be harvested. (Description of an encounter of *Wehrmacht* soldiers and Jews in Piotr Rawicz's *Blood from the Sky*)[2]

SPECULATIONS ON YELLOW AND IDEOLOGY

Although yellow is usually accounted a primary colour (i.e., one of the 'painter's primaries' that is the best known of the various sets of primaries), far fewer films associate themselves with it than with its cousin, red. This author's title search of the Internet Movie Database (accessed 7 April 2010) found 2,018 partial matches for red, and only 311 for yellow (with 1,459 for blue). Is this disparity solely attributable to

Cyclo: the Boss Lady's son in yellow

the strength of red's advertisement of passion and attraction, and hence to its headily seductive solicitation of an audience, which sanctions yellow's subordination to the red into which it can easily be shifted, or are there other plausible reasons, both cultural and natural? (Blue's relative primacy, as an opposite of red, both as part of a basic cultural binary and as 'distant' in terms of a retinal focus difference whereby red is 'close', is also obvious. Meanwhile, the opposition of the two colours becomes metaphysical in the colour schemes of two of the early Picasso's favourite Parisian haunts, the blue-ceilinged café Le Ciel and the adjacent red-lit café L'Enfer.)

One ground for contesting yellow's claim to primacy might be the malign Occidental tradition of its othering as the sign of the outsider, affixed to such groups as prostitutes and Jews. A later form of such othering, with the apparent alibi of visual accuracy, identifies yellow as a colour of 'the Orient', thereby linking it to a limited range of subjects, while yet another underlies Wassily Kandinsky's negative judgment: '[y]ellow, if steadily gazed at in any geometrical form, has a disturbing influence, and reveals in the colour an insistent, aggressive character'; worse still perhaps, '[i]t can never have profound meaning'.[3] The exotically attractive may be lit by gilding footlights, but may also be feared as the sickly, disease-inducing projection of Alexander Pope's 'jaundiced eye', to which 'all things seem yellow'. Of particular relevance in the cinematic context might be its use as a tint designating day-time in silent cinema, which taints it doubly, associating it with an 'obsolete' form of cinema and with a conventionality that denies it expressive power. (These identifications, with the Orient and silent cinema, intersect, of course, in D. W. Griffith's *Broken Blossoms or The Yellow Man and the Girl* (1919), though its diegesis – partly departing from the stereotypical as the film itself does from meleodrama in several key respects – employs *purple* as the Orient's sign.)

An ambiguous tribute to yellow marks the beginning of Eric Rohmer's *La Collectioneuse* (1967), when Daniel's friend comments that the dandy's elegance, like Daniel, creates a void – which may result also from 'a certain yellow' (that of Daniel's tie?). Yellow can appear insubstantial, always threatened by absorption into green, and then blue, or – conversely – by sublation into the 'warm' portion of the colour circle. Thus Goethe comments in his *Theory of Colours,* that 'one can very easily elevate and lift yellow into red, through thickening and darkening'.[4] Such an elevation shapes the end of Jerzy Skolimowski's *Deep End* (1971), as if echoing both Goethe's remark and Godard's designation of his films' red as paint, as the yellow of the dead Sue's discarded yellow plastic mac gives way to the spilled paint mingling with the rising pool-water as an image of her unseen, spilled blood. Yellow becomes the reverse of elevated when, in Voytech Jasny's *Az prijde kocour* (*Cassandra Cat*) (1963), the truth-seeing eyes of the cat Mokol reveal ill-matched newly weds in tell-tale colours, she red with ardour, he a yellow here connoting infidelity.

Yellow's downgrading may also reflect the relative rarity with which the world displays it occupying large expanses. Any such expanses are limited in time or space: wheatfields yellow only before harvest; deserts feature only in certain latitudes. By way of contrast, vast expanses of blue and green are visible globally, as if to divide and rule the visual field along the line of the horizon, the one generally connoting sky; the other, earth. Inasmuch as it evokes desert sterility, a Bachelardian reflection on yellow might even see it as designating a 'negative earth', as inhospitable as the sun's surface it recalls. Superimposing the wheatfield upon the desert might intriguingly conjoin signifiers of fertility and barrenness, but their incompatibility on earth renders this reconciliation questionable, artificially paradoxical. Beach yellow, meanwhile, suggests an excluded and exiguous mid-point between sea (blue?) and earth (green).

Negative evaluations of yellow may mirror its most frequent liquid appearance, as urine. The early 1970s' vogue for yellow lighting in American films surely matched the period's sense of American society as polluted, as in *The Godfather* (1972). Neither solid sand, the residue of once-fertile earth, nor liquid waste resonate positively.

Thus, despite its categorisation as a primary, yellow may not *feel* 'primary' in the sense of 'essential' or 'foundational', and many associations with it are not positive.[5] Yellow may seem disposable, even undesirable. If 'primary' entails primacy in life or landscape, it is more likely to appear subordinate, an *accent* within a work. Its association with the temporary or limited may evoke reactions against it – as if, enacting Kandinsky's remarks, Van Gogh's sunflowers revealed the mental instability behind them. Flowers too bloom only briefly.

This underprivileged status may appear paradoxical. After all, is not yellow conventionally the colour of the sun, upon which all life depends? This identification, however, would define yellow as the colour one does not look at: viewing the sun induces blindness, and close approaches risk the fate of Icarus. Moreover, yellow's claim to primacy as the sun's colour may be unmasked, as it is itself the cultural filter imposed upon sunlight, rendering the solar 'visible' in muted, distorted form. It cannot usurp the true primacy of white, with its dazzling fullness of colours, or the sun whose viewing is as taboo as that of the divine.

MASCULINE/FEMININE: *THE CURSE OF THE GOLDEN FLOWER*

One film that locates an ambiguous dialectic in yellow is *Man cheng jia dai huang jia jia* (*The Curse of the Golden Flower*) (2006), which thus represents an exception to the rule of colour univocicity in Zhang Yimou's films. Its profuse other colours – the pinks, purples, greens, blues and even reds of flowers, stained glass and doors – stud the yellow like jewels subordinated to a predominant gold. For much of its duration, as in Akira Kurosawa's *Ran* (1985) – and as in much of human history – the primary cultural function of colour is to identify warring factions. Here, for most of the time that war appears to

The Curse of the Golden Flower: Yin and Yang and yellow and black 1: the male

The Curse of the Golden Flower: Yin and Yang and yellow and black 2: the female

pit colour – the yellow of the chrysanthemums – against blackness. Yellow is particularly desirable because, as Joseph Needham notes, 'in Chinese culture yellow was the colour of the centre among the five regions of space … accordingly it was (for most of Chinese history) the colour signifying imperial might, mana and display'.[6] The war of the yellow associated with Yang, the masculine principle, and Yin, the feminine linked to black, threatens to consume all things. In the course of this struggle, each side seeks, duplicitously and imperialistically, to adopt the colour of its counterpart. Ambiguity is furthered by the cryptic colouration of a conflict pursued by every possible means. The Empress embroiders yellow chrysanthemums, and has the flower sent to the army that will support her against the Emperor who is gradually poisoning her. Black is the anti-colour of his guards and legion assassins, and of the fungus with which he is poisoning the Empress. Battle is joined on the eve of the Festival of Chrysanthemums, which carpet the palace courtyard with yellow. But although the forces of the Empress, led by her son Jai, and identified with the chrysanthemums, suffer defeat, the final note cannot be one of a predominance of the black that opposes yellow. Rather, it is that of the golden yellow worn by the Emperor, who dominates the last image. Yellow is not so much assumed by the Emperor as *retained* by him: it represents the power he said he might confer upon Jai, but would not let him take by force. That power has a source that can always trump the chrysanthemum: the gold of the sun. The golden yellow robe he sports covers darkness as the final, duplicitous sign of his successful concealment of his evil, and secrets, by murdering all who know them: as in the anthropology of Elias Canetti,[7] absolute power and absolute secrecy are one. For Zhang Yimou, meanwhile, colour serves, as so often, as the sign of surface opposed to depth. Beneath it lies the self-same abyss of nothingness covered by colour in Kurosawa's film, though the Japanese master's work is more resonant, plangently despairing over the triumph of the evil god who consumes his own children. Could the darkness of that abyss nestle within yellow itself? Since, as Needham notes, yellow is also 'the colour of the world beyond, for the place of the dead, somewhere underground, was called the "Yellow Springs" at least as early as the 8th century',[8] it would seem possible to argue that the film's ambiguous yellow dialectically encompasses the blackness associated not just with Yin and femininity, but also with negativity and death. (As so often, femininity is hardly privileged …)

MIDAS AND THE SAILOR: *IMMORTAL STORY*

It should be apparent from the very outset that Orson Welles' *Une histoire immortelle* (*The Immortal Story*) (1968), his first colour film, will be riddled with ironies: a man called Clay is seeking to assert his omnipotence. (He will do so by turning into a real event a widespread sailor's yarn of being invited by a rich man to spend the night with a beautiful woman, whom the rich man has paid to play the part of his wife.) Clay tells his clerk Levinsky that he hates prophecies, and yet – ironically – his scheme, with its hardboiled opposition to storytelling, turns this particular tall-tale into one. The irony extends deep into the work's colouration, undermining David Thomson's claim of a Wellesian indifference, even hostility, to colour.[9] The colour that interests the serial teller of tales of would-be omnipotence is, of course, that of fabulous money, of the Midas whose wealth destroys all it creates, including himself, like the double mirrors that endlessly multiply and diminish the ironically named 'Citizen' Kane, their diminuendo reducing him to mere citizenship indeed. The irony this colour emanates becomes glaring when Clay asks Levinsky whether the sailor hired for the role has ever seen gold (a five-guinea piece): even as he speaks the golden-haired sailor is gold-lit, a doubly golden boy, but Clay cannot see it. Later, in bed with the beautiful woman (Jeanne Moreau), the sailor declaims a poem composed at sea, likening the moon to a guinea. In other words, gold is no supreme value but only a translation of the lunar femininity at his side, the woman known in the night. And yet, having been paid by Clay to depart at dawn, he does so – setting the seal on her lunar existence. Despite their declarations of love, she makes no attempt to follow. After all, why should she? The fulfilment of Clay's vainglorious wish has killed him, avenging her for the house he had swindled from her father, and apparently leaving her in possession. Her triumph too is ironic, as the final shot frames her across the balcony against autumnal trees. Gold splits into two colours, those of youth and age: of the golden dawn into which the sailor walks, equipped now to buy a ship, while she, who has earned so much more, has the gold of autumn. Is it simply that revenge is bitter, tying one to the corpse of one's victim? Or is it just that, ironically, Virginie cannot go with Paul, for, unlike him, she is no virgin (this bitter fact underlined by the irony of naming)? Or is it just that the unification of the two is *another* story in the never-ending series?

If the yellow of gold, dawn and autumn is the polysemic leitmotif of Welles' film, one should not overlook its red. (After all, the word 'Adam', the name of the primal man in *Genesis*, also denotes the redness of the clay of which he is kneaded.) If both these colours suit the Chinese port setting (Macao), the red ironically links Virginie and Clay, being worn by both. Freudians would deem this the symbolic emblem of her maternal status, her pairing with Clay. One may imagine the sea-shell Levinsky proffers the dead Clay at the end being held subsequently by her, transfixed by its whispers of the place where the sailor has gone – an Oedipus who somehow escapes the Freudian version of 'the immortal story'. (Is this because he is 'really' Parsifal, the fool who is pure at heart, his heart of true fool's gold, and the *true* 'immortal story' is the Arthurian one? Is 'Clay' really – as in Hebrew – the old Adam, and the story one of his fall? If the story truly is immortal, it would have to reach back to the recorded beginnings of the human race.)

THE COLOUR OF MARNIE

Although red is blatantly the key colour of Alfred Hitchcock's *Marnie* (1964) – the colour of the suffusions that flash lightning-like across the consciousness of Marnie herself, and which are finally grounded in her recollection of the blood she shed in her childhood when killing a sailor who molested her

Marnie: duplicitous yellow and black, each hiding something

mother – yellow may be equally important, and certainly ramifies more subtly into multiple crannies of the work. The opening shot, at whose centre bulges a bag under the arm of a black-haired woman shot from behind, grants the colour an importance underlined when we discover it is full of banknotes. It is as if it has been suffused from within by the yellow that is the traditional colour of money: the yellow of gold. Although that bag is then discarded by Marnie, who changes her outfit and accoutrement along with her identity, yellow nevertheless arguably enters even more deeply into her identity, as she washes the black dye from her hair and first reveals her face to the camera when shaking out her golden hair. Similarly, although she drops through a grating the yellow-tipped key to the left luggage locker that houses a suitcase with her old identity, she is folded in yellow as she travels by cab to her mother's house in Baltimore. The persistence of yellow, through all these attempts to dispose of it, suggests that unsuccessful repression defines Marnie's identity. Even more firmly definitive of that identity, however, is the blonde she has dyed her hair; the most valuable hair-tint that may be called the colour of money. This identity is defined as conflicted and contradictory, however, for even though it is the 'colour of money', with which Marnie will seek to buy her mother Berenice's affection (she watches with hollow-eyed envy as it is lavished upon the golden-tressed young neighbour, Jessie), it is also the colour of the sexuality her mother abhors. Thus, the mother disparages her new hair tint with the words 'too blonde hair always looks like a woman's trying to attract the men'. When she criticises Marnie for spending so much money on her, Marnie replies that 'money answereth all things', a dictum she (deliberately?) mis-attributes to the Bible. Insofar as Marnie's own name – particularly as spoken by the mother whose diction diverges from standard correctness – could be heard as 'money', her self-definition through it is hardly surprising. When saying 'that's what money's for, to spend', Marnie is also saying 'that's what Marnie's for', speaking of herself in the third person in an unconscious echo and internalisation of the voice of the mother. If it is plausible to identify the film's yellows with a 'false freedom' – as did Raymond Durgnat[10] – it is because it subordinates the colour of Marnie to the colour of money, subjecting blonde hair to cherishing like a golden hoard. Money is utterly ambiguous, as money and men define the past prostitution of the mother, while 'men and a good name don't go together', she concludes. The yellow fridge in the mother's kitchen reiterates the motif of the persistence of an element consigned to the past.

Later, as Robin Wood noted,[11] the household of Mark Rutland is also associated with yellow: his father has a yellow waistcoat, and yellow flowers are among the first things seen there. This yellow reverberates across at least three registers, connoting the yellow of money, indicating the household's possible accommodation of the Marnie who was once associated with yellow, but also suggesting that her incorporation into it will involve her confrontation with things she has sought to leave behind. This yellow is, as it were, the initially welcoming, toned-down, disguised form of the related red that assails her. The imminence of the confrontation with red becomes apparent when Lil Mainwaring, who would have liked to marry Mark, appears in red to greet guests at an evening reception. Since we know that red threatens Marnie's stability, even before learning of Lil's surreptitious invitation of an old employer aware of Marnie's kleptomania, we suspect that Marnie's newly acquired, relative stability is due for an unspecified testing. She herself may once have been the red fox, travelling in the Red Fox cab company, but in the end she will be appalled by the rending of the fox and herself hunted by Lil. Her identification with that fox may be the symbolic death that prepares her rebirth through the final re-enactment of repressed memories.

VERTIGO AND YELLOW

Vertigo (1958) is seldom associated with yellow. After all, its key colours – as often noted[12] – are the red prominent on the walls of Ernie's, or the green that glows around Judy and Madeleine. However, if Hitchcock employs green to evoke Victorian associations with the ghostly, the yellow that stands so close to it may also figure a haunting. As in the case of green, this afterimage is that of a woman, whom Scottie never sees romantically, though she herself views him thus: Barbara Bel Geddes' Midge. On first appearance, Midge is associated with a yellow that is bright, sunny and pervasive both in her apartment and about her person. For one of my students, Jason Swiderski, this yellow breathes 'safety and comfort in the film; a chromatic sanctuary'.[13] He argues that as Scottie's relationship with Judy develops positively and safely: '[I]t is only natural that Hitchcock would evoke the ease and safety he has already associated with the colour yellow by making that the colour of Judy's blouse.'[14] The work's use of yellow echoes its general theme of women's absorption of one another: the false Madeleine's of the true Madeleine Elster, that false Madeleine's of Midge and Judy's of her own earlier incarnation of 'Madeleine'.

The absorption of Midge, a 'live burial', occurs through a triple displacement, triply dissociating yellow from her. First, after Scottie has fished Madeleine out of San Francisco Bay, she lies in his bed beneath a yellow blanket. That yellow then acquires a different valence by being woven into the red–yellow alternation Ornan Rotem terms the 'libidinal' strand in the work's colour scheme, and that flickers in front of Madeleine as she dries herself by Scottie's fire.[15] One could see this transformation adumbrated in the very décor of Midge's apparently restful apartment, where, although she herself may wear a yellow blouse, the blinds glow orange and the chairs are red; in other words, yellow can initiate the 'warning-series' whose importance for Hitchcock's films Richard Allen has described.[16] Second, yellow is established as no longer belonging to Midge – and hence free for appropriation – by its later appearance on yellow taxis and yellow roses (examples Swiderski also notes[17]). Third, because only a short step separates yellow from green, its absorption into green can seem natural, even inevitable. It can seem all the more so because the restfulness Midge wishes to embody is itself often linked green, and so its carrier, Judy, appears to Scottie as a haven from his trauma.

That haven appears all the safer for Judy's frequent side-on shooting, which suggests radical difference from Madeleine: her breasts also emphasised by a tight-fitting dress, her eros becomes physical and tangible. Ironically, this appearance makes her seem more readable than the Madeleine whose looks both spiritualised and repressed sexuality. When Madeleine had been shot side-on, at Ernie's, the focus had been on her head, suggesting a queen-like power over a Scottie reduced to a subject. (Since his head faces the same way, as it also does before driving her out to San Bautista's, the lover's profound identification with the beloved – and hence with her death – is suggested.) In one of the film's crowning ironies and signature images, Judy too is shot side-on in a manner that stresses her head: the green flowing in from the neon outside her apartment asserts her identity with Madeleine and counters her attempt to separate herself from her by wearing mauve when visiting Ernie's. Unlike Madeleine, with her floating mystery, Judy becomes an earth-goddess whose accentuated breasts indicate her ability to mother more comprehensively than Midge ever could. Moreover, yellow is further subordinated when, as Spoto notes, (unseen) yellow filters make Scottie's eyes look green.[18] And green itself, of course, is more widespread, and hence a better signifier of the natural, than yellow. As it conveys the chlorophyll of life, it can claim more convincingly always to be able to accompany one, never to leave one alone. As so often in Hitchcock, of course, this colour is duplicitous, suggesting both earth and the supernatural: in other words, in the hidden signifier linking the two, *the grave* into which Scottie stares and then falls. Insofar as green is haunted by yellow, the spectre of Midge underlies the appearance of Judy, and haunting succeeds haunting across a text that cannot come to rest.

GUILLERMO DEL TORO AND THE DIALECTICS OF YELLOW AND GREEN

An undecidability regarding the central colour characterises Guillermo Del Toro's use of yellow in *El espinazo del Diablo* (*The Devil's Backbone*) (2001). Here the ambiguity involves an oscillation within a single hue: thus, the uterine, orange underwater space inhabited by the ghost of Santi, the boy murdered by Jacinto, transforms, as if obeying a structuralist law of opposition, into the dry yellow-ochre of the road and the dirt of the countryside round the orphanage sheltering children of Republican parents. The vibrations of yellow constitute the polysemous centre of a work we finally learn has been narrated by another ghost, that of Dr Casares, who had helped run the orphanage, and whose opening voiceover likens ghosts to insects trapped in amber. The existence of varieties of yellow and orange both inside and outdoors, and associated both with wetness and dryness, embodies the instability of apparent opposites in the realm of matter. (In the moral sphere, however, such distinctions are clear.) And yellow is, of course, also the colour of the Republican gold held in trust, and in the safe, by Carmen, who co-heads the orphanage. Paradoxically, yellow designates both the worthless dirt outside and the fetishised treasure motivating all Jacinto's crimes. Meanwhile, the orange of the pool in which Santi has died, and where Jacinto himself will perish in the end, itself reappears as the colour of the alcohol in the jars containing the stillborn, one of whom has the exposed backbone that furnishes the film's title. That alcohol itself circulates as liquid gold, sold in the nearby town to support the orphanage. Thus, the colour functions on multiple levels, forming the lynchpin of Del Toro's rich metaphorical structure. Moreover, its interest in yellow might even constitute an intertextual homage to the honeycomb-coloured cinematography of the greatest of all Spanish films to filter the fascism of the 1940s through the fantastic, Victor Erice's *El espíritu de la colmena* (*The Spirit of the Beehive*) (1973).

Speaking of the colour scheme in his other, better-known film set at the intersection of fascism and the fantastic, *El labirinto del fauno* (*Pan's Labyrinth*) (2006), Del Toro distinguishes three levels: the real world of twentieth-century Spanish fascism, given in grey, green and blue; the world of the faun, who imposes tasks upon the young female protagonist, Ofelia, and whose association with green under-scores his link to the natural world, of which he is almost a gnarled outgrowth; and the warm colours of the fantasy world in which Ofelia performs the tasks. The prevalence of yellow in the one film, and green in the other, underlines their diptych status and emphasises the two colours' mutual transforma-bility, destabilising their fixed opposition. The colours' dialectics unfold both within and between them. Thus the fact that the faun exists in the fantasy world, but is associated with one of the colours marked as 'real', corresponds to our difficulty in reading him: he is majestic yet sinister, a helper in the girl's quest to escape oppression, but also a torturer. This overlap in functions may be deemed the source of the work's genuinely mythical impact – and in this respect it resembles Cocteau's *La Belle et la bête* (*Beauty and the Beast*) (1946), to which it owes much. The enigma he incarnates is also the one that drives the nar-rative: what does its process mean? Where is it going? Although outside a political reality steeped in torture, is he too finally a torturer? Certainly, his eventual command that Ofelia shed innocent blood, which seems to mean – which both he and the viewer take as meaning – the killing of Ofelia's baby brother, would suggest so. As Ofelia both fulfils the command and frustrates it, shedding her own instead, she takes charge of a process of which hitherto she has been the object, redefining the making of meaning by herself exploit-ing its doubleness. Even at the end, though, one cannot be sure whether the Faun, whose make-up has suggested a mask, is good masked as evil, or the Devil who serves the interests of deity despite himself, effecting the reunion of Ofelia and her parents in the true family romance in which she truly *is* a princess.

GRIEF AND GREEN: *SOLARIS, ELVIRA MADIGAN*

The atmosphere of grief pervading *Solyaris* (*Solaris*) (1972) is encoded in its opening shot: green fronds drawn out by a river's flow. The coded nature of even so apparently realistic an image measures the depth to which the film is steeped in dream. Although noting their resemblance to tresses, Philip Lopate[19] refrains from identifying them as coded thus in the unconscious of its protagonist, Kris Kelvin. However, they are surely signs of the form of suicide Gaston Bachelard deems 'the most feminine' in his analysis of 'the Ophelia complex'.[20] Tarkovsky's work may be seen to intersect here both with *Vertigo* and *Marnie*, through Judy/Madeleine's simulation of suicide and the real attempt made by Marnie. The iden-tity of fronds and tresses also encodes suicide as a turning away, a 'de-facing' and effacing of the hair's owner, reconjugating Tarkovsky's recurrent averted heads as signs of death and absence, transposing into another key (and gender) the turned heads of *The Hunters in the Snow*: in a sense, Hari is preoc-cupied with those turned heads because they repeat the gesture of her prototype, while their removal of the clear identifying features of the face then permits the serial misrecognition as 'Hari' of the vari-ous reincarnations bouncing back and forth between Kris's mind and the mirror of the planet. The averted face is turned to another world, earthly death doubled and mirrored by another planet. Whence the film's recurrent motif of forgetting the appearance of a face. The green is that of the mirror that

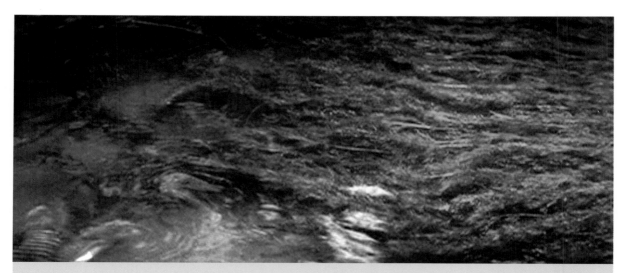

Solaris: river fronds as the severed tresses of a lost, unrecognised Ophelia

recurs across the film, its verdigris painting anticipated death on the face of its beholder. Meanwhile, the capacity of hair to outlive its wearer reveals that its encoding in the green fronds shows Hari as still alive in – still haunting, still capable of returning to – the mind of Kris from the very outset. That which is green is really still alive, photosynthesised by film.

That which is green must also die, however. Bo Widerberg's *Elvira Madigan* (1967) unfolds under the double sign of green and grief, its opening title informing us of the forest death of its two protagonists (Elvira and Sixten), and – as that forest setting indicates – its dominant colour is green: the green of the summer, before the autumn against which Elvira never manages to complete her knitting of a protective sweater. Shot, and held in a freeze frame, catching a butterfly, she is equally ephemeral. The studied melancholy of *Elvira Madigan* is that of the summer condemned to pass. 'Time held me, green and dying' (Dylan Thomas) might be its motto. The lovers' relationship to green extends into the repeated blurring of images and serves the eroticising – strictly speaking, in this context, romanticising – abstraction whose description by Brian Price was discussed earlier in this book, and which corresponds to the romantic gaze's exclusive, amplifying focus upon a single person. The centrality of green is noted by William Free, who comments:

[a]lthough the first lovemaking takes place in an open field seen through a long shot, we sense the lovers as encompassed by the grass, the trees, and the greenness of the field and as losing their individual existence as they merge simultaneously into each other, and into nature – an impression aided by the flat field of focus of the telephoto lens. Most of their walks together take place in the woods, tightly framed by trees which impart their greenness to the light.[21]

For Sixten's friend, Sixten's vision of the world as green, which is also Widerberg's, is distorted – as when one sees a single blade of grass close up and loses sight of the world beyond. Sixten's reply takes that blade as metonymising the world: 'I believe one blade of grass can be the entire world.' He rightly adds 'and the world is nothing without grass'. His friend might have retorted that a world that is all grass, entirely viewed through a green optic, is no world at all. (To take another possible epigraph, from Andrew Marvell's seventeenth-century poem 'The Garden', Sixten's view means 'Annihilating all that's made/ To a green thought in a green shade.') Such sheer exclusivity breathes self-destructiveness. A self-consciously 'European', tragic take on the 1960s notion of a 'summer of love', *Elvira Madigan* seeks to reduce the world to summer and youth alone, acknowledging – and knowing – only one season. And since youth must end, it too must die, prematurely, before shades of sere, or red, striate, then over-take, the leaf's contours.

(The inevitability of the death of green is the analogous conclusion of Zhang Yimou's *Shi mian mai fu* (*House of Flying Daggers*) (2004), when the death of the lovers – and, in particular, of Mei, who appears in her true guise near the film's end, dressed in the green costume of the House – is associated with the sudden, surreal onset of a winter whose snow engulfs her and her two feuding suitors. This final movement from green to white, from life to death, is foreshadowed by the way the green of the bam-boos associated with martial arts films discloses its deathliness: as the green arranges itself in rigid, regimented stalks, like the soldiers who climb them, or the bamboo spears split on impact to splay, revealing their inner pallor and hollowness. In Kawase Naomi's *Mogari no mori* (*The Mourning Forest*) (2007), by way of contrast, the overwhelming greens surrounding the old people's home relate ironically to Shigeki's feeling that he is no longer alive. Only when, having wandered away into the forest, he is able to find his wife's grave and dig down into the soil does he uncover the brown that is the companionable colour of death, of release from the agony of separation from her.)

NATURAL CAMOUFLAGE: JOSEPH LOSEY'S *THE BOY WITH GREEN HAIR* (1948)

After his orphaned grandson Peter's hair has turned green while taking a bath, and street wiseacres term this strange, Gramps indignantly avers: 'my grandson's hair turned green just as natural as the sun comes up in the morning'. A favourite teacher tries to naturalise the change by asking her class how many have hair of various colours – and since they include one redhead, alongside the green-haired Peter, the suggestion is that extreme minority status does not make him abnormal. (Indeed, since Gramps is Irish, and red hair is reasonably common among Scots and Irish, one might even consider the two boys related. The redhead's questioning look has the surprised bafflement of one who knows he has been tricked, but cannot grasp how, or how to protest.)

Problems and paradoxes arise in part because green is the colour most widely identified with the natural – but green hair is not. The question of Peter's relationship to nature arises repeatedly as he passes through the small town after his change, being exposed to public comment, and his head appears repeat-edly against its grass and hedges. If he blends in so easily, how can he be said to stand out? Indeed, this aspect of the film almost suggests a later Losey title: *Figures in a Landscape* (1970). One may wonder whether the local lawns are as artificial – being an often-used RKO set – as the hair of the boy passing them. Only when he runs out into the wild nature of a glade does he really fit in, a contrast Losey had intended to underline by having that glade differ as much in colour from the town as Oz does from the sepia opening of Victor Fleming's film.[22] For Foster Hirsch, the fact that 'the glade has the same studio quality as the town' means that 'the sequence doesn't have the tension and the visual flair that would have set it apart from the rest of the story'.[23] Nevertheless, this similarity may be a gain, as it reiterates the figural erasure of difference apparent already in the melting of Peter's hair into the background, thus anticipat-ing the town's ability to recuperate that difference – as it does when he allows his hair to be cut.

On entering the glade, Peter encounters incarnations of war orphans he had seen on school posters, who give the green hair a meaning and exhort him to tell others: 'I am a war orphan, and my green hair is to remind you that war is very bad for children.' Since a schoolmate had described the leading poster child as resembling Peter, and since he employs words also used by Gramps – calling the hair a medal – he is clearly a fantasy double. The medal metaphor is significantly suggestive that war continues, despite its apparent end. The film classifies green as the natural camouflage of an only apparently normal time (khaki, of course, would be that of acknowledged wartime). The need for camouflage in apparently normal times underlines their actual abnormality. As in that infinitely greater film, Alain Resnais' *Nuit et brouillard* (*Night and Fog*) (1955), where the growing grass of the concentration camps hides the possibility of war's renewed awakening, green is an illusory indicator of the normal. The sheer abnormality of 'post-war' conditions becomes apparent when the advocacy of cutting Peter's hair is pursued by the milkman, who has been losing business. Even the most natural and nurturing fluid may be contaminated, like the 'black milk' of the 'Death Fugue' of Paul Celan – who, of course, did the German translation of the commentary of *Night and Fog*.

The inexplicable trigger of a politically allegorical fantasy, the green of Peter's hair may be the consequence of a dream-like overflow from the plant Gramps says he likes to keep (its floppy leaves like hair pushed up by a sweatband), for it signifies spring and hope. It is as if green is unnatural, or certainly unusual, in the interiors that epitomise any space shaped by humans: whence its absence from the school's war orphan posters, which primarily feature red, blue and yellow. It is also pointedly denied by the yellow and blue markings of the plane with which Peter toys after his haircut, which underlies his loss by its colouration as well as, of course, by being an instrument of war. Its 'absent presence' between blue and yellow suggests its simultaneous negation on the level of the visible and persistence as a concept; or, if one likes, its status as the repressed that is bound to return (Peter, after all, says his hair will grow back green). If, as Peter tells the psychologist, 'it seems there wasn't any place where a war orphan could settle down', is his green also an ironic sign of identification with the outdoor spaces of the town, as if in the hope that at least he might belong in a place of symbolic exclusion? It is as if, unacquainted with local rules for the regulation of colour placement (children do not know the rules), he overidentifies with the town's most pervasive colour, reproducing it in an inevitably inappropriate context. Is the green hair also an oneirically displaced fruit of identification with the grandfather who is Irish, Peter himself becoming a 'little person' who is green? Green is everywhere outside; and, for that very reason, nowhere really at home. Similarly, the Irishman who worked in the circus could be at home in many places, and yet none in particular. Beneath its banal, awkward surface, *The Boy With Green Hair* secretes an overdetermined meditation on a variety of forms of exclusion. Could the green hair itself be due to the radiation of the next war, and the bald, shorn head a sign of the impossibility of any 'return to normal'?

GREEN UNSEEN: THE POETICS OF ABSENCE IN *THE FLIGHT OF THE RED BALLOON*

Although it may seem perverse to consider the presence of green as the key element in a film entitled *Le voyage du ballon rouge* (*The Flight of the Red Balloon*) (2007), Hou Hsiao Hsien's tribute to Albert Lamorisse's much-loved 1956 short children's film *Le ballon rouge* (*The Red Balloon*) (1956), approaching it through the optic of green usefully foregrounds the most remarkable aspect of its treatment of

The Flight of the Red Balloon: a bus window's balloons take flight in a Muybridge-like stutter, overseen by green

colour: its concern to film *both* the colour that is ostentatiously present, and privileged by its title, *and* another one – green – which it invites us to deem possibly present even when invisible, and which insistently shadows its reds, as of course only the deployment of the green screen permits the red balloon to seem self-moving.

Although such suggestions of absent presence and invisibility might seem to imply the mystical, Hou's film grounds them firmly in the technologised texture of contemporary life. As Megan Ratner notes, '[t]echnological devices that allow us to be simultaneously absent and present – computers, cell phones, PlayStations and video cameras – make cameo appearances in nearly every scene'.[24] Central to both the film's style and the meanings it makes is a technique of digital film-making mentioned half-way through the film by Song Fang, the Taiwanese nanny of Simon, whose harried mother, Suzanne, is played with improvisational verve by Juliette Binoche. When Suzanne asks Song, a film student, why the footage she watches on her digicam includes so many shots of a boy in green carrying a red balloon on a string, Song replies that the green clothing facilitates his erasure in digital editing. The final effect, of course, will be the magic of an apparently self-directing balloon. And although that balloon may indeed drift, self-willed or wind-willed, above Parisian streets, its movements closer to ground (for instance, round a metro platform, and then a train containing Simon, with which the film begins) do indeed suggest an anthropomorphic quality stemming from the suppression of its human guidance. It is perhaps a metaphor for Simon himself, cut loose by his mother's self-absorption. Song's remark has the modernist consequence of injecting into our memory of all earlier images of the balloon the possibility that its string is an uncut umbilical cord linking it to a human, of contaminating its later appearances with a possibly unseen human presence. As if parodying and criticising the martial arts films whose invisible wires permit the spectacular tricks that have brought fame to a particular genre of East Asian cinema, Hou leaves the wire visible, modernistically and wittily baring the mechanism, even if only in the mind's eye. But to ensure that we make the connection, Hou shows Song's footage of Simon carrying a red balloon up a public steps, then wearing green as he goes upstairs. When, shortly after Simon's climb up to bed, we see a red balloon drift over buildings, we may wonder whether he might be walking rooftops somnambulistically, and are not surprised to see Song go up to his bedroom, as if acting upon our own suspicions that he may in fact be outdoors. It is surely significant that Suzanne should speak of footage with a boy in green – causing us to wonder whether she recognises her own son, or whether perhaps Song has used another child.

This difficulty of recognising a child is thematised itself, late in the film, in another moment of modernist self-reference that makes us think Suzanne might well have made such a mistake. In the scene in question, which occurs during a class visit to the Musée D'Orsay, a teacher discusses with her pupils Félix Vallatton's 1899 painting *The Ball*, informing them that because of the period's conventions for children's clothing the child's depiction from behind means it might be a boy or a girl. Suzanne's non-seeing of Simon, who is in any case associated with the invisible, may even reflect her desire to see another child of another gender, whose image she projects in his stead: that of her daughter Louise, whom she wishes would move to Paris, the desire to facilitate this motivating her plans to evict the downstairs tenant – thus making space for Louise. In Vallatton's painting a red ball lies to the right of a child, probably bouncing away from it in a park, but the nature of the green within this image interests the teacher just as much: the invisibility of the tree trunks, she remarks (again, a telling invisibility) shows the painting's angle to be a high one. Because this mention of a high angle suggests the presence of a force looking down, it is hardly surprising that Simon should then lean back and see the red balloon bobbing above the ceiling's panes of glass. The balloon becomes as it were a playful stand-in for the framer of the image, the director himself, who looks in unrecognisably, possibly playing with identifications of 'Chineseness' and auspicious red. The uncertainty with regard to the child's gender extends to the painting's two distant white-robed adults, whom one child identifies as ghosts. This indeterminacy includes the relationship of the child to the red ball, as the high angle makes it hover like a balloon. Similarly, the painting's mood is split: the teacher calls it a mixture of sadness and happiness. Like Hou's film, it is bitter-sweet. The fact that the class is reflected in the protective glass that renders the painting behind it a ghostly presence typifies Hou's film, which repeatedly shoots people and things through glass that also reflects another reality, dramatising perception as a process of double exposure, and indicating the continual shadowing of presence by absence. The distant figures in the painting are seen as possibly either parents or ghosts, reminding one that one of Simon's parents is absent, in Montreal. The teacher even comments that it may contain other children we cannot see – like the erased carriers of the red balloon in Hou's own film. The unseen green, that colour the Victorians associated with ghosts, is the appropriate emblem of such absent presences. Could the insistent double focus in Hou's use of reflections also be an image of his own foreignness in Paris, and of the double exposure of a film that is itself a guest and a ghost haunting such originals as those of Vallatton and Lamorisse?

The importance of the red balloon foregrounded in the title should not be downplayed, of course. Yet even at the outset a green–red dialectic shapes subtle geometries of colour, prefiguring the red–green dialectic made explicit in Song's remarks on digital effects. The red rear lights of the car in front of Suzanne's are balanced by shards of green dancing round her dashboard and windscreen. When Simon is shot from a low angle playing pinball through glass that reflects a balloon-like traffic light at the top of the image, the lights behind him include a green pharmacy cross. Having been red, the green traffic light near the screen's top enters into alignment with a girl in a green T-shirt at a café table below. As it observes Simon through the plate glass, the film waits for the reflected traffic light to turn green before it cuts. An image of a street is framed between a car's red rear lights to its left and the green bin by a courtyard door on its right. The absence pervading the film correlates with its title's non-mention of green, which may be construed as one of the peacefulness associated with that colour; Song may radiate calm, but Simon's own mother is perennially overwrought. The green of summer is merely a realistic background, not picked out, like the red of the balloon, and yet the two go together. The absence the balloon trails around with it, in the form of the usual invisibility of its green carrier, extends into the way the balloon passes unnoticed by the characters in scene after scene. Again and again Song stares down at the footage on her camera or laptop, not seeing the red balloon that hovers outside the apartment window, as if wishing to enter. Similarly, it had answered Simon's invitation, at the film's start, to come down to him from the greenery of the trees – though unfortunately too late, as the train doors close before he can see and reach out to it. His inability to do so may be hardly surprising, of course, as the balloon on the platform is doubtless being twitched by another – erased – little boy. The film's motto could be Tristan Corbière's 'Je suis là – mais comme une rature'. It is the absent presence toasted in the final bitter-sweet melody, 'Chin-Chin', as a drinker ruefully sings 'Chin chin à toi, mon balon rouge'. Is there any way of infusing a red balloon with absence more effective than linking it throughout with green? (And it has been absent, displaced, on its travels from the very outset, as the ovaloid multicoloured forms – unsurprisingly running from green to red – seen upon a bus window moving off suggest a flock of balloons, condemned to wander.)

FROM YELLOW TO GREEN (VIA BLACK): *THE DOUBLE LIFE OF VÉRONIQUE*

Colour; female liberation; uneven development; a privileging of music; doubling; and the relativity of point of view that accompanies doubling: if all these phenomena cluster in one complex – particularly during the *fin de siècle*, as argued in Chapter 2 – their assembly within Krzysztof Kieślowski's *La double vie de Véronique* (*The Double Life of Véronique*) (1991) may be expected, even if his film appears at the end of a different century than the one in which they first constellate.

Yellow filters may laminate Kieślowski's with a single colour, but there is no differently coloured or monochrome domain representing a reality from which it might stand apart, which might frame it. The only other colour to achieve any prominence – the red suffusing the screen after the guttering of the anamorphic image of Weronika inside a candle flame – is itself classifiable as a derivative of yellow, and hence merely as its transformation, not as an alternative to it. The move from yellow to red simply echoes the work's theme of transformation. And since the only other colour to occupy the entire frame is the black that follows Weronika's death, the linkage between a whole-frame colouring and death suggests that not only is red not its opposite (not the 'life' red so often connotes), but that it is linked to it.

Shortly after the death of Weronika, we see Véronique attending a puppet show at the school where she teaches. As she sits among schoolchildren staring rapt at the show, she alone stops looking ahead at it and both her gaze and the camera travel leftwards, away from the spectacle, across a stretch of black, to arrive at the face of the puppeteer. It can only be a reflection, as it is located far away from the hands we see along with the puppets they manipulate. Among other things, the moment suggests a willingness on Véronique's part to probe the visual field even when all that occupies it is blackness; and it also suggests that her reaction may flow from our association of the dead Weronika with the blackness of a screen, as a shot from her coffin's position had shown soil thud down upon it until all was black. (It is also as if the colourless space Goethe posited as the desired accompaniment of a colour (see Chapter 1) here becomes not the expected white but its opposite.) The roving of Véronique's gaze may also be prompted by the incompleteness of the hands, which withhold the sign of the directing consciousness mirrored in the face. Her gaze travels across black towards a reflection: both things associated with Weronika. In essence, it moves across death towards life. The intuition that connects her to Weronika sensitises her to the possibility of something existing beyond the normal frame of vision, and she moves outside the frame to find it. As the frame itself expands here into the emptiness of blackness, to end up revealing – in displaced form – the something behind that emptiness, it could be read as an allegorical or microcosmic image of the movement of the film itself. It is as if Véronique is seeking a reflection to replace the one whose loss she intuits: that of Weronika. The placement of this new reflection outside the frame corresponds to Weronika's persistence beyond the bounds of her conscious awareness. It is also as if the reflection is itself a personification of the emptiness of blackness, in the form of the *Doppelgänger* whose appearance foreshadows death.

If the yellow wherewith Sławomir Idziak's colour filters laminate this world becomes red at one point – through the candle flame within which Véronique's dead (Polish) soul-sister Weronika appears – this may anticipate Kieślowski's later *Trois couleurs: rouge* (*Three Colours: Red*) (1994). (Is the appearance of a full-frame red in this film, meanwhile, the reason why no such image is found in *Three Colours: Red*, Kieślowski being averse to repeating the effect?) If Kieślowski declared during this phase of his work that his interest was in the inner life, its termination in red may be unsurprising also: not just because Goethe described red as totalising; not just because flame travels upward, beyond the realm of representation, like the final movement of the script for *Heaven*, which he never filmed; not just because the sun's dilation, and augmented fullness, is red when setting – a moment on which *Three Colours: Red* focuses; not just because flame sets the seal on the end of representation by engulfing objects it might have conveyed. It is also because red figures life, and – as the Old Testament teaches – 'the blood is the life'. It is a *secret, interior* principle of life, however. The moment that ends its occultation within the body sees it flow, and life ebb away. The moment the sun becomes visible, ceasing to issue the dazzling interdiction that renders its seeing taboo, is the moment of its death. The deepest interior has been reached, and breached. Dialectically, therefore, red becomes black: the black sun of depression superimposes upon the yellow–red reality the blackness that enshrouds any eye intrepid enough to view it directly. That movement is adumbrated in miniature in *The Double Life of Véronique*.

Although I have followed Kieślowski himself and described the primary colour of this film as yellow, the matter is nevertheless more complex, and it is possible that just as there are two endings of *The Double Life of Véronique* – according to whether one considers the European version or that for the American market – so there may even be two colour schemes. It would be strangely appropriate if the film were double in this respect also. This possibility is suggested by the following extraordinary interview statement by Sławomir Idziak:

I felt we shouldn't allow any latitude for Eastman Kodak to decide how the colour looked on-screen.
There needed to be a common denominator between these two worlds. I invented a system of yellow

filters, some of which I made myself, in order to control the colour. It was very important to work with the set designer to avoid specific colours that, translated through these filters, would give a completely different effect. This was a somewhat Sisyphean labour. I have a tendency towards using green. Yellow–green was the colour shift. But the copies I was getting were a warm yellow. This process always takes place, and is always painful, but in this film it was downright dramatic. When I started to make prints of the film, and I returned to my original colour scheme, I suddenly and unexpectedly encountered producer's protests. But I didn't care. I was sure Krzysztof would side with me. Unfortunately I got a surprise, because when he saw my version, he didn't like it. He wanted warm yellow. I felt thoroughly betrayed. I thought it was an unbelievably nasty thing to do. I wouldn't talk to him. I told them, 'Do what you want! I don't agree with warm yellow here. It's maudlin, bad, wrong for the film.' Then came Cannes, where there's a whole circus around film screenings. The night before each screening, the film-makers have the opportunity to set the conditions for the projection: to make it darker or lighter and set the sound level to their satisfaction. Since it was very late at night, I came practically in my pyjamas. There was no-one there except me and my wife, who speaks French and translated for me. As the Americans were leaving in their tuxes, I walk into the screening room in my pjs, and what do I see? My colours that they earlier had made a warm yellow had again gone back to green. So I called Krzysztof and said, 'It's back to my way!' And he said, 'I guess you were right.'[25]

The mysteriousness of this process, and the disagreement between Idziak and Kieślowski, cannot but make one wonder whether Idziak himself engineered a switch – as his visit to the projection booth suggests he may have intended to do. If Kieślowski did indeed let matters rest there, it would have matched his customary generosity towards co-creators, and a lesser willingness to make an issue of the disagreement than that of his cinematographer, whose Polish films of the period habitually privilege green.

The degree to which green figures systematically in the work is a moot point, however. Insofar as the play of shot and counter-shot between Weronika and her environment sometimes involves an alternation between her image against a red background (in the train, at her aunt's house) and her field of vision in green (e.g., her aunt opposite her), the latter resembles a negative afterimage, like the green precipitated after looking at red. This may mean that the second image derives from the first in a manner suggestive of a primary narcissism precipitating otherness out of itself, and persisting even after its departure, with green less an independent colour than a 'haunting by red'. As in Hitchcock's *Vertigo*, green might be construed as the ghostly colour. Several other uses of green are not easily reconciled with this, however. One may wonder why the photograph of Weronika herself on her bedroom wall is green, why she is lit green during a conversation with her father, and why green is associated with performance spaces both in her life and in that of Véronique (the concert at which the former dies, the puppet performance attended by the latter). If these moments of green resist integration into a system, this may mean simply that Idziak was working independently of Kieślowski and that his lighting and filter work were not always subservient to the intentions of a director known in any case – as noted above – for bestowing considerable co-creative leeway on his main collaborators. Alternatively, it may enhance the work's mystery, and so serve the directorial purpose of tuning ellipsis to enigma. If green is to be identified with counter-shot, it may even embody such forms of otherness as negativity and evil. If direct green lighting is associated more with Weronika than Véronique – for all the Polish girl's simultaneous association with red backgrounds – this may indicate the seriousness of the threat to her life. The fact that she can

The Double Life of Véronique: one of the greens haunting the film (Sławomir Idziak's bid for authorship?)

be illuminated green whereas red and yellow colours directly light the face of Véronique may suggest both greater fullness of life than her French counterpart and greater endangerment. In other words: if a system exists, it is extremely subtle, and – appropriately – only partly visible.

FROM YELLOW TO BLUE: *THREE COLOURS: BLUE*

The strangeness of the title of Kieślowski's next film, *Trois couleurs: bleu* (*Three Colours: Blue*) (1993), which mismatches singular and plural, may be entirely attributable to its heading of a work inaugurating a trilogy based upon the French flag, but it can be read less mundanely as suggesting the title colour's inherent multiplicity (just as the flag itself is triple): its tendency to shade or break up into other colours, to summon them dialectically. Thus, in its first moments a little girl holds a lollipop wrapper outside a car window, and the wind's suction flips it back and forth between outer blue and inner white. This tiny whipping movement microcosmically adumbrates the film's larger dialectic of inner and outer, a more obvious cognate dialectical image being the one placing almost all the (white-coated) body of one person (a doctor) within the black of another person's eye, *pupilla* within pupil. If the film's status as the first in a series based upon the tricolour sensitises viewers to appearances of the other key colours, white and red, Kieślowski's colour play goes further, however, as *Three Colours: Blue* includes fades to blue, black and white. It is as if these other colours (or perhaps those complementary forms of vacancy, black and white) might be the inner lining of blue, like the white secreted inside that lollipop wrapper. White and black might then become possible opposed *termini* of a narrative trajectory unfolding under the sign of blue: one more positive, the other more negative. (One might recall Alexander

Theroux's statement that '[p]aradoxically, it [blue] is the only one of all the colors which can legiti-mately be seen as a close neighbor to, as well as essentially symbolic of, dark and light both, oddly black in the night and almost white at the horizon by day'.[26]) The strength of the threat of negativity manifests itself in the greater frequency of fades to black, which also raise the question of when an end might supervene, reminding one thereby of the similarities between this film's widowing and that in the earlier *Bez końca* (*No End*) (1985).

Matters become more complex still when one notes the frequency of the appearances of another colour: green. In this context, the close thematic relationship between *Three Colours: Blue* and *The Double Life of Véronique* signals a dialectic between them echoing that between black and white at the heart of blue in this film, as if the two films pursue a series of branching, self-replicating and self-mir-roring possibilities. In each case, 'green' seems to represent an outcome too negative to be named, be it the green playing over the concert death of Polish Weronika, or the green stained glass so frequently present in the apartment Julie rents as she seeks to expunge all reminders of the life with husband and child destroyed in a car accident. If Julie is moving away from blue, the presence of green may abet that move. However, if the film's blues are to be evaluated positively,[27] green may represent a negative counterweight. Several things lend weight to this idea. First, as pointed out by Lisa di Bartolomeo, Kieślowski had already structured *Dekalog 1* (*Decalogue 1*) (1988) around an opposition of blue and green, associating green with a computer designable as a 'false god'.[28] Second, the green of this film is often darkish, as if inlaid with black, or representing its seductive disguise: as if the peace so often associated with green, and sought by Kieślowski himself, were that of death. Moreover, throughout the 1980s the cinematographer on these two films, Sławomir Idziak, had given green negative connotations, particu-larly in works shot for Kieślowski's colleague at the Tor film unit, Krzysztof Zanussi – *Paradigmat* (*The Power of Evil*) (1985) and *Wherever You Are …* (1988) – not to mention Kieślowski's own *Krótki film o zabija-niu* (*A Short Film About Killing*) (1988). Given Kieślowski's long-standing interest in alternative scenarios, the 'mismatch' of plural and singular within the title expresses the implicit multiplicity of a singularity that is only apparent.

In the context created by the title, an absence of blue, or a strong presence of another colour, becomes noteworthy. The frequent presence of yellow and green underlines absence, as if blue could have been there, but is not. With characteristic pertinacity, John Orr notes the importance of these other colours for one of the film's central environments: '[t]he yellow and green walls of the apartment echo through proximity the blue which she sees everywhere and simultaneously loves and hates'.[29] The echo, however, is only in the mind of the spectator, for whom this proximity measures the depth to which Julie's being has been riven, as blue collapses into its neighbours on one side of the colour circle. The proximity also breathes an irony, as it prolongs a colour combination that first appears when Julie is hospitalised after the accident, thereby belying her assertion of happiness in the apartment. The appear-ance of red tones in the hospital environment shows blue as not merely absent but negated, a negation deliberately prolonged by Julie herself.

If Julie can indeed be said to 'love and hate blue', it might be because of the transcendence it con-notes in many symbolic systems: the absence of sky from a film entitled *Blue* is conspicuous. It is an absence of the heaven negated by the death of her daughter Anna. More important, however, than the way this general absence, based on a widespread association, overarches the story is the way spe-cific objects – the uneaten lollipop, the crystal ornament and the blue room – unbearably recall Anna.

Three Colours: Blue: Kieślowski's play with expectations: Julie against green and yellow

Banishing blue seeks to cauterise grief, to render Julie a Niobe, turned to stone so as not to weep continually. On arriving home after the accident, Julie asks whether the blue room has been emptied: unable to bear Anna's loss, she clearly hates any reminders of a lost happiness. Nevertheless, she cannot resist the impulse to take its predominantly blue crystal ornament with her: perhaps because that object is as much a sound – a tinkling – as a sight, allowing it to appeal to the musician still alive within her; perhaps because Julie sees in its crystalline fragmentation a metaphor for her own condition, hard, shattered, held together by suture-like threads: a totality made up of fragments. The blue room's association with Anna is underlined when Lucille says that in her childhood a similar ornament hung above her, which she would dream of reaching up to clasp. If Julie's focus during the funeral is primarily on Anna's small coffin, whose image she touches with a finger, the child's linkage to the lollipop and the ornament is to a blue that is *frozen*: the antithesis of life. Thus, Julie's plunges into the swimming pool embody an unconscious dream of return to the past, of submerging herself in an enveloping blue of maternity in Anna's room, of revoking her traumatic death. It is a dream of the expansion and liquefaction of blue, of frozen essence becoming all-pervasive, screen-filling. The liquefaction of enclosed, dammed-up blue is also one of the music Julie resists, slamming down the piano lid or casting the incomplete score into the garbage truck in order to transform it into noise (and so blue appears on her face when a literal disturbance occurs, when the street altercation bubbles up her stairwell to burst forward loudly on the far side of her door, as a man seeks refuge from assailants). That blue had been associated hitherto with music: blue slivers of light dance around Julie's head as synaesthetic renditions of slivers of recurring music; and blue momentarily floods the screen when her eyes close, a fantasy regression to the happiness of creativity and life with Anna. The liquefaction of blue is, of course, that involved in the writing of notes in blue ink:

what lay frozen in the marker spreads out along the staves. The moment of her recovery is indicated by the camera's rise from the room in which she has been composing to view it through the ornament: blue now covers the screen, emanating from a real, concrete object, not a fantasy projected within Julie.

Thus, the moments at which the screen fills with blue are less likely to designate traumatic memories, which Kieślowski tactfully leaves unrepresented, than a negated upsurge of an irrepressible, but repeatedly repressed, creativity. The moments at which it darkens entirely appear therefore to have a function other than the non-representational representation of inaccessible trauma. Rather, they register the strength of a negation directed outwards, as Julie cuts off conversational advances, first by the would-be interviewer, then by Antoine, Lucille and Olivier. The moment with Lucille is particularly telling, as Lucille's departure to tidy up the bodies of the dead mouse and her young in Julie's spare room immediately precedes children leaping into the swimming pool. The combination of their white costumes, red water wings and the pool's blue foregrounds the colours of the entire trilogy, for which children thus acquire an importance matching the one accorded them in Kieślowski's *Decalogue*.

The work of Gaston Bachelard throws further light upon the use of colour in *Three Colours: Blue*. Bachelard's reflections on the blue of the sky and Kieślowski's use of blue resonate with one another. For Bachelard, '[b]efore a sky from which objects have been banished, there will be a born an imaginary subject whose memories have been banished':[30] the close match between this 'emptied' experience and that of Julie underlines the relationship between her trauma and a blueness separated from the sky, which she never contemplates, as if the colour's point of origin had been destroyed along with all the other sources of Julie's life. Thus if 'nothing' is a keyword for Julie, it is because it forms a continuum with blueness: '[f]irst there is *nothing,* then there is a *deep* nothing, then there is a blue *depth*'.[31] Since Julie's movement back and forth along this continuum places her in the ranks of those Bachelard describes as 'willing to take [a] stand in the realm of the imagination rather than in that of representation',[32] it is worth adding that the abstraction in question is augmented by the abstraction of music itself. This correlation of blueness and music may prompt an amendment of the following otherwise relevant statement from Bachelard's meditations on the imagination of blueness: 'The blue sky, meditated upon by the material imagination, is pure feeling; it is emotionality without object.'[33] Rather, for Julie the object of meditation is a blueness detached from the sky: an emotionality without object, indeed, for all its key objects are dead. Highly relevant therefore to Julie's condition throughout is Zola's description of the convalescence of Serge Mouret:

> In front of him there was a broad expanse of sky, nothing but blue, an infinite blue. In it he bathed his
> pain and abandoned himself as if to a gentle cradling; from it he drank in sweetness, purity, and youth.
> Only a branch, whose shadow he had seen, stuck out past the window and made a bold green spot on
> the blue sea. And that was already too much for his delicate condition, as a sick man who was wounded
> by the dirty spots that swallows, flying on the horizon, made.[34]

Only in the mind's eye does such blue exist. In reality, blue can be corroded by green or yellow, losing the purity of its isolation.

Just as each of the three sections of Kieślowski's trilogy can be said to activate, in an undertone, the watchword of the next (with equality entering *Blue* through the creativity obscurely shared between

Julie, Olivier and Patrice, for instance, or *Red*'s note of fraternity entering *White* through the brotherhood of Jurek and Karol Karol), so each may foreshadow the key colour of the next. Kieślowski may have been particularly happy therefore to find for Julie a box to transport her mobile stamped with the word 'blanco' in blue letters, or to locate a telephone with red plastic through which to shoot Karol as he listens to Dominique's love-making – to say nothing of wrapping Dominique herself in red sheets in the Marriott hotel (an intensity of red suggestive of the imminent ending of this particular film, as another signals from the wings its impatience to appear fully).

Also relevant is Julia Kristeva's essay 'Giotto's Joy', which provides Emma Wilson with the context for her discussion of *Blue*.[35] Wilson's is a valuable critical move, as Kristeva's text intersects with Kieślowski's film in ways even more far-reaching than the ones discussed in her reflections on the politics of its colour use, as I hope to show.

One point of intersection involves a purposive use of colours both resembling and contrasting with blue, as mentioned above. If Kieślowski frequently employs colours that either lie close to blue, or stand radically opposed to it, his practice resembles that of Giotto – as if all art experiencing colour's liberation (abstraction) underwent a similar succession of phases. After all, Kieślowski's film is one of the first to have employed colour with such freedom and imagination, even while retaining one foot in a realism that, for Giotto, still lay in the future – for all its partial adumbration in such strategies as his use of colour variation to suggest volume, which Kristeva also discusses.[36] Kieślowski's achievement of artistic freedom from *both* the realism *and* the non-narrative film-making whose codes he taps means that although Julie cannot achieve freedom, perhaps preferring love, her artistic double can.

Most remarkable and fruitful, however, is the parallel between Kristeva's account of a development within Giotto's *Last Judgement* and the final sequence of *Blue*. Kristeva writes: '[i]t seems as if the narrative signified of Christian painting were upheld by an ability to point to its own dissolution; the unfolding narrative (of transcendence) must be broken in order for what is both extra- and anti-narrative to appear'.[37] A few lines later she adds: '[o]nly in this way is the *signifier* of the narrative (i.e. the particular ordering of forms and colors constituting the narrative as *painting*) released here, at the conclusion of the narrative'.[38] But if, for her, this 'becomes symbolized as the reverse, negative, and inseparable other of transcendence',[39] Kieślowski presents a transcendence that sloughs off images of Heaven and Hell, and floats free of the Christian context, even as its project of reconciliation refuses to repudiate it, quoting 1 Corinthians 13, which speaks of love, but not of God. God may be love, of course, but neither the Pauline text nor the film dot that particular i, thus creating a 'Concerto for Unification' acceptable both to secularists and believers. The result is the near-aleatory set of images that may revolve around and return to Julie, but also encompasses all the primary denizens of the filmic world around her, reconciling the values of both centring and decentring.

THE DESERT AND THE BEACH: DELEUZE, ANTONIONI, ZHANG KE JIA

Somewhat obscurely, but as usual suggestively, Deleuze describes the dream sequence located shortly before the end of a Minnelli musical like *An American in Paris* (1951) as 'only the absorbent form of colour'.[40] One might parse this as referring to a colour that absorbs individuals into itself and so becomes primal, like the matter that pre-exists form (a reading possibly corroborated by Deleuze's subsequent reference to an 'amorphous set'[41]). Conceived thus, colour becomes a matrix that either has not yet allowed forms to emerge, or is sucking them back into itself. However, such an idea is surely less well illustrated in the

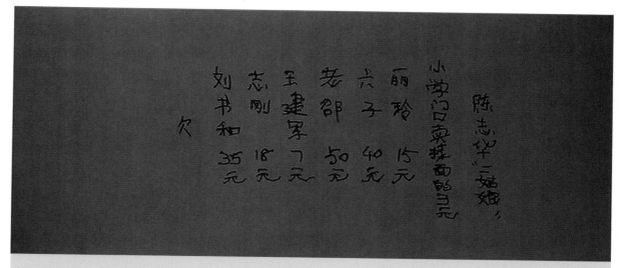

The World: the hospital wall as Little Sister's tombstone, displaying his debts

colourism of Minnelli than in that of Antonioni, of whom an adjacent passage says '[c]olour elevates space to the power of the void'.[42] This too might be rephrased, to state that colour becomes a void that emanates power. In other words, this void is not emptiness, but rather is augmented by negation in the manner described by Bergson (an appropriate figure to connect with Deleuze, of course), for whom negation always *adds* something to what it negates. One might call this a move from 'object' to 'object plus shadow', enriched with additional virtualities of being. The object is both a bearer of colour and itself a colour, or ante-colour (when literally shadowed). Obvious examples would be the sun and/or whiteness, both of which often figure in symbolic systems as representing totality, life, even infinity or eternity. (The black sun, conversely, is the eclipse that, for Antonioni, functions as a punctuation mark presaging colour's emergence, presaging *his first colour film*.) To be more specific: the white and yellow of the sun conjugate into a desert that is not simply empty but bordering on a future paradigmatically represented by *the beach* in the story Giuliana tells her son in *Deserto rosso* (*Red Desert*) (1964). Where the desert might seem no more than the sign of water's lack, here it leads to it, in imagination (the story) and reality (beaches frame seas). Giuliana, who spoke of a singing pervading the beach-side world inhabited by a lone girl in the story she told her son Valerio, might have used Paul Celan's words: 'there are still songs to sing/ Beyond mankind'. Beyond red, this yellow (beach) leads automatically to blue (water). (Another full-screen colour possessing 'the power of the void', which in this case is death, is found in Zhang Ke Jia's *Shijie* (*The World*) (2004), during the dying of Little Sister, who was named thus because his parents had wanted a girl as their second child. His statement of his debts is superimposed upon a blank green stretch of hospital wall, as if inscribed upon a tombstone.)

THE PAINTER'S PRIMARIES AND TOTALITY: *LE MÉPRIS*

If the presence of colour in a film is justified only when it demands a particular attentiveness to it on the part of spectators, the example of Godard's *Le Mépris* (*Contempt*) (1963) – as of many of his 1960s films – becomes highly resonant for, by employing various coloured filters in the film's first scene, he underlines their significance from the outset. Moreover, the subsequent frequent juxtaposition of white walls with the three 'painter's primaries' (blue, red and yellow) draws attention to colour by emphasising the possibility of its absence, and by framing each for separate consideration. If the red filter appearing at the start of the first scene of a nude Bardot on a bed broaches the film's themes of eros and commerce and their unification within cinema – which becomes metaphorically anchored in a red-light district – the triangulation of red with one more closely related colour (yellow) and another often opposed to it (blue) raises issues of relationship and opposition, fidelity and belonging, that also pervade the film. The central position of Camille's Bardot is emphasised by her successive 'wearing' of all three of the painter's primaries. She briefly escapes into green, the space between the yellow and the blue in that series, but just as that series has to unfold from red to blue, so does the film of which it forms a microcosm, moving from its title in red to the word 'fin' in blue. The end recaptures Camille for the tragic, first mentioned on the first appearance of blue, when Paul asserted that he loved her 'totally, tenderly, tragically'.

Although Camille appears straightforward, Godard uses colour to suggest (impose?) the ambiguity that is a common feature of his female leads, and manifests itself also in her use of a black wig. Thus he moves her from an initial outstretched nudity in red, in a widescreen proving apt for something other than snakes and funerals, and in the interior red-light district of intimacy, to her wearing of a blue dress shortly thereafter at the rushes for the fictional film-within-the-film, Fritz Lang's version of *The Odyssey*. Within those rushes Penelope appears against a yellow background. Since Penelope figures fidelity, Camille's non-wearing of that colour at this point may question her future loyalty to Paul. At this stage, yellow is worn only by the assistant of Jerry Prokosch, the dutiful and subordinate Francesca (Georgia Moll). Later, Camille will don yellow when she and Paul visit Prokosch's Capri villa, and Fritz Lang will comment on the 'schöne gelbe Farbe' of the bathrobe she sports. This yellow may be deemed deeply ironic, as by now Camille is contemptuous of Paul and flirting with Prokosch. The irony is underlined as she and Francesca pass one another at the villa, sporting identical yellow robes. Since the rushes also associate red and blue with the gods – these being the colours of their painted eyes and lips – one may wonder whether the advent of yellow means entry into a lower world variously figured in the film as one of commerce, humankind and betrayal. From Paul's viewpoint, meanwhile, yellow may signify femininity. Over and above the widespread identification of colour and femininity, the shifting nature of its meanings subtends its association here with a femininity conceptualised as ambiguous. Paul's trademark hues, by way of contrast, are the black of his hat and the white of the robe he wears – parodying the dignity of the classical toga – for part of the long apartment scene midway through the film. That whiteness may also correspond to the recessiveness of Paul's identity, as he fails to confront Prokosch either over his proposed vulgarisation of Lang's film or his designs on Camille. This chameleon poet is colourless, his identity negative not in Keats's sense of entering into a multiplicity of things, but in being washed-out.

An analysis of the implications of the colour patterns of *Le Mépris* might begin in quasi-structuralist fashion, by mapping them onto oppositions of masculinity and femininity, and interiors and exteriors. Although the traditional symbolism cross-referenced by Freud identifies interiors with femininity, and although in this film the most prominent red is associated with the producer Prokosch (masculinity) and his sports car (exterior), paradoxically the interior here is also where the work's two contrasting feminine figures – Camille and Francesca – don red. The only female figure to wear red outside a domestic space is incidental, the Italian singer at the audition the main characters attend. In the exteriors, Francesca first appears sporting a yellow top, and Camille in sober navy blue. When she allies herself with Prokosch near the film's end, Camille starts wearing the yellow associated hitherto with Francesca – a bathrobe – and the two are linked ironically and tellingly as they pass one another in those yellow bathrobes. As they pass one another, becoming doubles, it is as if Godard is alluding also to Rossellini's *Vanina Vanini* (1961), prompted by Francesca's family name of Vanini. Their linkage is deepened by the use of yellow behind Penelope in the *Odyssey* rushes – and Paul's modernising interpretation of Homer's text parallels Camille with Penelope by making both despise their husbands. The difference between the colours the women wear inside and outside reinforces the film's general thematisation of the separation of interiorities and exteriorities, of the impossibility of rendering visible the inner world of emotion, and of explaining the grounds of one's actions. For Paul, this means above all else the difficulty of knowing whether or not Camille is telling the truth, although what he terms her mendacity might be her method for discerning whether he really knows her. If Francesca is effaced by Prokosch, so – ironically – is Camille by Paul, though his lack of Prokosch's brazen, naive self-conceit limns his actions with irritable self-hatred. Since yellow and red are usually seen as related, Francesca's inner and outer selves do not conflict (she can wear yellow in both places). Camille's social and private being lack this unity: indeed, the film may be said to dramatise a couple's failure to find a way of being outside what they are when alone. This failure is only partly due to, or reflected in, their alienation, as French speakers, from the outside that is Rome. It is also linked to the way in which the first scene's use of filters with three primary colours establishes their inner world as their only true – fully-coloured one – so each step outside becomes fraught with possible betrayal. That private paradise, with its sense of totality, cannot but be lost, just as the world itself cannot but fragment into a disarray of colours. The Eden of Camille's nakedness cannot but become contaminated by hints of pornography when it appears later in the film, in the social world, and it is surely significant that the two later, centrefold-style images of her rump cut off her head, placing her against two colours – blue and red – rather than clothing her with them, as the initial filters had done. These later images are hard-lit, wordless, depersonalised, and seem to exude the contempt Paul himself displays when he says that when a woman is shown cinema she shows her rump. (Is that perhaps also a sign of her contempt for it, though, embodied in an age-old gesture of insult?) Also telling is the absence from these centrefold images of yellow – the colour of Penelope and thus, in the film's system, of fidelity. The yellow robe is something she casts aside as she swims away from Paul, naked, becoming one of the water-nymphs Prokosch lusted after in the projection room. The step outside the totality of the polychrome beginning then reacts poisonously with their subsequent interior relations. Camille and Paul have no outdoors where they can relax, as Francesca can at Capri: no outdoors that is also 'indoors' in the sense of a private retreat, place of relaxation, sunbathing and swimming.

Thus it is only in an interior and – significantly – before the narrative has begun that the opposites of Camille's colour experience are overcome, as red, yellow and blue play successively over her naked body, in the film's first declaration of interest in correlating colour with characterisation. (The second such declaration occurs in Lang's rushes, with the blue-eyed and blue-mouthed Neptune, red-eyed Minerva and Penelope against yellow.) Consequently, at the film's outset Camille can 'wear' colours – the sign of social being – while wearing nothing, simply lying with Paul. As the last of the three colours plays over her, he states that he loves her 'totally, tenderly, tragically'. The totality is apparent in her association with all three primaries. Since such totality of being is identified with interior experience, however, entering the world involves tragic splitting – a denial of self reflected in the way the wearing of only one colour at a time shows one as manifest subsequently only partially, as a fragment.

Le Mépris: Penelope made up like the gods, but also associated with the yellow background

As outer denies inner, in Camille's case the colours become contradictory. She can wear the yellow associated with Penelope and fidelity precisely when she is at Capri – though the superficiality of her liaison with Prokosch (after all, in the end she plans to leave him in Rome, and return to a secretarial job) may be suggested by her non-wearing of any of the three key colours as she kisses him.

The potential for self-contradiction is linked to colour in the couple's apartment, whose key colours are red and blue. Also present, however, is yellow. As Camille sits in the bathroom in a red robe, with a yellow towel hanging nearby, the camera's approach to her body makes her seem naked, removing the red but leaving the yellow towel visible, left-of-screen. She is associated with the yellow of Penelope – but it is not the colour she is wearing. Moreover, she only appears to be nude, as she had been at the outset. Is Godard linking cinematic framing to the question of mendacity? Does the removal of one of the scene's key colours ask us to think about the fluctuations within the couple's relationship? Does the disappearance of the one colour suggest that of the quality often associated with it (passion)? Similarly, as Paul sits on a sofa which is visible only as a thin line of red along part of the bottom of the screen, does its marginal presence within the scene indicate that the passion has almost drained out of the relationship?

In a further turn of the screw, the tenderness initially associated with Camille's bare body drains from the film as nakedness becomes the sign of commerce and pornography in Prokosch's Roman art coffee-table book. The Roman becomes a degradation of the Greek, spawning references to Neptune and Minerva rather than Poseidon and Athene. (With the gods themselves degraded, what hope for humanity?) Or is the degradation the revenge upon the Greek pantheon of the Italy founded by the descendants of Greece's enemies, the Trojans? Decline is doubled in the subsequent movement from the Classical world to Cinecittà. There may be gods (after all, Neptune destroys the modern Odysseus who is Paul), but their agency is enigmatic in a modern world from which they appear to be absent, where the only hope is the Hölderlinian one mentioned by Lang: that, paradoxically, that very absence may help. After all, modernity's statues – the one in the apartment, for instance – are not of them. There may be gods, but Jeremy Prokosh is deluded when he thinks himself one: the red with which he is associated is not the colour of Neptune the destroyer, and he himself dies at the film's end.

Le Mépris: the epistemological dilemma deepens: is Francesca the true Penelope?

The development of Camille's three-coloured, unified totality into a set of separate, potentially contradictory strips of colour appears to conjugate into narrative the contradictions within the rushes' image of Penelope. For whereas Neptune, Ulysses' opponent, is associated with blue through the colouration of his eyes and mouth, not to mention that of the sea, and Minerva – conversely – with red in the same places, Penelope, wearing blue eye-shadow and red lipstick and posed against a yellow wall, is contradictory to the point of unreadability. This unreadability, of course, bedevils the female leads of early 1960s Godard. But while women are at least still capable of passion, Paul's final appearance, in yellow suit and blue shirt, indicates only confusion, a failure to make clear-cut decisions, the very paleness of his attire suggesting one of self-assertion. Camille resembles Penelope more than he does Ulysses. Closer to the world of the gods (the stars?), she is finally beyond him. The pale colour of his suit is not only washed-out but washed-up.

LE MÉPRIS, 2: THE TRIUMPH OF BLUE

At one point in the long, virtuoso circling dialogue in the apartment Paul shares with Camille, he stands in blue before a blue chair, and she in red before a red divan. The opening scene passes various colour filters before Bardot's bare body and concludes with Paul's avowal that he loves her 'totally, tenderly, tragically'. Is there a relationship between these two textual moments? If there is one it may well lie in the way the purity of a single colour bespeaks a *totality* of separation: one is completely one thing, set apart from all others. So it is appropriate that the colours identified with Paul and Camille at this moment in their apartment are opposed ones, their separation emphasised by the intervening white of the walls; it is appropriate also that the three colours that most interest that acerbic social critic, Godard, should belong to the French flag. Indeed, the extent of the opposition of blue and red is marked by the need for white to hold them apart and together. But although at this stage of the film Camille is steeped in red, earlier on she has worn blue, just as she has 'worn' successive colours in the opening scene. During that scene blue occurs as she asks Paul if he loves her face, and as he says 'yes' the blue darkens it to near-invisibility. At its end he says he loves her 'totally, tenderly, tragically'. Are these three words just a *littérateur*'s daintily alliterative self-indulgence (an alliteration also present in Godard's French), or is there more to it than that? Blue, of course, emblematises Poseidon, the foe of the Odysseus with whom Paul aligns himself. Paul's self-alignment with the colour is one both with Camille and with the force of his own destruction. Blue will also be the tragic colour of the self-destructive Pierrot le fou (again, a fictional character of Godard's fashioning is aligned with a pre-existent fictional character, Pierrot, whose name provides a shorthand clue to his nature,[43] while Camille recalls 'La Dame aux Camélias', for whom colour was of particular significance, and who also died young).

In the opening the sliding camera seeks to encompass the totality of Bardot's body (to give producer Joe Levine *everything* he asked for, even as the filters withhold it), while Georges Delerue's music breathes tenderness and tragedy. All and nothing enjoy a clandestine relationship, even identity. For Godard, giving Levine all he wanted meant, in fact, giving him nothing: questions of nudity, paganism, divinity and 'naked truth' (Bardot-as-personification standing for *La Vérité*, as women so often have done, and as she herself had for Clouzot) swirl through the film. Later Paul will respond to Camille's enquiry 'What makes you think I don't love you?' with the word 'Everything'. To say 'everything' is to forgo the effort of specification Camille seeks here, as she had at the film's outset, when enumerating her body parts – from toe to top – and asking Paul if he loved them. Surveying the totality is god-like, and so humans' aspiration to such vision is impossible, leaves them with nothing, with nothingness in fact, a sequence allegorised in that key early camera movement that slides on a long rightward diagonal down and away from the blue sky to the deeper blue of the sea. The opening sequence, ending on blue, is a microcosm of the film, which also concludes with blue. At its very outset Godard's second colour film proclaims its status as, among other things, a *Farbenlehre*, and an essay on the impossibility of total possession (even a colour does not invest its wearer entirely – unless, of course, like Pierrot, one paints one's face too, a totality of immersion that may be the sign of death – and this is one overdetermined cause of the film's interest in neck-up shots). Since the Greek statues of the gods were originally coloured – our belief in their whiteness being false – Godard's interest in the relationship between white and colour mirrors that in modernity and myth. In his film's desacralised world it may be impossible to have Lang's desired opening 'in which the gods discuss the fate of men', but Paul's opening dialogue with Camille fittingly prefaces a film which will plunge individuals into the single blocks of unadulterated colour that signify their total inaccessibility to one another. For Łucja Demby the chill pervading the film embraces even Godard's reds (Godard himself, perhaps with Prokosch's car in mind, identified the film's red with death). Demby describes the colours of Prokosch's villa as 'cold, pure and lurid, with no admixture of other hues'.[44] One colour's refusal to admit any other becomes a form of cold, an absolute separation homologous with contempt, icy white separating them. Similarly, ostensible dialogues are really monologues; their repetitious self-enclosure matches the colours' continual tautologous self-identity.

When Camille is doubled by Francesca Vanini near the film's end, each sporting a yellow bathrobe, among other things the doubling may well prefigure death, as so often in legend and myth. And yet the film's last moments also suggest a utopia in which opposites fuse within blue, as they have earlier revolved around Camille, the bearer of various colours, in a sense the source of the world's colour per se. In the end, sea and sky fuse in blue, virtually indistinguishable, with no downward movement, merely a long unblinking stare. The moment's unattainability for Paul and Camille is marked by its placement beyond her death, and blue itself becomes death as the colour has the last word, FIN, the word that follows the diegetic word 'silenzio'. In this utopia colour does not separate, as it always separated

Camille, whether with Paul or after, wearing a blue set over against the red of Prokosch's car and sweater. The final blue is mourning for her, who began and ended the film in that colour, and hence for the world (the film), all of whose colours begin with her. As blue supervenes, we enter the world of Dante's Ulysses, whose final words describe the sea closing over him: 'Infin che il mar fu spora noi richiuso' – words spoken to Rheingold by Moravia's Molteni.[45] He and Emilia, Moravia's equivalent of Camille, have long inhabited that depth:

> At lunch we scarcely spoke. Silence seemed to penetrate inside the villa together with the strong light of noon; the sky and sea that filled the big windows dazzled us and gave us a feeling of remoteness, as though all this blueness were a substantial thing, like a depth of water, and we two were sitting at the bottom of the sea, separated by luminous, fluctuating liquid and unable to speak.[46]

Whether consciously or not, Godard's 'silenzio' takes these words from Moravia's nineteenth chapter as the epitaph on the relationship he mourns. The return to the sea is one to western culture's Mediterranean womb – and the philosophy of Thales. Godard's colour separation is also a radical separation of (Grecian and Brechtian) elements. In the words of Andreas Kilb: 'the most extreme abstraction of the visible is the sea; that is why, as the film's *ens realissumum*, it merits the camera's last look. Things emerge from the pure element and in the end are submerged in them again.'[47]

Although the 'painter's primaries' of red, yellow and blue appear to be the triangulated coordinates of *Le Mépris*, the blue–white–red combination dominating Godard's more explicitly socially conscious late 1960s works may also be in play. The argument for the co-presence, even primacy, of this later combination rests on the whiteness of the light in the middle of the sequence of Bardot's initial nude illumination, and on the walls of the unfinished apartment Camille and Paul share.[48] However, because the film's Italian setting does not cue the French tricolour obsessively present in late-1960s Godard, this argument may project later patterns into an earlier phase. Moreover, the 'yellow–white' portion of the sequence focuses primarily upon Bardot's rump and legs upon a yellow blanket, with the white bedsheet above it present only briefly, just before and after the camera slides down to yellow. Throughout the film, white is more an everyday background than the blankness whose centrality to the French flag later suggests a gaping hole in the national identity, while yellow is particularly privileged, in traditional cinematic fashion,[49] by its sporting by both female protagonists. On the other hand, if Juliette, in *Deux ou trois choses que je sais d'elle* (*Two or Three Things I Know About Her*) (1967), can muse that blue may possibly have been called green, the lability and arbitrariness of colour names make 'yellow' potentially 'white', and vice versa. After all, if the fully effulgent sun is defined as that which one cannot view, its 'true' colour can only be guesswork.

BLUE ANGEL, BLUE DEVIL: *GOYA IN BORDEAUX*

Although red, white and black saturate Carlos Saura's *Goya en Burdeos* (*Goya in Bordeaux*) (1999), not one of them is a strong candidate for its key colour. Red is important for the infernal intensity it lends the face of Goya as he informs his daughter Rosalita of the terrible things he hears, despite his deafness. Black and white interact dialectically, as Goya dies in a white bed under a whitening light, but engulfed by a black shadow whose shape suggests that of the work's key female figure, Cayetana, the Duchess of Alba. The black–white dialectic of these two figures at the work's end recalls Goya's early dream-pursuit of the Duchess down a black-and-white tiled corridor, emphasising the fact of ending by bringing the visual scheme round full circle. The fact that he is in white and she in black measures the absolute nature of the separation between them, which compounds that of male and female with that of living and dead. The stark alternation of the tiles in that early dream sequence had suggested a series of footprints left by one or another of the passing feet, rendering the corridor a frozen diagram – or script for – the movement of a ghost, of the haunting so central to a film that repeatedly lets us see through figures to the walls behind them, or shows us that the transparent figures were moving along a wall's far side.

Thus, for all their prominence, red, black and white cannot claim dominance (this is not *Viskningar och rop* (*Cries and Whispers*) (1972)). Rather, the dominant is blue. Even more than black, its cousin blue is associated with Cayetana. It suffuses her phantom face as her image floats flatly out of a painting, as it does Goya's own face as he contemplates her in his old age at the film's beginning; it is the colour that pulses in and out with the rhythm of his breath during that contemplation; and it is identified with art itself, as all the *Cappricios* appear bathed in a blue light. Blue is the colour of the angel-devil of obsessive love, who is also a muse. Goya may say that he paints at night because the colours then are warmer and more beautiful, but the colour of night – and, of course, of cinematic 'day for night' – is blue. As Goya sketches Cayetana, she stands against a blue background. When his wife Josefina enters, speaking nervously, as if taken aback at the sexual charge connecting Cayetana and her husband, Goya's intimidating allegiance to Cayetana is underlined by the blue background behind him too as Josefina looks at him. Seen alone by Goya, at one point Cayetana appears in blue. Only as she recedes, and people then appear in the room behind her, does this colour cease to surround her. Subsequently, however, a blue sheet descends upon all. Blue therefore is the mixed colour of art and eros. If for Sławomir Idziak the key colour is green, for that master painter-in-light Vittorio Storaro (recall the blue light on the bare upper body of Dominique Sanda in the ballet room in Bertolucci's *Il conformista* (*The Conformist*) (1970)) that status belongs to blue.

TRAPPED IN BLUE: *LA RELIGIEUSE*

One might presume that the first colour film of so serious a cinéaste as Jacques Rivette would reflect a considered application of colour, and it does. The prevalence of blue in *Suzanne Simonin, la Religieuse de Denis Diderot* (*The Nun*) (1966) might be read as saturating it with the depression of Suzanne, who is consigned to a convent because family funds have been expended on marrying her elder sisters. Its primary, indubitable function, however, is to embody ineluctability, as the recurrent blue-lighting metonymically echoes the blue habits of both the orders Suzanne enters – be they austere or licentious – tinting all difference with an imprisoning, tormenting sameness. Each scene as it were reconjugates the public viewing through bars of the first attempt to make her swear a nun's vows. Once her lack of other options has made her swear nevertheless – though her apparent unconsciousness renders it like the rape of Clarissa in the Richardson novel that so impressed Diderot – she may occasionally enter an outdoor space and experience other colours, but only in the company of her Mother Superior, also in blue. Only in a blue-lit night is she alone in the garden, and even then only momentarily, as other nuns appear. Her appeal for release having failed, her escape is engineered by a renegade monk who expects payment in sexual favours: as in the case of Clarissa, departing one prison leads her to another. This should not surprise one: the inn where the monk seeks to force himself on her is blue-lit, and her secular dress

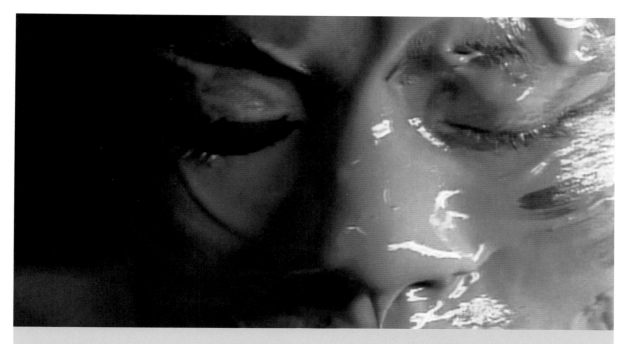

Cyclo: Kien turns his face into a mask of blue paint

blue. A paler blue then colours the laundry where she works briefly. Still hunted by the authorities, she begs on the street, but the older woman offering shelter is recruiting for a brothel. Its world may be delusively multi-hued, its inhabitants wearing dresses of different colours, but Suzanne's is of a blue whose pallor suggests a mocking proximity to freedom. Moreover, even here she is masked – in the costume of dalliance – as if still being hunted. Realising where she is, she opens the window and drops to her death on the street below: Diderot's Enlightenment anti-clericalism melts into a 1960s existentialist preoccupation with suicide and choice. The last shot shows her spread-eagled body lit a rich blue, deep-dyed still in the colour of her fate.

NOTES

1. Johan Wolfgang von Goethe, *Theory of Colours*, trans. and notes by Charles Lock Eastlake (London: John Murray, 1840).

2. Piotr Rawicz, *Blood from the Sky*, trans. by Peter Wiles (New Haven and London: Yale University Press, 2003 (1964)), p. 46.

3. Wassily Kandinsky, 'Reminiscences', in Robert L. Herbert (ed.), *Modern Artists on Art: Ten Unabridged Essays* (Englewood Cliffs, NJ: Prentice Hall, 1964), pp. 37–8.

4. Goethe, *Theory of Colours*, p. 235. Similarly, for the King of the Lower Congo, '[t]he lexical term for "red" … is *ambwaki*, which also signifies "yellow"'. (Anita Jacobson-Widding, *Red–White–Black as a Mode of Thought: A Study of Triadic Classification by Colours of the Ritual Symbolism and Cognitive Thought of the Peoples of the Lower Congo* (Uppsala Studies in Cultural Anthropology; Uppsala: Almqvist and Wiksell, 1979), p. 154.

5. Patricia Valdez and Albert Mehrabian, 'Effects of Color on Emotion', *Journal of Experimental Psychology* vol. 123 no. 4 (December 1994), pp. 394–409.

6.   Joseph Needham, *Science and Civilisation in China Vol. V: 2 (Chemistry and Chemical Technology)* (Cambridge and New York: Cambridge University Press, 1997 [1974]), p. 13.

7.   Elias Canetti, *Crowds and Power*, trans. C. V. Wedgwood (London: Gollancz, 1962), pp. 290–6.

8.   Needham, *Science and Civilisation in China*, p. 13.

9.   David Thomson, *Rosebud: The Story of Orson Welles* (London: Little, Brown and Co., 1996), p. 385.

10. Raymond Durgnat, *The Strange Case of Alfred Hitchcock* (London: Faber and Faber, 1974), p. 365.

11. Robin Wood, *Hitchcock's Films Revisited* (London: Faber and Faber, 1991), p. 192.

12. Donald Spoto, *The Art of Alfred Hitchcock: Fifty Years of His Motion Pictures* (Garden City, New York: Doubleday/Dolphin, 1979), pp. 316–17.

13. Jason Swiderski, 'Colours of Obsession, the Supernatural, and the Past: Chromatic Definitions in *Vertigo*', mid-term essay for Film 311F, Department of Film Studies, University of Western Ontario, 2007, p. 2.

14. Ibid., p. 3.

15. Ornan Rotem, 'The World as One Whole: The Syntactic Role of Colour in Film', Kinema (Spring, 2003), <www.kinema.uwaterloo/rotem031.htm> (accessed 29 May 2009).

16. Richard Allen, 'Hitchcock's Color Designs', in Angela Dalle Vacche and Brian Price (eds), *Color: The Film Reader* (New York and London: Routledge, 2006), pp. 137–41.

17. Swiderski, 'Colours of Obsession', p. 3.

18. Spoto, *The Art of Alfred Hitchcock*, 317.

19. Philip Lopate, liner notes to Criterion DVD, 2002.

20. Gaston Bachelard, *L'Eau et les rêves: Essai sur l'imagination de la matière* (Paris: Libre José Corti, 2005), pp. 96–100.

21. William J. Free, 'The Film as Poem', *The Georgia Review* vol. 23 no. 2 (Summer 1969), p. 132.

22. Foster Hirsch, *Joseph Losey* (Boston: Twayne, 1980), p. 34.

23. Ibid.

24. Megan Ratner, '*Flight of the Red Balloon*', *Film Comment* vol. 44 no. 2 (March/April 2008), p. 72.

25. Slawomir Idziak, interview, disk 2 of Criterion DVD, 2006.

26. Alexander Theroux, *The Primary Colours: Three Essays* (New York: Henry Holt, 1994), p. 2.

27. Herb Eagle, 'Color in Kieślowski's Film Trilogy: *Blue, White, Red*', *Periphery: a Journal of Polish Affairs* no. 4–5 (1998–9), pp. 138–45.

28. Lisa Di Bartolomeo, 'No Other Gods: Blue and Green in Krzysztof Kieślowski's Dekalog 1', *Studies in Slavic Cultures* no. 1 (February 2000), pp. 47–59.

29. John Orr, *Contemporary Cinema* (Edinburgh: University of Edinburgh Press, 1998), p. 64.

30. Gaston Bachelard, *Air and Dreams: An Essay on the Imagination of Movement*, trans. Edith R. Farrell and C. Frederick Farrell (Dallas Institute of Humanities and Culture: Dallas, 2002), p. 168.

31. Ibid. (emphasis in original).

32. Ibid.

33. Ibid., p. 165.

34. Ibid., p. 164.

35. Emma Wilson, '*Three Colours: Blue*: Kieślowski, Colour and the Postmodern Subject', *Screen* vol. 39 no. 4 (Winter 1998), pp. 349–62.

36. Julia Kristeva, 'Giotto's Joy', in Kristeva, *Desire in Language: A Semiotic Approach to Literature and Art* (New York: Columbia University Press, 1980), pp. 229–31.

37. Ibid., p. 214.

38. Ibid., p. 215 (emphasis in original).

39. Ibid.

40. Gilles Deleuze, *Cinema 1: The Movement-Image*, trans. Hugh Tomlinson and Barbara Habberjam (Minneapolis: University of Minnesota Press, 1986), p. 119.

41. Ibid., p. 120.

42. Ibid., p. 119.

43. See Pauline Kael, *Going Steady* (Boston and Toronto: Little Brown and Co., 1970), p. 78, for a discussion of this aspect of Godard's work in general.

44. Łucja Demby, 'Skąd się bierze Pogarda? (O 'Pogardzie' J. L. Godarda)', *Iluzjon: kwartalnik filmowy* vol. 2 no. 50 (1993), p. 25.

45. Alberto Moravia, *A Ghost at Noon*, trans. Angus Davidson (London: Secker, 1955), p. 187.

46. Ibid., p. 180.

47. Andreas Kilb, 'Abschied vom Mythos: Über *Le Mépris* von Jean-Luc Godard (1963) und über den Wandel in der Filmkritik' in *Die Macht der Filmkritik: Positionen und Kontroversen*, ed. Norbert Grob and Karl Prumm (Munich: edition text + kritik, 1990), pp. 186–7.

48. Steven Woodward, 'The Picture of Marriage: Godard's *Contempt* and Kieślowski's *White*', in Steven Woodward (ed.), *After Kieślowski: The Legacy of Krzysztof Kieślowski* (Detroit: Wayne State University Press, 2009), p. 144.

49. Steve Neale, *Cinema and Technology: Image, Sound, Colour* (London: BFI/Macmillan, 1985), pp. 151–5.

C : TOUR/DÉTOUR D'AMÉRIQUE

6 Melos, Drama, Melodrama: From Demy to Sirk to Antonioni

INTRODUCTION

In the first chapter of this book I mentioned the relationship between colour's licence to roam free and the practices of both modernism and fantasy. In each case, the elements of which the film is composed may be peeled apart, either explicitly and following a programmatic purpose (as in modernism and the avant-garde), or implicitly (as in the genres of fantasy, whose overtly 'composed' status differentiates them from realism). One of the most patent 'additives' to cinema is, of course, the music that originally was not canned together with the image-track, but potentially dissonantly 'live'. In early and silent cinema, colour, like music, figures as an additive, being achieved through processes of tinting, toning and frame-by-frame hand-colouring applied to the exposed negative. Indeed, one of the most noted silent uses of colour was genuinely an 'addition', in the sense of an after-thought: Lillian Gish reports that Griffith adopted the blue and golden colour scheme of *Broken Blossoms* (1919) only after seeing the screen lit thus during rehearsals of the Carol Dempster dance he had decided to film as its prologue.[1] Silent cinema's reliance upon a combination of melos and drama would be underlined by the Hollywood trade papers' habit of designating almost all films 'melodramas'. The affinity of colour and music in the period is evident in the proliferation of processes jostling to become the dominant means of registering each. This affinity of filmic elements deemed 'secondary' is cemented in classic cinema by the employment of a language of 'harmonisation' to define the role each is assigned. The point is not to harmonise colour and music with one another, in the sort of synaesthetic translation execrated by Eisenstein, and certainly not to permit any counterflow against the drama, but to recruit each into reinforcing the film's legibility. The use of the language of 'harmony', however, suggests repressed awareness of the possibility of the homogenised elements claiming independence, becoming fugal, centrifugal, or even dissonant. After all, both colour and music are relatively 'open' signifiers, each often perceived as offering a separate invitation to fantasy. Each can intimate the existence of dimensions beyond the concrete, that heartland of the realism both modernism and fantasy abjure. Of all the genres, the musical and melodrama appear to solicit fantasy most fully; and although the embedding of the word 'melos' in melodrama might suggest their convergence primarily upon the ground of music, both also intensify the quality known as 'colour'. In a sense, they play out a dialectic, the musical giving licence to dream, and melodrama foregrounding the constraints upon dreaming (and on those figures whose dreams have traditionally most often been sealed off hermetically from the sphere of action: women). (The European musical meanwhile – as will be seen again in Demy's *Les Parapluies de Cherbourg* (*The Umbrellas of Cherbourg*) (1964) – may superimpose these forms, as the dream is frustrated). The shared commitment to music and colour in musical and melodrama motivates the following chapter's focus upon these two forms, as a prelude to consideration of other forms of fantasy in Chapter 7. If the book's 'detour' from the predominantly European to the American may join Dorothy in concluding that there's no place like home, 'no place' is of course utopia, utopia is no place and neither is what anyone knows as 'home' yet.

SINGIN' – AND DANCIN'? – IN THE RAIN: *LES PARAPLUIES DE CHERBOURG* AND *SINGIN' IN THE RAIN*

Since an alternative title for Jacques Demy's *Les Parapluies de Cherbourg* could have been *Singin' in the Rain* (1952) a comparison of these two much-loved and intensely pleasurable films might be in order. Taken together, they can illustrate some of the similarities and differences between the normative practices of the most inventive musicals produced both in Europe and Hollywood – particularly with reference to colour. In these cases colour figures as a sign of the presence of pleasure, even though in Demy's film the candy is hard and bitter-sweet. However, a glance towards that glowingly coloured film by Demy's wife, Agnès Varda, *Le Bonheur* (1965), might prompt one to abandon Film Studies' habit of inflating the idea of pleasure and use another term instead: happiness.[2]

Les Parapluies de Cherbourg begins with an orange-tinged shot of the port of Cherbourg itself, before the camera pans down to give an overhead view of cobblestones. Upon their natural grid, after a yellow-shirted cyclist has passed, umbrellas pop up successively like mushrooms, unfold like flowers. A red one opens up on the left-hand side of the screen and floats vertically through the screen's top; a cyclist dressed in red then passes from the upper right to the lower left; a blue umbrella slides horizontally from the bottom right to the bottom left; two cyclists in nondescript, dun garb move in parallel and opposite directions between the top left and the bottom right; a bluish-green umbrella descends from the top right to the bottom right; a reddish-purple one tracks just above the central horizontal axis of the frame from left to right; as if to illustrate the title that comes up at this moment, a mix of blue-and-white umbrellas lines up across the screen and descends in phalanx; with other combinations of cyclists and umbrellas following for the remainder of the credits. All the time rain is pouring down into the centre of the image, as the work's affecting theme song – 'I will Wait for You' – plays uninterruptedly. After a set of black umbrellas has moved in line from left to right across the centre of the frame, the show ends: black clearly signifies ending. The camera then swings back up to recover the opening view of the port.

This credit sequence wittily interweaves order and randomness (and is itself wittily recreated in relation to a wet Tokyo in Chris Marker's *Le mystère Koumiko* (*The Koumiko Mystery*) (1965)). Red, with its attention-catching capacity, is unsurprisingly the first umbrella's colour, signalling the title the spectator should know but has not yet seen on screen, and black the last. The red-to-blue movement between the first two umbrellas is one between the two contrasting valences of colour experience: between the colour that approaches the eye and the one that withdraws. Their combination with the initial yellow announces the film's will to exploit all three of the colours usually declared primary. In terms of the film as a whole, the yellow associated with a male may seem anomalous, as it will usually be associated with Catherine Deneuve's blonde Geneviève. Demy's decision to allow yellow to migrate thus, however, may hint that it will not be his male protagonist who makes events happen, he being their object, as women have been so often. At the same time, though, the combination of yellow and a bicycle announces a traditional masculinity, and 'Frenchness', through the Tour De France significance of the yellow jersey. 'Frenchness' will then be reiterated in the red, white and blue of the garage where Guy is a mechanic.

The umbrella movements in this opening sequence map out a geometry, even as their floating beneath falling water suggests a flocking of urban jellyfish across a seabed-wharf. The geometry will not be dehumanising, however, as every now and then the movement involves humans. Its dance may be seen as also an abstract one of the sexes, bright umbrellas being associated with femininity, and the cycles pushed by males with no free hands to grip an umbrella. As so often, the coding of the circle as feminine is reinforced by the fact of its colouring. When the umbrellas turn black, a line is crossed in a manner that symmetrically inverts the line-crossing of the first appearance of ('feminine') colour on a cyclist: here the 'feminine' form is filled in with the 'masculine' (pleasure-ending) black of a reality principle bringing down the curtain on the credits' playfulness. It is almost as if the meeting of opposed signifiers parodies the synthetic conclusion of a Hegelian dialectic. If the colour is associated less with the male pushing the bicycle taking a line for a walk than the circle connotative of femininity, a primary interest in the feminine surely characterises a film that has no subject more photogenic than Deneuve: the overwhelming quality of her image can be gauged by its association with three colours (pink, green, yellow) upon her first appearance in the umbrella-shop window, and, of course, also by the melancholy muting of colour by the whiteness of snow in the finale's registration of her definitive loss at Guy's petrol station. Guy may have dreamed of buying a station and painting it station white, but its overpainting by snow simply underlines his lack of control of a life that has had to settle for only a partial fulfilment of dreams. The sequence shows that although the umbrellas may be primary protagonists, they are not the only ones. Despite its temporal and spatial colour patterning and quasi-dialectical alternation, this will not be a Busby Berkeley musical relying heavily on patterns perceptible only from above (the ways in which it is not a musical like *Singin' in the Rain* will be considered shortly). The contents of the frame see-saw in a delicate *pas-de-deux* of human and abstract, real material being and stylisation, and signifiers of masculinity and the feminine.

A combination of music and dance is a staple of the musical: in the musical many view as prototypical, and in its best-known sequence, Gene Kelly is 'singin' *and* dancin' in the rain'. Song suggests the presence of considerations of harmony, an element also associated with pleasing arrangements of colours within the frame; and dance usually involves pattern: at its most essential, the symmetrical revolutions of male and female dramatise cosmic balances. Consequently, strong forces within the musical operate to fuse song with the spectacle of dance. If the pattern involves colour, it will usually appear in single blocks shifting within the kaleidoscope that is the model distillation of the shape of dance. Identified with a single colour, the individual is cast in the lyric mode of simple, strong assertion, thereby becoming song-like. The verbal combination 'song-and-dance' may be proverbial; it is not universal, however. The song-and-dance combination and alternation is, in fact, the essence of the American musical, reflecting the centrality of kinesis to its cinematic norms in general, and the fundamental abandonment of realism in the utopian assumption that breathtaking physical moves will not preclude the taking of breath necessary to inflate the voice. Here *Les Parapluies de Cherbourg* differs: characters may skip, or run, across streets (though, tellingly, in its latter part its war-wounded male protagonist limps), but they hardly dance at all. As in an opera – for all the up-to-date jazziness of passages of the score, a pre-Wagnerian one, with much recitative – they stand and deliver themselves. The pervasive yearning is intensified by this lack of dance movement, and the early frustration of the pairing-off impulse of the dance may hint at the frustrations of relationship ahead. Characters may sing in the rain, but they do not climb the walls of the sets, as does Gene Kelly. The mechanic planning an evening dancing is not the protagonist. After seeing Bizet's *Carmen* Guy and Geneviève may indeed go to a red-walled dance floor, but their dancing is conventional, subordinated to conversation, and presented in medium shot; not a long shot showcasing the pyrotechnic movements of the big number executed by agile bodies. (Throughout the film, Demy's camera is more prone to moment-to-moment movement than are his protagonists.) Guy and Geneviève resist the tango's invitation to spectacular moves, and soon sit down. Even though the mambo draws Geneviève to her feet, the sight of the couple is blocked almost immediately by other dancers, and the sequence ends a few seconds later.

Both *Les Parapluies de Cherbourg* and *Singin' in the Rain* place their key songs in the credits. Each set of credits also revolves around umbrellas – which themselves sometimes revolve, as if the swirling would generate a colour circle, colours flying centrifugally like sparks, or rather droplets. Of the two sets of credits, Demy's is longer and more intricate. That of *Singin' in the Rain* lines up its three main protagonists, backs to us, but with umbrellas turned towards us in a way that causes anticipations of a dramatic turnaround and revelation whose imminence is underlined when the names of the three main actors appear on the umbrellas; it is no surprise that they then turn around to allow the names that function as trailers satisfyingly to become realities. In terms of the film as a whole, this trailer is also a spoiler, as the centrality of Debbie Reynolds shows her importance to the coming movie. There is no interest in employing the umbrellas to create abstract patterns perceptible only from unusual angles. The camera views the characters at their eye-level, further justifying audience expectations of rapid revelation of the individuals behind the umbrellas.

The Kelly/Donen film also differs from Demy's in its treatment of colour. Colour is not foregrounded throughout the work, as it is in his film, but in set pieces, the most spectacular being 'Broadway Melody'. If bright colouration is central to the American musical, it is as a declaration of the fulfilled intensity and presence of its world. It will eschew any colour abstraction that might suggest that the colours themselves, rather than the colourful characters, make things happen, or constitute a level of events of equal interest to those generated by the characters. This abstraction surely reflects the wistful melancholy of Demy's film, in which events do not follow the script of the characters' wills: Geneviève, for instance, in the end does not go against her mother's wishes.

Only in three sequences of *Singin' in the Rain* does the colour patterning approach autonomy. The most interesting of these is the least typical: the quickfire montage of musical excerpts accompanying the song 'Beautiful Girl' dramatises the studio's speedy adoption of a 'sound-is-musical' formula inspired by the unexpected success of *The Jazz Singer* (1927). This montage includes female soldiers in red, black and white uniforms against a yellow background; three green-dressed male dancers against another yellow background; and a man with a megaphone against a light purple background. Not surprisingly, it begins with party girls and multicoloured balloons against a red background. This sequence is marked as anomalous, for it is not sung by any one of the three main protagonists (indeed, its main narrative function is to allow the primary threesome to be constituted, as Debbie Reynolds' Kathy Selden is spotted as part of the 'Beautiful Girl' chorusline), while the use of montage further underlines the absence from these shots of the figures who really matter: had they been present, the camera would have tracked their movements in respectful long takes. If the sequence foregrounds colour to a frenzied extent unusual in this film, this appears to underline a film-historical thesis of some importance to a work whose plot turns upon one of the key technological transitions of cinematic history. It demonstrates that although the addition of sound in the late 1920s might seem to bring the mocked and indulged past perilously close to the present, for which sound is of the essence, present-day moviemaking nevertheless possesses a trump card of which that period could only dream: the Technicolor flaunted so ostentatiously here.

Technicolor need not be used for such brash assertion alone, however much it may adopt that mode, wishing to put early sound musicals in their place. Consequently, the two other sequences foreground colour in a long take that foregoes the buttonholing quality of montage. In the first, Gene Kelly's Don Lockwood paves the way to his declaration of love for Kathy by setting up a stage with a beautiful sunset before her and, behind her, in the blue, red and green of three-strip lighting. The protagonists glide and sing between red- and blue-coloured areas to indicate their complementarity as ideal couple.

Only in the 'Broadway Melody' sequence does *Singin' in the Rain* approach the wistfulness of Demy's film, and then only briefly, in the near-abstract ballet of lost love projected in the mind of Gene Kelly upon re-encountering the Cyd Charisse lured away from him by a gangster. Up to this point, the sequence has besieged the audience with a plethora of reds, blues and yellows that renders Charisse's green special. It begins with Kelly extolling Broadway against a background of yellow, before the camera pulls back to leave him spotlighted by yellow in the middle of a black space within which blue and red then erupt; a blue light enfolding the central yellow, and red emblazoned on Broadway signs around it. Beginning as a bumpkin who has 'Gotta Dance' and finally finding one of the impresarios' yellow doors welcoming, Kelly then serenades a Broadway crowd in a colour scheme foregrounding the primaries: himself in yellow hat and waistcoat at the top point of a triangle, his foremost spectators are a man in a blue-striped coat left of screen and a flapper in red bottom right. Absent is the green that marks out Charisse as sought-after and seductive. After losing her, during a reception Kelly sees her again in white at the top of a staircase. The crowded reception dissolves into a two-person dance across a near-surrealist (Dali-esque, Tanguy-like) flat, blue-, red- and white-lit landscape. The modernity of this dance places it closer to ballet than to musical, and the rendering of loss in balletic form can be seen as a way of placing it 'outside' the film even as simultaneously it buries it deep within it, framing it doubly as a projection in the mind of the character Kelly plays within the description he himself is giving his producer of the choreography for 'Broadway Melody': the American musical is allowed to demonstrate mastery of effects and styles more often deemed disconcertingly 'European' or 'sophisticated', but on the precondition of suppressing any true longing for such a style, disavowing it as a technical feat, a projection and, worse still, a 'Broadway Melody'. A dream-like, long floating train of white suggests the possibility of securing the girl even as the unreality of the setting locates her, in her whiteness, even more firmly outside the coloured world Kelly inhabits. On his disillusioned return from this fantasy, only the sight of a bumpkin replica of himself at the sequence's start, also singing 'Gotta Dance', restores his spirits and reintegrates him with the crowd of dancers. In essence, the moment turns the clock back twelve minutes and fifty-seven seconds (I owe the timing to Gerald Mast, who describes the sequence as a summa of 'MGM's entire *Broadway Melody* series'[3]). It is as if the whole sequence has become a dream, and the abstract ballet a dream within a dream, played out in the unconscious that knows no history but recycles endlessly the obsessive trauma of a wound (the wound of modernity?).

COUPLING AND UNCOUPLING COLOURS: *UNE FEMME EST UNE FEMME*

If *Une femme est une femme* (*A Woman is a Woman*) (1961), like *Les Parapluies de Cherbourg*, begins by stressing the relationship between colour and the umbrella, the doubling of the quotient of femininity in the title of Godard's first colour film probably dictates its carrying by a woman and its redness, that colour stereotypically associated with western female self-display. The umbrella–woman combination, however, suggests a leitmotif of Godard's future work: colour is arbitrary, for one could always carry a different-hued one, while an umbrella, not being 'worn' in the same way as clothing, cannot be deemed as directly expressive of its bearer as is clothing. Its red can do double duty, both ensuring that Anna Karina (Angela) is noticed in her Godardian debut, and inaugurating another Godard theme that follows from the idea of the arbitrariness of colour: that of paradoxicality (Angela is no 'scarlet woman', unlike Bette Davis in the famously shocking red dress of *Jezebel* (1938)). Just as faces resist decipherment throughout his work, so signs are not only unrevealing but possibly even flatly contradictory of an inner essence, assuming there is one. The arbitrariness and paradoxicality are underlined when, immediately after Angela has folded up her umbrella and ordered white coffee, the next customer playfully orders a green one. In line with the self-consciousness and retrospective decoding that would be key devices of art cinema, calling a coffee green declares the white of white coffee a colour. At the same time, the customer may be suggesting flirtatiously that he and Angela belong together like colour complementaries (forgetting perhaps that this may also make them incompatible).

Once Karina has left the café, the next sequence raises the question of the relationship between people and the spaces they inhabit – a theme explored more insistently in *Deux ou trois choses que je sais d'elle* (*Two or Three Things I Know About Her*) (1967) – as Angela's red stockings and white raincoat prompt us to perceive her as forming momentary patterns with the red street signs, particularly because one (like her) is red and white, while the 'No entry' sign suggests a flash forward to her frustrations over not getting pregnant. The same question is posed with regard to indoor space also, threatening the distinction between interior and exterior: in the apartment, the red lamp against the white wall recalls the umbrella, as in each case red is placed slightly above her. It is as if the red lamp is a displaced image of the umbrella, or each is simply a transformation of an abstract red located at a particular height (the unattainable one of 'real passion'?).

A Woman is a Woman prefigures other Godard habits too. The lights playing over Angela's face at the strip club anticipate the multiple colouration of Bardot at the start of *Le Mépris* (*Contempt*) (1963). The paradoxicality mentioned above extends to language, foreshadowing many Godardian word-games. Thus, upon hearing Angela refuse to go to Marseilles, a man at the strip club observes wittily 'bas rouge, bas bleu': the redstocking is a bluestocking, in fact. (The paradox being that blue is more self-assertive than red …) Paradoxicality being pervasive, Godard's main interest is in twinning colours usually considered incompatible, a process that echoes the one of human couple formation and reformation, as Angela hangs frustratedly between her love Emile (Jean-Claude Brialy), who is unwilling to inseminate her at the drop of a hat, and Alfred (Jean-Paul Belmondo), who is. Of these colour pairs, red (the colour of Angela's sweater, and her colour in general) is the constant. Red and white appear in Angela's clothes and the apartment; red and blue, on Alfred's coat sleeve, in the stocking combination and on Angela's face as she strips; and red and green, in the bathroom to which she retires with Alfred. The constancy of red underlines the film's primary focus on the woman who wears it, even though it does not express her. The interrelationship of colouration, coupling and splitting is well caught in Edgardo Cozarinsky's comment that the film 'has a beauty that is brash and pathetic, like splintered coloured glass, fragments that somehow compose a picture while refusing to hold together'.[4] It thus becomes like a stained-glass window, an entity that is always a collection of splinters held together by leaden strips that also hold them apart. Perhaps because they are placed under the aegis of language, and naming serves separation, it is as if colours are inherently disjunctive, naturally pulling away from one another. (The final unification of the bickering couple can thus seem a particularly sickly, cutely willed resolution.)

TOTALLY? TENDERLY? TRAGICALLY?: *AN AMERICAN IN PARIS, LE MÉPRIS* AND *MOULIN ROUGE* (WITH A POSTSCRIPT ON *THE GOLDEN COACH*)

If, as Steve Neale among others has noted,[5] Hollywood has long identified femininity with colour, the most consistently ecstatic version of that identification is found in the musical. If a girl means the world to a guy, she ought to wear all its colours. It thus becomes intriguing to correlate the presentation of Leslie Caron in *An American in Paris* (1951) with a Godardian work that also identifies its female lead with all colours: *Contempt*. The most interesting comparison of these films, however, concerns the degree to which each mobilises a sense of the totality, tenderness and tragedy cued by Paul's initial statement in Godard's work, that he loves Camille 'totally, tenderly, tragically'. Totality is present, of course, in the female's opening association with the full range of primary colours. Filters project them onto Bardot's body at the start of *Contempt* (as noted above, they had played upon the face of Anna Karina's ostensibly stripped body part-way through *A Woman is a Woman*, which thus becomes a candidate for classification as one of those Godardian beginnings famously displaced from the actual start). And, in *An American in Paris*, as Henri Baurel describes Lise Bouvier (Leslie Caron), she dances in various costumes against backgrounds of the primaries, finally waving as a ballet dancer in blue from a lozenge inserted in between all her other incarnations (upper left: in white against a red background; lower left: in yellow against green; upper right: in pink against blue; lower right; in black against yellow; is she absent from green because so restless?). The doubling of blue amid these five images is the hinge between this 'vignette totality' and another totality unfolding across the narrative: the red, white and blue of the two countries' flags, whose colours dominate Jerry's fantasy ballet (an ironic echoing of the imperialisms of those two flags would, of course, pervade Godard's later 1960s work in colour). Beginning with blue rather than red indicates her non-vampishness, a red rose symbolises her in Jerry's fantasy ballet, while her final white is the hinge of a narrative door swinging open from the white of the New Year's ball to admit the image of a wedding held briefly in suspension between the Frenchman Henri and the American Jerry (Gene Kelly).

Both films therefore construct femininity as totality, conceiving it as a metonym of a world one could safely enfold in one's arms. Equally obviously, both treat their protagonists tenderly. The issue of tragedy is the point of division. *Contempt* is indeed tragic, documenting the break-up of Paul's relationship with Camille and her subsequent death. Only the epic still being filmed by Fritz Lang serenely survives the wreckage. *An American in Paris* comes surprisingly close to tragedy, in the Hegelian sense of a collision of irreconcilable goods. These goods would be the marriage of Henri to Lise and of Lise to Jerry. On hearing the name of Jerry's beloved, his composer friend Adam shakes nervously at the thought of imminent disaster. Henri's sacrifice of Lise is a germ of tragedy nipped in the bud by the automatic mechanisms of the film's overwhelming identification with Jerry. If the musical's lodestar is pleasure, its insistence upon satisfaction is surely the dark side of its infant-like innocence. The final mood is exultant, unlike that in the red-, white- and blue-tinged, hauntingly bittersweet close of *Les Parapluies de Cherbourg*. Henri's tragedy is elided, repressed by a logic of sacrifice that may well give the viewer pause – as it does in Demy's delicately balanced, pensive final counting of the cost.

It may not be irrelevant to note that both films are also preoccupied with brightly coloured posters. (Do the film posters that proliferate across Godard's early films draw some of their inspiration from the ones decorating the street walls during the 'Swonderful' routine?) And those posters may lead one to a

Moulin Rouge: femininity as the totality of colour

work concerning the great *fin-de-siècle* master of the form, Henri de Toulouse-Lautrec. Femininity, total-
ity and tragedy converge again in John Huston's *Moulin Rouge* (1952), deemed at the time one of the first
Hollywood films to deploy colour significantly, albeit doing so most convincingly in its early scenes.
Initially, a sense of colour totality is evoked by the sweeping camera survey of the interior of the Moulin
Rouge. Moving from the entrance and up and down steps to and from a band on the balcony, the
camera passes backgrounds that are predominantly blue, red, yellow and green in turn, embracing all
the colours classed as primaries. Subsequently, however, an even fuller totality is identified with femininity, as Can Can dancers swirl across the floor in these four colours, plus black and pink (the white of
flounced drawers continually underscoring the flaring presence of each colour). The verve of these
early scenes would be linked to the closeness with which they follow scripts laid down in the lithographs
of Toulouse-Lautrec.[6] When he falls in love with Marie Charlet, however, the lack of any linkage between
her and a full colour spectrum may foreshadow her loss, after which he turns on all the gas taps in his
apartment. Viewing his incomplete design for his Moulin Rouge poster, however, he starts touching it up
– and, as he does so, his true, compensatory love is established as one for painting; a shot of his palette
shows all the colours, a distilled essence of femininity never to be encountered in a person. He turns the
gas off again.

Postscript: *The Golden Coach*

If *A Woman is a Woman* presents colours in terms suggestive of a stained-glass window, while that film, *Contempt* and *An American in Paris* are united in identifying the female with a totality of colour, a more enlightening example of this trope is Jean Renoir's Technicolor *The Golden Coach*, a film so full of performers singing and dancing as to bid for classification as a musical. Before moving onto this film though, a word or two about Renoir's attitude to colour in general.

Although Renoir was one of the first French directors consistently to film in colour, from *The River* (1950) onwards, before – with characteristic independence – reverting to black and white precisely when others were adopting colour, the degree of his commitment to it can be doubted. He decried chemical and optical effects ('I'm too egotistical to rely on a chemist for my film's final results'[7]), seeing film-makers as primarily photographers ('If we arrive at a set saying "I want to be Rubens or Matisse," I am sure that we will wind up making big mistakes'[8]). The relationship between this attitude and that of his Impressionist father Auguste is, of course, endlessly debatable, for although Impressionism foregrounded colour, Auguste's paintings were not experimental in the theorised manner of a Monet or Seurat. It is hardly surprising, therefore, that the terms of his son's work on *The Golden Coach* appear more tasteful than innovative:

> Claude [Renoir, his nephew] and I were able to study colour contrasts with a great deal of care.
> Sometimes, for example, we didn't shoot because the costumes didn't work with the set background.
> Sometimes we had the sets entirely repainted, had the wigs changed, had the makeup changed.[9]

This approach appears entirely consistent with the Technicolor consultant's concern for harmony, matching rather the 'classical' strain in his work than the modernist one, for all the film's echoes of *La Règle du jeu* (*The Rules of the Game*) (1939).

Consequently, although Renoir's painstaking colour harmonisation should be noted and, of course, appreciated, it seems to me that with regard to colour its main interest lies not in the *mise en scène* but in the presentation of the alluring female protagonist. For although Anna Magnani is presented here as, indeed, the unattainable object of desire, pursued by three men, and consequently finally removed from them into the regret-stained heaven of an art transcendentally cut off from life, her wearing of all colours is no trick of *mise en scène* or directorial subjectivity: rather, it derives matter-of-factly from her playing a character for a living in an Italian *commedia dell'arte* troupe visiting South America, Columbine. Her costume is like a stained-glass window of cloth, colourless lines separating and uniting its coloured diamonds. Magnani's Columbine may stand out, and as Magnani, of course, she cannot but do so, but similar costumes are worn by the majority of the other players in the troupe. Her harlequin garb renders her both extraordinary and ordinary, the dizzying alternation between them fuelling the film's mapping of this dialectic onto those of art and life and the plebeian and the aristocratic. The diversity of colour becomes part of Renoir's fascinated seismographic tracking and analysis of the sheer lability of the moods and fates to which humans are subject. In many respects, therefore, this film becomes a colour counterpart of *The Rules of the Game* (albeit one concerned to contrast classes in terms of a horizontal separation of their allotted spaces, rather than a vertical (upstairs, downstairs) one). Her costume its locus, Columbine/Magnani is as much the sad, bemused catalyst of the confusion as the Christine of that earlier film, the simultaneous presence of all colours rendering her as unreadable as Christine's Austrian background had done.

A NOTE ON MELODRAMA AND MODERNISM

The logic of sacrifice mentioned above in connection with *An American in Paris* is, of course, central to another genre often opposed to tragedy: melodrama. Although melodrama and modernism are often defined antithetically also, the degree to which both emancipate colour from context (a development discussed at length in Chapter 2) permits a questioning of the absoluteness of this opposition. The remainder of this chapter considers two works linked by their foregrounding of a female protagonist – another often-noted feature of melodrama – and by differing degrees of imbrication with modernism. The foregrounding of colour in each may indicate identification with the femininity so many cultures have conceptualised as a 'second sex', that is, a sacrificed or sacrificeable one. Since colour is often cast as secondary in the sense of subordinate to a putatively 'masculine' line, a preoccupation with colour invites characterisation as 'feminine'. If 'melos' too is often deemed secondary to a drama, whose meanings it does not so much establish as underline, the significance of colour in a melodrama would amplify that of its music. If each performs 'the same' semiotic work, however, each is disposable: in other words, secondary. Secondariness and sacrificeability, in turn, suggest a term central to the Freudian theorisation of the family romance of melodrama, with its late revelations of 'true', unknown parentage: the repressed, which can include the sensuality associated with colour. As is suggested in the theorisation of Sirkian melodrama by Geoffrey Nowell-Smith,[10] by analogy with the Freudian aetiology of hysteria, this forces its repressed desire into the insistently present but secondary positions traditionally accorded colour and music.

Inasmuch as melodrama is held in place through another binary, the one opposing it to 'realism', the fact that its arch-enemy in this scenario is also modernism's may not suffice to make the two forms actually 'friends'. After all, in the history of artistic forms, yesterday's realism is often denounced today as 'melodrama', its erstwhile realism trumped by an even greater attention to overlooked details, or mores, in its successor. In the context of a debate around modernism, *All That Heaven Allows* (1955) becomes relevant because of the frequency with which it is described as practising a variety of Brechtian alienation from its deluded, bourgeois protagonists, and hence possibly pursuing a modernist 'dehumanisation of art', to use Ortega y Gasset's term. However, the intensity of the emotion washing round its ironies suggests a greater sympathy with Brecht's practice than with his theories, whose purity of anti-emotionality neither Sirk, nor his closest imitators – Rainer Werner Fassbinder and Todd Haynes – ever sought to achieve, while Brecht's own most powerful plays (the late ones) slip through the fingers of alienation again and again. Perhaps only in Antonioni's remarkable experiment *Il mistero di Oberwald* (*The Oberwald Mystery*) (1981) does a declared modernist pursue melodrama. And here the key question, to be discussed later, is whether the modernism and the melodrama fuse, or one of them overwhelms the other.

MELODRAMA, REALISM AND *ALL THAT HEAVEN ALLOWS*

In most Film Studies writing on melodrama, the emancipatory potential traditionally ascribed to the genre inheres as much in form as in socially activist content: in particular, in an 'excess' that is often colouristic. The foregrounding of bright, even garish, colour, is described as anti-realist, genuinely populist in its commitment to excess, and hence subversive of the putative transparency of a Hollywood style described as 'realism'. A scrupulous analyst approaching Douglas Sirk's *All That Heaven Allows*, however, finds herself encountering a mismatch between the theoretical terms of reference and the phenomena she notes on screen. Thus Mary Beth Haralovich writes:

In many instances where colour is 'excessive' or has the potential to disturb concentration on the story, the color is doubly motivated by realist narrative space and by the conventions of melodrama. Color in *All that Heaven Allows* is, then, within the conventions of normalcy at the same time that it 'complicates' the narrative space.[11]

As so often, inverted commas round keywords mark a problem in the discourse, the presence of a term requiring further (theoretical) definition (what exactly is involved in this 'complication'?). The problem lies in the characterisation of Hollywood films in terms of a 'realism' that is viewed as opposed to melodrama, rather than as involved dialectically with it, or as occupying positions on a continuum between absolute, 'total' realism and an equally absolute melodrama. In fact, although narratives may place characters in environments the audience is cued to consider real, that 'reality' rapidly undergoes heightening or enhancement by practices associated with melodrama: in particular, by distinguishing clearly between positive and negative figures; by underlining those distinctions through music (as the etymology of melos plus drama would decree); and by using that music to intensify the work's emotional appeal. 'Realism' is little more than a shaping of *mise en scène* and – yes – narrative space to render the characters' world initially continuous with, and so accessible to, that of the audience, granting the work's dream the status of a plausible alternative version of their lives: a *family* romance indeed, 'the same but different'. Realism may be the sugar of familiarity coating the pill of the difference of the stars' fates, but it is also a drab wrapper peeled off – as the female star removes her bifocals – to reveal sparkling, magical otherness.

The problems generated by use of the standard theoretical apparatus for discussion of Hollywood films and melodrama become glaring when Haralovich considers the costuming of Cary Scott in the period of her attempted renunciation of the love of Ron Kirby:

In the last area of color I would like to consider – the role of the female lead in relation to the film's color system – *All that Heaven Allows* splits the primacy of the female lead in color planning between Jane Wyman and Agnes Moorhead. In his analysis of the role the female star plays in the development of color aesthetics, Neale observes that 'whether conceived and articulated in terms of the discourse of "natural beauty" or the discourse of "glamour", color aesthetics ensured that the female lead would provide spectacle to be looked at at the same time that she carried out her function within the narrative' (Neale, 151–55). In *All that Heaven Allows*, however, Moorhead functions more strongly as the source of color spectacle than Wyman does.[12]

Haralovich's remarks universalise a single model of female star function, ignoring the variety of codes utilised by the very genre under consideration, melodrama. Where one variety of melodrama relates the suffering of the female protagonist to a self-destructiveness expressed in part in flamboyant dress, Cary Scott's relinquishment of the flaring red worn at an earlier stage of the film, by way of contrast, taps the codes of another melodrama that links suffering to humble, self-sacrificial virtue (with the wobbling between strong colour and colourlessness encoding the contradiction between a (young) widow's right to hope for new love, and her continued obligations as a mother). Thus the context and consequences of her initial donning of red become particularly significant. The older, resigned Harvey escorting her may say approvingly that the colour becomes her, but the remarks of the notorious gossip Mona are the ones that prove prophetic. Mona states on seeing Cary that 'there's nothing like red for attracting attention, is there? I suppose that's why so few widows wear it – they'd have to be so careful.' Sara may criticise Mona's cattiness, but immediately afterwards the philandering Howard reads red as a sign of availability and forces himself upon Cary. This occurrence shows the advisability of a retreat from bold colour statements. Cary's donning of red at this point indicates not the brazenness projected by Mona and Howard, but the unworldliness of someone who neither calculates nor fully grasps the effects of her costume: who is not governed by outward show, and so will be a fitting match for the Ron who is very much his own man. Her red dress may express a longing for companionship that – unlike Harvey's – includes passion, but it does so unconsciously and symptomatically. Her unworldliness and slight disorientation render her more appealing as an identification figure, but also condemn her to the habitual form of suffering endured by melodramatic heroines: a public misreading of motives.

If red is defined as the colour that draws attention most signally, it is hardly surprising that the film should associate it with the figure whose attractiveness is noted most often by swooning women: Ron. However, although Ron's red lumber-jacket may indicate his desirability and warmth, and correspond further to his moral quality of standing apart from the conformist crowd, its primary realistic status as working attire that can be, and is, worn by other men, makes it as much a trade uniform as a sign of separation. This day-time, workaday wear is in no way 'feminising', unlike the red dress reserved for evening. These varying associations are mobilised subtly in the scene in which Cary seeks to purchase a Christmas tree. A red-jacketed, foregrounded salesperson is helping Cary pick a tree when Ron appears on the other side of the screen, in the background. Although the image is plausibly realistic, the repetition of red suggests a doubling that emphasises Cary's distracted, unfocused condition after renouncing Ron, her haunting by signifiers of his possible presence. Irony underlines the distraction by placing the man himself in the background, his signifier in the foreground and borne by somebody else.

The importance of colour to this film is first suggested by a *mise en scène* that, although realistic, might have prompted Godard to formalise it into the method of isolating primary colours against white backgrounds that dominates his colour films of the 1960s. Whiteness may be a real element of the environment – of the white clapboards on the New England houses, or of snow – but it allows saturated blocks of primary colour to stand out from the very outset, when Sara arrives in a blue car and walks up to Cary's house, where a meal awaits under a yellow sunshade also seen in *Magnificant Obsession* (1954). Colour is not named in the dialogue, however, until Ron clips a sprig of the golden Chinese flower. His action is accompanied by a first snatch of understated, romantic piano music, indicating the extent to which colour and music function as doubles in mood-setting, as required by the Technicolor aesthetic established by Natalie Kalmus.

Thus the function of colour fluctuates across two registers: an initial one tied to realism and the everyday; and a symbolic one expressive of love and (melodramatic) dream. As so often, realism may be the legitimising alibi that is the starting point of the mainstream Hollywood film, but melodrama is its destination and lure. The blue and the yellow stand out but fulfil no obvious function at this point in the film, and consequently may be deemed signs of the probably self-indulgent decorativeness of Sirk himself, for whom they encode his (unrecognised) artistry and tastefulness. (They would, of course, be staples of the later auteurist praise of Sirk as a deviser of figures within the carpet of orthodox 1950s Hollywood.) The blue–yellow combination sustains a variety of uses across the film, however. One – to distinguish between lit and unlit spaces at night-time – is simply realistic. Nevertheless, a climactic moment in the film sees Ned berate Cary for her intended marriage. Here the blue and yellow, hitherto compatible components of a realistic space, suffer separation by a shot-reverse-shot mechanism that places a blue background behind Ned and a yellow, lit one behind Cary. The status of the exchange as a traumatic possible turning point renders the blue–yellow separation significant, though the range of its meaning is not allegorically clear-cut but amplified melodramatically to overwhelm the regime of restricted signification. Insofar as colours that have previously accompanied one another within a single image are now opposed systematically, their distribution between separate images might correspond to the unnatural quality of the rift between mother and son. The blue behind Ned may also signify his coldness, with the yellow behind Cary recalling the golden flower associated with love at the film's beginning. Since the colour circle does not present blue and yellow as direct opposites (the direct opposite of blue being orange; that of yellow, blue-violet), it is as if up to this point a realistic code has de-emphasised the potential opposition between them, something played up in this scene's application of the intensities of the melodramatic code.

The point at which colour explodes across its full potential range, though, is the subsequent scene of Kay's lament that the marriage would ruin her life. It unfolds before a major light-source suggestive of stained glass. As Cary sits on the bed, Kay tosses back and forth distractedly across the room. Roger McNiven has argued that the green projected onto Kay's face from the light-source bespeaks envy of her mother's condition as a person who is loved.[13] The association of green with envy may be conventional, but this hardly renders it irrelevant to the narrative genre film that is *All That Heaven Allows*, however unconscious such an envy would have to be. A more serious objection to, or necessary qualification of, this reading may be that other colours also pass across Kay's face: how to account, for instance, for the simultaneous presence of blue on her forehead face and green on her lower face. It surely does not signify the cold conventionally associated with it, which has already been linked to the 'cold

All That Heaven Allows: Kay's disintegration like a prism's splitting of light

anger' of Ned. The primary function of the colours seems to be rather the establishment of an opposition between a confused, distracted and mobile Kay, whose disturbance is as it were objectified in the unpredictable play across a literalised 'emotional spectrum', and Cary, whose self-possession and possible simultaneous shock are suggested by her immobility and the absence of any colour-movement across her face, which has a natural flesh tone. As in the preceding scene with Ned, the colour usage underlines the unnaturalness of the children's words and behaviour. The only colour associated with Cary here is a red on the lower part of her nightdress: the sign, surely, of her warmth, as she supports and consoles her distraught daughter.

MODERNIST MELODRAMA? *THE OBERWALD MYSTERY*

Michelangelo Antonioni's *The Oberwald Mystery* – a work of pathbreaking experiment with colour-console mixing from the early 1980s – begins with an apparently firm modernistic commitment to abstraction. A tongue of forest may extend greenly into the centre of the image, but the sky above is unnaturally red, and the reddish birch forest entered subsequently may feel like a negative. Crickets may declare it night-time, but the rusty branches are very unlike 'normal', bluish cinematic 'day-for-night', and lightning flashes pure red. Meanwhile, the sky periodically sheeted by the lightning has become predominantly purple. Once inside a castle, we see a hearth that has clearly been coloured, its fire not flickering, as one would expect, but a solid red. As the film proceeds, however, moves of this kind become increasingly infrequent, gradually assuming the status of subservient flourishes decorating the margins of the royal, *Mayerling*-like melodrama of Jean Cocteau's characteristically swooningly death-obsessed screenplay, in which a Queen (Monica Vitti) protects a young poet (Sebastian) charged with her assassination, falls in love with him, then provokes him to kill her indeed once his taking of poison has raised the prospect of her remaining alone. Colour modulation loses its bid to be the engine of the work's progression. As the colour becomes predominantly naturalistic, the modulations come to seem finicky, falling away from a consistently modernist stylisation. Uncertainty over the degree of the colour's motivation loses the centrality it seemed to possess at first. A promising early example of such uncertainty is the bright green flooding the castle room when the Queen's maid of honour Edith opens windows to counteract the stifling effect of the fires. One may wonder whether this green is motivated by its frequent conception as the opposite of red, the colour of the fires; whether it represents a near-synaesthetic 'blowing in' of the abstracted colour of the surrounding forest (for closing the window appears to shut it out); or whether it appears for other reasons, or none at all, except as a modernistic tearing of the skein of habit. Unfortunately, the momentariness of such strong modulation, and the frequent lengthy reversions to a simple realism, make it seem to matter little whether or not one knows. More disappointing still are the subsequent occasional lapses into a predictably melodramatic colour-coding of characters. Thus when an unnatural colour – a blue lighting, modulating into lavender-violet – is associated with the Queen's nemesis, Police Chief Foehn, it seems simply to label him, snuffing out the flares of modernism. It may be intriguing to see blue flood a room as the Queen, seated in a chair, draws a blanket over herself and then disappears, like Thomas in Antonioni's earlier *Blow Up* (1966), leaving only the blanket visible, its shape unchanged; and it is surely significant that a similar pale blue heavily veils and abstracts the library where the Queen and her would-be assassin restate their love, underlining the strength of their desire to blot out the world. But in each case naturalistic colour soon reasserts itself, rendering the stylisation half-hearted or finicky, and implying the futility of the sort of subjective war on reality both modernists in general, and these lovers in particular, pursue. Antonioni's work on the surface of the world becomes insufficiently thoroughgoing to convince. Only in the natural world does the principle of colour modulation prevail: a moon viewed by the Queen shifts from yellow to red to purple to blue; a field outside the castle becomes deep green, then blue, then desiccated, then purple; while the landscape through which the Queen rides has a green sky above, a blue forest below, and its sky is first yellow then grey in the end. Unfortunately, this metamorphic natural world is merely a backdrop for the slow-motion, fatalistic Wagnerian interior chamber-drama. Perhaps because the film's world is pre-industrial, its transformation by the human (including changes in its colouration) is not integrated into its themes and diegesis, as it had been in *Deserto rosso (Red Desert)* (1964). Instead, it points to the doodling, absent-minded presence of a bored demiurgic narrator. Moreover, the motif of the world's variable perception, correlated so powerfully with mutations of colour in the earlier film, also vanishes from *The Oberwald Mystery*. Instead of the blending of 'subjective' and 'objective' viewpoints in the 'free indirect subjectivity' whose centrality to *Red Desert* was noted first by Pasolini, one has a simple alternation between them. In the scales that balance melodrama and modernism, the weights are placed disproportionately on the side of the former.

If colour and music harmonise with drama in classic Hollywood, it is hardly surprising that the score should rise to a sentimental climax as the flowers in front of the Queen briefly redden as she mentions the assassinated King's blood. This harmonisation, which extends to the use of a *fin-de-siècle* score featuring Richard Strauss, Brahms and early Schönberg, discontinues the experimentation with sound and colour relationships that had pervaded *Red Desert*: modernism colours only form, while content remains resolutely melodramatic, and the colour lacks the indirect 'expressiveness of the repressed' that forms a ground-bass of the best of Sirk. However, the restriction of colour experimentation to one screen-section in the scenes involving dialogue (e.g., Foehn's lavender tinting) becomes interesting and powerful at the film's end, as pallor passes from the lovers after their death, golden sunlight now illuminating them as the onlookers gather in a pallid group at the end of the tunnel of the frozen frame. With the departure of the lovers' idealistic energies, life itself becomes moribund. Nevertheless, this formally satisfying logical conclusion to the occasional division of the frame between realistic and non-realistic colouration (realism for the Queen and Sebastian, non-realist for Foehn) cannot redeem its earlier uses.

For Seymour Chatman, the film becomes problematic by attempting to deploy televisual colours for subtle effects.[14] In other words: subtlety is introduced where none is expected (for reasons including the conventionality of the material, the frequent lengthy periods of realism and the size of a television screen, which makes subtleties less easily discernable). It is as if colour acquires the insubstantiality of the ghostly phenomena conjured up in the film's occasional trick effects involving mirrors and portraits. Antonioni himself described a need for a cinema 'freed from the limits of realism' and revealing 'truths which everyday reality no longer gives us'. He added: 'I am convinced that the fantastic world of which my film has disclosed a mere glimmer is at our door and that that door will open itself if we do not ourselves open it.'[15] But if these remarks suggest a quest to unify the separate anti-realist traditions of modernism and the fantastic, the fundamental solidity of the detail of a costume drama world compromises both modernism and fantasy. Nevertheless, Antonioni's intuition of the imminence of a door's opening was indeed visionary: when it opened, however, what entered was neither modernism, nor a modernist-fantasy amphibian, but the fantasy melodrama of the Hollywood CGI whose primary addressees would be adolescent.

NOTES

1. Lillian Gish, with Ann Pichot, *The Movies, Mr Griffith, and Me* (San Francisco: Mercury House Inc., 1988 (1969)), p. 221.

2. The intensity of Varda's fascination by colour can be gauged by its mention even in the black-and-white *Salut, les cubains* (1963), whose commentary draws a distinction between a decorative colour use and a socialist one. As for the question of terminology, another relevant partial equivalent for 'pleasure' and 'happiness' is, of course, 'utopia', as brought into play in relation to the musical by Richard Dyer ('Entertainment and Utopia', in Bill Nichols (ed.), *Movies and Methods II* (Berkeley and Los Angeles: University of California Press, 1985), pp. 220–31).

3. Gerald Mast, *Can't Help Singin': The American Musical on Stage and Screen* (Woodstock and New York: Overlook, 1987), p. 261.

4. Charles Barr, Stig Björkman, Barry Boys *et al.*, *The Films of Jean-Luc Godard* (London: Studio Vista, 1987), p. 27.

5. Steve Neale, *Cinema and Technology: Image, Sound, Colour* (London: BFI/Macmillan, 1985), pp. 151–5.

6. Carl Theodor Dreyer, 'Colour and Coloured Film', in Donald Skoller (ed.), *Dreyer in Double Reflection* (New York: E. P. Dutton, 1973), p. 170.

7. Jean Renoir, *Renoir on Renoir: Interviews, Essays, and Remarks*, trans. Carol Volk (Cambridge and New York: Cambridge University Press, 1989), p. 50.

8. Ibid., p. 51.

9. Ibid., p. 245.

10. Geoffrey Nowell-Smith, 'Minnelli and Melodrama', in Nichols, *Movies and Methods II*, pp. 190–4.

11. Mary Haralovich, '*All that Heaven Allows*: Color, Narrative Space, and Melodrama', in Angela Dalle Vacche and Brian Price (eds), *Color: The* Film *Reader* (New York and London: Routledge, 2006), p. 149.

12. Ibid., p. 151.

13. Roger D. McNiven, 'The Middle-Class American Home of the Fifties: The Use of Architecture in Nicholas Ray's *Bigger Than Life* and Douglas Sirk's *All that Heaven Allows*', *Cinema Journal* vol. 22 no. 4 (Summer 1983), pp. 38–57.

14. Seymour Chatman, *Antonioni, Or the Surface of the World* (Berkeley, Los Angeles and London: University of California Press, 1985), p. 210.

15. Ibid., p. 212.

7 Colour and/as Fantasy: The Rainbow and the Jewel

INTRODUCTION

Positing that films use colour to establish a sense of an entire world, Stanley Cavell describes them as doing so in three ways. The first, and simplest, yields 'a consistent region of make-believe'.[1] Unsurprisingly, the primary examples of such a practice are films whose main protagonist is a child, or that might be deemed 'child-like' themselves, though Cavell eschews this term. Also unsurprisingly, given the licence technological progress appears to offer to an evolutionary notion of historiography, the simplest form of fantasy is the earliest of the three in cinematic history, identified with the 1930s and 1940s. Another, arguably a later derivative of this, gives 'a premonition that the world we inhabit is already the world of the future'.[2] More often than not, this futurity inhabits the genre known as science fiction. Finally, a film like Alfred Hitchcock's *Vertigo* (1958) utilises different colour spaces to enable a passage aimed at 'establishing a world of private fantasy'.[3]

The fantasy worlds of Cavell's third category might be described as 'expressionistic', as they radiate from a single individual's gaze, not from the futurity that envelops a whole world. Nevertheless, Cavell himself might not accept this extrapolation, as he uses *Das Kabinett des Dr Caligari* (*The Cabinet of Dr Caligari*) (1920) as an example of his first category. If *The Cabinet of Dr Caligari* and *The Wizard of Oz* (1939) exemplify the same category, it may well be one dependent upon a framing device. Another interesting case of border-slippage might be the brief early scene in Martin Scorsese's *Mean Streets* (1973) in which the orange light of the bar entered by Harvey Keitel's Charlie breathes an almost expressionistic privacy of fantasy, a subtly infernal welcome, as 'Jumpin' Jack Flash', by Their Satanic Majesties, the Rolling Stones, fills the soundtrack, accompanying the display of female flesh on the club's stage. In this context, the orange light resembles a magnification of the church candle into which Charlie had dipped his finger earlier, musing of damnation. The steeping of the world in a single colour might correspond therefore to the Last Judgment's determination of a final destination with the definitiveness of a single state: in this case, that of a fire of perdition.

The possibility of such an analysis of this moment in *Mean Streets* indicates the use value of a set of categories such as Cavell's, which are not defined rigidly and rigorously but slide into one another. Consequently, Scorsese's scene might even be described as combining all three categories: a childishness of primal, libidinal colour; a projection of fantasy; and the hallucinated advent of a real futurity in a flashforward to the afterlife. In this chapter, however, I will consider closely the colour patterning in Cavell's two key films, *The Wizard of Oz* and *Vertigo*. Should one read Hitchcock's film in the manner proposed in Chris Marker's *Sans soleil* (*Sunless*) (1982), however – as a science-fiction work about Scottie Ferguson's creation of an alternative temporality – it too might spill over into another of Cavell's categories, the one founded on futurity. Meanwhile, if the creation of a blank dream woman as the screen to entertain projections lies at the heart of *Vertigo*, as many have thought, it may seem hardly accidental that two of the 'future films' Cavell cites (*Fahrenheit 451* (1966) and *Petulia* (1968)) revolve around Julie Christie, whom Pauline Kael described controversially as 'extraordinary just to look at – lewd and anxious, expressive and empty, brilliantly faceted but with something central missing, almost as if there's no woman inside'.[4] In this description, Christie becomes a victim of alien body-snatchers, her post-1960s career readable as an heroic effort to recover that body for herself and demonstrate the presence and persistence within it of a warm and thoughtful person.

If colour is associated with fantasy, it is partly because the very idea that humans could control the world's colours has been felt to be fantastic by most societies throughout history. Hence the association of bright colour with the Other World, as discussed by Aldous Huxley.[5] When this finally occurs, during the Industrial Revolution, it fulfils age-old dreams and equally inveterate nightmares: the rainbow may descend to earth, but so does the thick cloud of the accompanying storm (in the case of *The Wizard of Oz*, that of a hurricane in the Dust Bowl).

THE WIZARD OF OZ: COLOUR AND THE ACCIDENTS OF TRANSFORMATION

If the signature tune of *The Wizard of Oz* is 'Somewhere Over the Rainbow', whose yearning is intensified by its singing before any colour has been seen, its breakthrough into colour – after Dorothy's twister-borne house has landed and she opens the door – suggests that the rainbow has been broken apart. The first, and most obvious, sign of this is the appearance of the Munchkins dressed in a multiplicity of colours. More interesting, though, are two other relevant images. The first involves the gradual materialisation of Glinda, the good witch. At first, one sees a predominantly greenish ball's floating approach, a mist of different colours suffusing it. It becomes red at its point of largest expansion, before melting into a figure whose pink dress and wand approximate a good fairy rather than a witch. The spiralling movement of the ball and the colours within it grant it the status of a rainbow folded upon itself to become a world: a rainbow whose unusual behaviour ramifies into its approaching the viewer, rather than representing the unattainable, the endlessly receding. It is after this rainbow has landed that Dorothy can be sent on her way: to the Emerald City.

The rainbow is the arch down which one walks to the jewel whose symbolisation of the Other World is discussed by Aldous Huxley.[6] That walk may follow the famous Yellow Brick Road, but it begins as a spiral at an angle to another spiral nested into it at its outset: a spiral of red. The two roads become, as it were, two strips of the rainbow, separated out, yet each representative of the positive tonalities of colour, each related. Since Dorothy is wearing the ruby-red slippers, a combination of colour contrast and relationship appears to dictate her taking of a yellow road. (When the Wicked Witch extends her green hand towards them, their electrical spray of yellow sparks suggests a magnetised emission of the dust of the Yellow Brick Road.) In a film that defines itself as a dream, is it possible that its signifiers have a truly dream-like condensation and multivalence? If so, the movement of the yellow towards green may be read as suggesting an alchemical progression from the precious metal that is gold to the precious stone of the emerald that is also an allegorical movement from a more primitive, mythical form of value (gold) towards a more modern one (the green dollar).

All the above-mentioned manifestations of colour involve magical transformations. Just as the sepia of Kansas can become the colour of Oz, so the green of Glinda's ball can metamorphose into red. Glinda's status as a witch may be related to her ability to run the gamut from one end of the spectrum to the other – from a colour associated with calm to one linked to passion – but her goodness correlates with the fact that she is never linked with two primary colours simultaneously, and so never becomes ambiguous. The red and the green co-present in the Wicked Witch of the West, with her green face

The Wizard of Oz: the rainbow rolls up like a ball

and the red sand in the hourglass she holds up beside it, are troubling because they manifest simultaneously phases Glinda's appearance codes as requiring separation.

The very greenness of the Wicked Witch's face shows her particular perversion of a colour usually associated with the natural. If the essence of colour is its ambiguity of meaning, and interesting colour use acknowledges that ambiguity, however, green becomes the work's key colour, being associated both with the Wicked Witch's face and with that of the Oz who is presented as a wizard expected to perform good deeds. If both the witch and the wizard can appear as green-faced, terrifying, unnatural figures, the wizard is redeemed, of course, by the revelation that his green apparition is the mask of a hidden, retrievable human. In terms of the code whereby green connotes envy, each becomes secretly envious of the true power Dorothy ascribes to herself in her dream-like fantasy, where her sole possession of a dress of blue indicates her singularity. (And although one may doubt that this blue could be related to that of the Madonna, who is also 'small and meek', or that the red, white and blue she wears render her singularly American, the polysemy of dream elements makes it hard to rule out these possibilities nevertheless.) In the case of the wizard the sinister connotation of the green face dissolves with the demonstration that he is not really green (only *symbolically* so – a distinction of relevance to my remarks below on text's subterranean entertainment of signifiers associated with 'Irishness'). The wizard becomes redeemable through the separation of essence and image, and the moment at which the work acknowl-edges the principle of this duality is also the one at which an off-stage mechanism is able to recast the transformed images of the farm hands – the Scarecrow, the Tin Man and the Cowardly Lion – as their human counterparts and return them to Kansas, along with Dorothy herself. Another element that ren-ders the wizard redeemable might be designated as the 'crypto-Irishness' of some of the work's components, which come into focus around him, the Emerald City suggesting the Emerald Isle, and his blustering verbal gifts the effects of kissing the Blarney Stone. Retrospectively, the dwarfish Munchkins, with their predominantly green army, become a version of 'the little people'. If such 'crypto-Irishness' represents a source of redemption it is, of course, through the popular cultural linkage of Irishness with fantasy and magic. In this context, *The Wizard of Oz* exemplifies less explicitly a Hollywood habit expressed more openly elsewhere: one whereby a film foregrounding green may well also include an overtly Irish element, and possibly a fantastic one (both are found in Losey's *The Boy with the Green Hair* (1948), where the grandfather of the boy whose hair greens is Irish). In *The Wizard of Oz*, an ambiva-lence vis-à-vis green is managed through its separation into a green associated with malign magic and an emerald as sparkling, as light-bringing, as the ruby slippers.

Somewhat surprisingly in the light of its identification with yellow brick roads and ruby slippers, the dominant reading of *The Wizard of Oz* charges it with chromophobia. This reading revels in the colours of Oz and decries the return to home as not only sentimental, but as betraying the film's own pow-erful fantasy.[7] In extenuation of a much-loved film, Batchelor adds '[p]erhaps the implications of not returning, of not recovering from the Fall into colour, were too radical for Hollywood to contemplate'.[8] Without wishing to underestimate the strength of Hollywood's drive to conformity, I would suggest that another aspect of the ending permits a different reading (one probably not intended by the makers – though the plethora of makers in this case renders the discernment of intention a matter of guesswork). This feature is the final absence of Miss Gulch, which Peter Van Gelder deems a loose end.[9] This absence allows one to read the ending not as a capitulatory return to reality but as indicating the productiveness of fantasy, which engineers Miss Gulch's destruction by the 'accident' of a dream-event. Significantly, both destructions of the witches are performed by Dorothy, but through the two innocence-preserving accidents of the unpredictable landing of her tornado-borne house and her dousing of the Wicked Witch of the West with water intended to save the Scarecrow. The epigraph to this film of 1939 might have stemmed from the last moments of Jean Renoir's *La Règle du Jeu*, (*The Rules of the Game*), of the same year, when Saint-Aubin categorises Robert de la Chesnaye's description of André Jurieu's shooting by his gamekeeper as 'an accident' as 'a new definition of the word "accident"'. Thus the film does not pass from reality to fantasy only to return to reality. Its movement is arguably more Hegelian than that: from reality to fantasy to a reality–fantasy fusion. Was the possibility of that fusion always present *in nuce* in the work's beginning *not* with the grey Kansas of L. Frank Baum's book, but with a *sepia* from which colour could germinate credibly, and which could therefore accommodate the effects of subsequent events in the coloured world?

COLOUR, INDETERMINACY AND FANTASY IN *VERTIGO*

Early on in the other key film Cavell marshals to define fantasy, Alfred Hitchcock's *Vertigo*, its male protagonist Scottie sits in his green sweater, in the left background, with Madeleine, whom he has just fished out of the San Francisco Bay, in red. Earlier still, however, Madeleine herself had been associated

Vertigo: Scottie's first sight of Madeleine at Ernie's

with green, through the magnificent, almost imperial green dress she wears at Ernie's restaurant. The mutual substitutability of Scottie and Madeleine first suggested by his donning of 'her' colour reaches far beyond a simple colour exchange into a far deeper one. Its primary source is in the visual vocabulary of profiles, silhouettes and shadows linking them. Scottie's first sight of an iconic Madeleine – in the above-mentioned scene at Ernie's – is side-on: her image is held like that of a monarch on a stamp or coin, a half-view that suggests a hidden side, anticipating both Scottie's difficulties in knowing her thoroughly and the mystery that intrigues him (and, of course, this too is monarchical, as none dare view the monarch directly). But Scottie himself appears side-on at this moment, facing *in the same direction*: the shot-countershot is reversed to intimate a fantastic identity between the two, over and above the realistic code whereby Scottie views her with a sidelong, shifty look. When Scottie first sees Judy on the street, the fact that she is in green, and in profile, doubly recalls the first appearance of the Madeleine-icon, for all the difference – which includes the way that very first appearance had shown Madeleine in a black only edged with green, that is: primarily invested with the colour of the underworld. When, in her hotel room, Judy asks Scottie whether he is drawn to her 'because I remind you of her', the camera dollies in towards her as she is silhouetted in green against the hotel window. The green connotes the ghostliness it signified in the Victorian theatre to which Hitchcock was alluding consciously, and the association is reinforced by the use of a profile that here suggests her need of the other half for which she can only be substituted, as she can never be a complete person: the 'Madeleine' whose jewellery and clothes she has retained, as if only waiting for the opportunity to 'become' her again.

If Scottie and Madeleine are linked from the outset by their presentation as profiles, they are further linked – at the apparent 'end' of their relationship – by their shooting as silhouettes as they emerge from the stable at the San Bautista mission. At this moment, both are about to lose their loves, to be rendered

insubstantial by the mechanism of a plot within which they are no more than cogs. The sense of their identity as silhouettes or shadows is cemented when Scottie's dream projects him as a shadow on the roof
of the mission, in the position of the Madeleine whose death has rendered him a shadow. Since the
roof then melts away to leave him still falling, it is apparent that he has achieved the insubstantiality of
the ghost of Carlotta, passing through solids to enter one time after another, always 'falling in love'
beyond death. This is one reason why he sees Carlotta, not Madeleine, in the arms of Elster in that
dream; another is that as yet he has not disentangled Madeleine, Carlotta and Judy, who are all mutually substitutable at this point, which means – among other things – also *all versions of himself*
(subconsciously, he seems to be aware of his own 'feminisation', be it by acrophobia or his subordination
to Elster). Only at the end will he be able to envisage a condition in which he is no longer 'haunted' (his
word) by the past, though its infernal repetitiousness means that he only overcomes one haunting
through subjection to another, by the death of Judy.

Throughout the film, the indeterminacy of the shadow or silhouette is a driver of fantasy, as it seems
to solicit the projection of a clarifying image into its blank, black space. The most deadly such projection is the final one: when Judy sees a black shape arise out of the tower stairwell, its indeterminacy
enhanced by its viewing through the sidelong look that is more important for this film than the direct gaze
described by Laura Mulvey,[10] she projects its identity as that of a ghost – probably that of Madeleine –
rather than the nun as which it is revealed later. Her step backwards reflects guilt, fear and a possible super-
stitiousness that corresponds to her powerlessness (where Elster cynically manipulates the illusion of the
supernatural, Judy appears to be ready to believe it real). The nun's deadly indeterminacy may then be
seen as pointing forward to that of the disguised Norman Bates in the shower-murder scene of *Psycho*
(1960), that darkest of all conjugations of the image of a Mother Superior and the theme of a man's
substitutability by a woman.

Of the two key colours that play out across the film – red and green[11] – only one is strongly associated with a character, and it is not the red conventionally ascribed to 'the female lead' in mainstream
Hollywood colour practices:[12] it is the green worn by, and appearing around, Judy. Given Gavin Elster's
desire to seduce Scottie to remain within Madeleine's orbit, thereby sealing his fate as the 'made-to-order
witness' of her apparent suicide, one might think he would clothe her in the red that is deemed the
most magnetic of colours. However, only at Scottie's apartment, after he has rescued her, does she don
red, and it is in the form of the bathrobe he has left out for her. If anything, red is thus associated rather
with Scottie, and his potential passion may be declared by the red door of his apartment. Madeleine's
usual 'colours', meanwhile, are black, white and grey. The non-advisability of any attempt to use red to
attract Scottie becomes apparent when Midge, who feels he is slipping away from her, dons a red
sweater. Her colour choice accompanies the spectacular failure of her attempt to win him by painting
her own face onto a copy of the portrait of Carlotta, a return to her 'first love' (painting) that also
implicitly recalls the youth in which she was briefly engaged to Scottie.

Madeleine's monochromaticism can be explained in two ways: according to viewers' assumptions
concerning the realistic grounds of narrative events; and in terms of polyvalent symbolism of the grey
that is her most characteristic tone. Interpreting the narrative events purely realistically, the viewer may
see the black, white and grey as the real colours worn by Elster's spouse, and speculate that these may
reflect a presumed character trait (modesty), a wealth that is tasteful and has no need to flaunt itself
and/or her married status. Continuing these considerations in terms of realism, Elster's monochromatic

clothing of Madeleine may betray his subtle knowledge of the bachelor who is Scottie, who may withdraw from women with evident designs upon him – as he does from Midge.

Alternatively, the monochrome may have symbolic import. It is in these terms that Richard Allen reads the black-and-white combination worn by Madeleine: '[w]hen Judy Barton as Madeleine leads Scottie Ferguson to the bell tower in *Vertigo*, she wears a wool speckled black-and-white coat. The mingling of black and white here suggests the blurring of moral boundaries, as in the suggestion that something is not black and white.'[13] Ornan Rotem's suggestion that the monochromatic combination connotes contrast and determination in the film's colour scheme might also be relevant here, with contrast spurring action,[14] and the possible blurring of boundaries causing a detective's action to reestablish their separation, or uncover the opposite hidden beneath the appearance (woman as the mystery constructed by Elster). Read symbolically, Madeleine's grey would correspond also to her fading towards a non-differentiation equivalent to non-existence, and also to yet another layer of self-hood, beneath the upper ones of white and black. The ambiguity of grey would intrigue and, of course, be even less threatening to Scottie, and so potentially more attractive still than black and white. If, as my student Jason Swiderski has observed,[15] black and white appear frequently when Scottie and Madeleine kiss, this is in part because the black–white strand running through the film is accompanied by red, as Rotem notes. If Rotem is right to link this particular colour complex to decisive action, the action in question would be erotic, a rupturing of the protagonists' sense of separation, and so overlap with the red–yellow 'libidinal' complex he also discerns.[16] The monochrome backgrounds underline an association of the libidinal with a 'love–death' that goes beyond the swooning Wagnerian one cross-referenced by Bernard Herrmann's score, becoming literal death; a draining of colour. The occurrence of two of these kisses in or near the San Bautista tower, whose phallic connotations need no spelling out, emphasises the presence of a death that is feared as well as ecstatic, as Scottie looks down and his world shudders.

Judy's key colour, however, is green. The meaning of the thin strip of green within the black robe she wears on her first appearance as Madeleine at Ernie's may not be entirely clear, though it may indicate the presence of a residue of Judy within the upper-class woman whose performance is not yet fully into its stride. If Madeleine's first appearance is in profile, lit brightly and turned to the right of the screen, Judy's profiling is against the green of the Empire hotel's neon. The visual rhyme is also an inversion, as Judy looks left of screen, and her features are almost thoroughly shrouded in darkness. The wedge of red behind the green-lit Judy as she begins to break down before Scottie's importunity, agreeing to cancel going to work the next morning, hints at the danger the concession involves, as well as recalling the red background against which the other woman had appeared at Ernie's. It is as if she is already sliding down the slope that ends in an identification with Madeleine that includes one with her death. In many respects Judy is indeed the systematic inversion of Madeleine. This inversion may be a matter of class and character, or of disguise, lest she be recognised subsequently as a strange reincarnation of the dead woman. As it is, only Scottie's obsession is able to excavate that image hidden within her, like the grey Madeleine suit concealed within the wardrobe, and which Judy intends at first to leave behind when planning to flee after meeting Scottie again. Judy's green is intensely ambiguous: it may be that associated with ghosts in late-nineteenth-century theatre, as Hitchcock himself averred, but her appearance is also intensely physical. One learns far more about Judy's bodily contours than one ever did of Madeleine's: her green dress is tight, emphasising the amplitude of her breasts, and the side-on shots of her standing in the apartment reinforce this effect. That green may be restful, as it is conventionally, and therefore earth-motherly, but of course 'mother' is never a simply positive term in Hitchcock's work, even before *Psycho*. The rest may be that of death, further justifying Rotem's association of the work's dominant red–green spectrum with Thanatos.[17] Its ambivalence renders it potentially deceptive, and it may well be an unconscious suspicion that this is the case that prompts Scottie to reclothe her in a manner that paradoxically strips away appearances to recover her incarnation of pure appearance. If green is ambiguous, it is also because it fuses and confuses the two colours that dominate the apartment of Midge, who has been for Scottie the image of a woman with whom he has felt at home. The analytical separation of those colours leaves him unprepared to deal with their fusion, as Judy/Madeleine's green lures him into that 'non-homely' place known as the uncanny, *das Unheimliche*. Ultimately, grey is the colour generated by the fusion of red and green implied by the mutual substitutability of Scottie and Madeleine discussed at the beginning of this piece. That mutual substitution is a mutually assured destruction akin to that of the red and green that converge in grey. As Johannes Itten notes, 'two complementary colours are a strange couple. They are opposed, enhance one another, achieve their highest luminosity in juxtaposition, and destroy one another in mixing to grey – like fire and water.'[18] Grey becomes the duplicitous disguise of deadly darkness, its presence veiling the viewing Scottie's awareness that his attraction is one to death. It may also be understood as implicitly demystifying the colour opposition whose most melodramatic, and primal, form is, of course, that of black and white. This demystification is accompanied by the presence of a double body. If, as Tobin Siebers argues in relation to representations of Medusa, '[t]he evolution of the Gorgoneion suggests that the seemingly antithetical figures of Medusa and Athena are really only two different expressions made by the same face',[19] the opposition of the characters Madeleine and Judy is unmasked by the latter's gravitation towards the grey of the former, as Scottie-as-author (Scottie possessed by his author?) taps his knowledge that both are Kim Novak to subvert their apparent difference.

One scene, of course, represents a seeming exception to my statement that Judy's body is better-known than Madeleine's: when the former appears bare-shouldered in Scottie's bed after her rescue from San Francisco Bay. The relationship between this scene and the remainder of the work, however, suggests the operation of a censoring dream-work which falls well within the parameters of 'a dream of fair women', as the narrative unfolds primarily in the unconscious of its main protagonist. (After all, a fully conscious Scottie would surely have commented on the physical identity of Kim Novak as Madeleine and as Judy.) Within that dream, the memory of the strapless bra displayed on Midge's desk can underpin a credible, fetishistic disavowal of Madeleine's hidden nakedness. After all, the onlooker may say, she could be wearing just such a bra. The fetishistic 'now you see it [in reality in the past, and in the memory that is the mind's eye], now you don't [in present reality]' obeys the visual doubling and double-taking that pervade Hitchcock's film.

Vertigo's narrative unmasks the supernatural elements of its early sections as a hoax, props in Gavin Elster's conspiracy to persuade Scottie that Madeleine is obsessed with her ancestor Carlotta Valdez, believes herself possessed by her and so is suicidal. Nevertheless, the film's colour use taps symbols of other-worldliness in a manner that infuses its cynical story of enlightenment with a genuine undertow towards myth. Most obvious, and most renowned, is the association of Madeline – and then Judy – with the green that accompanied ghosts on the Victorian stage. The persistence of ghostly green even into the story of Judy, whose existence as the impersonator of Madeleine theoretically dispels all supernaturalism, suggests its uncanny prolongation. Her story becomes the ghost of a ghost story. (It is as if the true uncanniness of green lies in its demonstration of the other world's ability to simulate – to double – the colour that most often signifies life and growth.) The diffused green surrounding Judy as she appears in a doorway in her hotel room, consummating her makeover by Scottie in the image of Madeleine, suggests the magical dust-shower of a fantastic transformation, even if only in the eyes of Scottie himself. Equally important as a portal to the other-worldly is the red ruby necklace Carlotta wears in her portrait, whose 'other world' of art spills its otherness into reality as Judy dons it also. The moment at which Scottie notices the jewel and remembers its origin in the painting begins the text's final slide back towards another world which, this time, is that of death: the San Bautista mission, the past, and the supernatural. It marks a key turn in a text whose recurrent spirals are a *mise en abyme* image of its own cunning movement.

Particularly relevant to the meaning of this moment are reflections on the symbolism of jewels such as those of Aldous Huxley. After describing how visions display a plethora 'of what Ezekiel terms "stones of fire", of what Weir Mitchell describes as "transparent fruit"', Huxley adds that '[t]he material objects which most nearly resemble these sources of visionary illumination are gem-stones. To acquire such a stone is to acquire something whose preciousness is guaranteed by the fact that it exists in the Other World.'[20] His conclusion is that 'precious stones are precious because they bear a faint resemblance to the glowing marvels seen with the inner eye of the visionary'.[21] And since, as he notes subsequently, flowers adorn the images of heaven of people unacquainted with jewels or glass, Scottie's vision of Madeleine in the flower shop – and Carlotta's continual association with a bouquet that flies apart in his nightmare – assumes great significance. It is as if the bouquet is a set of jewels disintegrating through the impact of the woman's fall to her death. Scottie's attraction to Madeleine, like his desire to recreate her after her death, is not simply erotic, but has religious overtones also. The erotic and the religious intertwine, separating only when the nun appears at the end as the final double – final because an inversion – of Carlotta. Like the jewels of so many myths, particularly the Wagnerian ones invoked by the score, in the end Judy falls away from Scottie into the abyss. The Other World may manifest itself at points in this one, through colours, but ultimately it is unattainable. And, despite the final presence of the nun, which is that of another signifier of the Otherworldly, Hitchcock's traumatic ending offers no hint that it may be unattainable only if sought in this life: that, although the path towards it might begin in darkness, further movement along the spiral of rebirth would take one to the turning at which the coloured Other World becomes visible again, not as a reflection but in the fullness of its own light.

'THE COLOUR OF HOPE', OR A FRAGMENT OF THE RAINBOW: *LE RAYON VERT*

… hope that is seen is not hope: for what a man seeth, why doth he yet hope for? But if we hope for that we see not, *then* do we with patience wait for *it*. (Romans 8.24, emphasis added)

At one point in Eric Rohmer's *Le Rayon Vert* (*The Green Ray*, aka *Summer*) (1986), green is described as the colour of hope. Rohmer's film is worth considering here because, like Hitchcock's, it is concerned both with green and the idea of the supernatural, while it is also – as will become apparent – Hitchcockian in another respect. For Rohmer, the key question seems to be whether green means anything, or is just distributed randomly across the environment. Another form of the question concerns whether calling this film one in a series of 'Comédies et proverbes' ensures its status as a moral parable framed realistically, rather than – one of its keywords – a 'conte', in the sense of a fairy tale, fulfilling the dreams of its protagonist, the lonely Parisienne Délphine. Rohmer, the reader of Pascal, might have used pensée 19 as an epigraph: 'All our reasoning ends in surrender to feeling. But fancy is akin to feeling, yet contrary thereto, so that we cannot distinguish between these contraries.'[22] Central to Rohmer's work therefore – and the reason for its inclusion in this section – is its preoccupation with hope, the disenchantment often known as 'realism', and fantasy ('la fantasie' being the French word translated 'fancy' in the Pascal quotation given above). Another reason lies in the relationship between the procedures of Hitchcock-enthusiast Rohmer and those of 'the master of suspense', particularly as understood by Slavoj Žižek. Rohmer's film may well be classified as suspended between, and dialectically uniting, Hitchcock and *The Wizard of Oz* – the two key films of this chapter.

About two-thirds of the way through *Le Rayon Vert* viewers are cued to prick up their ears and attend closely to the dialogue: no longer is it, as usual, Délphine digging herself deeper and deeper into a hole, but a set of words signposted as possibly particularly revelatory by its quotation of Rohmer's title, which turns out also to be that of a Jules Verne novel under discussion by some characters Délphine passes while trying to holiday in Biarritz. The green ray, an older man explains to an old lady and a group of young women, is the last ray of the sun occasionally visible at the end of summer days of exceptional atmospheric clarity. Although all the colours of the spectrum figure in the curved beams the sun emits as it slips below the horizon, the wavelengths of blue and green are more elevated; however, of these two, green is the more discernable, and hence the last one seen before the sun's disk disappears. As the spectrum that is the rainbow curves over the horizon, only this portion of it is seen. Verne describes the moment as a magical one during which viewers' feelings become comprehensible to them, along with those of all other people. Since such an experience would fulfil Délphine's idealised, romantic dream, it is tantalising that Rohmer places her at a slight distance from the conversation, withholding certainty whether she has heard and will use this information. This suspense is resolved near the film's end. Having met a sympathetic young man at the Biarritz station, she walks with him and is struck by the sign of a shop called 'Le Rayon Vert'. Hope that something of mystic significance may be in train prompts her to ask him to watch the sunset with her. As it does so, she emits a semi-suppressed yelp of happiness, apparently thinking she has seen the ray. The shot-reverse-shot mechanism leaves viewers uncertain whether or not she has.

A similar uncertainty concerning sign-interpretation has marked both the experience of Délphine herself and that of spectators throughout. Knowing the film's title – the shop-sign hung out by Rohmer, as it were – spectators may take note when early on, and in this order, there appear a green tablecloth and an Irish girl, and Délphine herself passes a green lamppost, picks up a green and yellow-backed playing card, and passes a green car. Rohmer thus forces spectators to muse on how much of this is random, how much possibly significant, and how much possibly simply a manifestation of deadpan directorial archness. Shortly thereafter spectators learn that Délphine herself has discerned a pattern, on the basis of a different cue: a medium's statement, which she recounts to friends, that green would dominate her year. One friend suggests that if she goes on holiday (despite the frustration of her plans by the withdrawal of another friend with whom she was to have visited Greece) perhaps she will find a green man (her boyfriend being unsatisfactory). Another simply adds: 'the colour of hope'. Is Délphine possibly simply superstitious, to be patronised by spectators who may consider her a pain, or does this mean something?

However, green then slips out of the picture. For although it may be the colour of many of the landscapes Délphine traverses, weeping, at the various unsatisfactory holiday spots she samples, she herself usually sports blues and red. Green's slide into the background swings the narrative pendulum away from medium-inspired fantasy and towards realism. It also measures the depth of Délphine's loss of hope, her abiding sense of worthlessness. Nevertheless, shortly after this she finds another playing card, one whose black back might have dissuaded her from doing so. (After all, the first one, ominously, had been the Queen of Spades.) Its status as the Jack of Hearts allows Rohmer to continue his play with our expectations, as we wonder whether this will be significant. And then, near the end, she meets the sympathetic young man at the station. Does she see the green ray as she sits beside him? Is it so momentary as to be lost to us in the gap between shot and reverse-shot, as the camera alternates between her and the horizon? (If it is indeed lost, that would give the lie to the suturing pretensions of the shot-reverse-shot mechanism, which purports to include everything important.) Might the earlier Rohmer of *Ma nuit chez Maud* (*My Night with Maud*) (1969), more explicitly engaged with Catholicism, have deemed her one of the poor in spirit to whom the Beatitudes promise that they will see God, aligning her with Prince Myshkin in *The Idiot*, whose reading by her is therefore not coincidental? We are unsure what she has seen, and whether or not it constitutes a wish-fulfilment.

It is thus hardly surprising that, even though, reportedly '[i]nsistent that no trick photography be used, Rohmer posted a cameraman on the Atlantic coast who, for weeks on end, scoured the horizon each evening at sunset in the hopes of capturing this rare atmospheric phenomenon,'[23] the ray's existence and visibility were questioned upon its initial dissemination, via TV. Derek Schilling adds:

> Though the director's entourage maintained that the ray was filmed off the Canary Islands, it is likely that
> a lab technician intervened in the end. In any event, the morning after the broadcast première, some
> viewers remained unsure whether Delphine had in fact seen 'son rayon vert' … A minor conspiracy
> theory developed suggesting that Rohmer had instructed the lab to create an effect all but imperceptible
> on video, so that television viewers would head to the theatre for a second opinion![24]

The mention of conspiracy would surely warm the hearts of both Hitchcock and Žižek. The most important point to note is surely that on this occasion – as if a consequence of the extensive use of improvisation in the dialogues – Rohmer's film partly escaped his control, itself becoming a 'second nature'. For, as in the case of Dorothy, bound for Oz, the spectator cannot dismiss the possibility that the strength of Délphine's desire, and not reality, may have taken her 'over the rainbow'. The film that apparently marginalises and possibly even gently mocks the fantastic (itself like a dream in sidelining an element to hide its *governing* status?) places a large question mark in the margin beside the image of fulfilment. After all, how could one realistically hope for something so rare? And yet, whether she sees the green ray may not matter. Viewers themselves may or may not recall that after the old lady recounting her brief experience of the green ray ('it lasted a split second') had described as a form of clairvoyance the emotional enlightenment Verne associates with it, a younger woman had responded: 'that's what happens to the heroine, who never sees the green ray but who finally reads her own feelings and those of the man she's met'. These words had been spoken over an image of Délphine, to whom Rohmer had just cut in an editing move whose significance becomes clear only retrospectively.

It is in his concern with the relationship between the seen and the unseen – visibility at the end of a clear day, and projection – that Rohmer is most Hitchcockian, and apparently in the manner of Slavoj Žižek's reading of Hitchcock. As the old man notes, pointing to the sun as it nears the horizon, 'the sun is not exactly where you see it'. Indeed, 'when the sun seems to touch the horizon, it's already below the horizon'. The green ray recalls what Žižek terms the Hitchcockian 'stain', a detail that 'has no substance in itself' but 'is, so to speak, "substantiated", caused, created, by the transfixed gaze itself'.[25] However, Rohmer's presentation of the moment of vision remains compatible both with Catholicism and with mysticism in general, as Žižek's atheistic version of Hitchcock is not, as the film's seeing may be *either* an inner illumination that is real, even though no external reality corresponds to it, *or* a 'stain' in another sense: that of a mirage, that seepage over the horizon of something whose reality is actually invisible. The former possibility would correlate with Rohmer's interest in Kleist, whose *Marquise of O* he had filmed a decade earlier. The latter, meanwhile, matches his interest in the mirage, displayed both in the speech of the old man who describes the ray as one, and in Rohmer's own penetrating 'Reflections on Color'. Indeed, a passage from that piece links these alternatives:

> To insist on the subjective character of color would be to forget that an optical instrument, the mirror, gives us an absolutely perfect copy of reality and that another, the lens, reproduces in a darkroom an image whose colors differ from the real ones only in their concentration, owing to the smaller surface that they cover. To create a complete mirage, it would suffice for this image to be preserved on film.[26]

In apparent obedience to this dialectic, *Le Rayon Vert* connects subjectivity and the objective in a way that both thrills us and leaves us scratching our heads.

POSTSCRIPT: SKETCH FOR A THEOLOGY OF COLOUR: THE RAINBOW AS THE BROKEN BODY OF LIGHT

One might develop further the considerations regarding the Other World running through this chapter by noting how in the New Testament, in the Book of Hebrews 10.19–20, the death of Jesus Christ is described as opening a way through the veil before the Holy of Holies in the temple, that veil itself being also his body: 'through the blood of Jesus Christ we have a right to enter the sanctuary, by a new way which he has opened up for us, a living opening through the curtain, that is to say, his body'.[27] In this context, what is the meaning of the fact that the fabric of the veil was coloured crimson, violet and red? I can only scrape at the surface of its meaning, which may well be depthless, encompassing many things, and even possibly all things. First, the red is the blood of Jesus himself, and of his torn body, as his death tears the veil apart to give access to the Holy of Holies to all believers – not just a male priest approaching it, doubtless with trepidation, on the Day of Atonement, bearing the blood of an animal sacrifice. The toning of red between crimson, violet and red suggests the mystery of the Trinity, the conjoined suffering in Jesus's crucifixion of all three members of the Godhead. The violet suggests the regal purple robe that is Jesus's due, and with which he was dressed in mockery before his death. Jesus's own blood is the stain that corrodes the veil, and also the colour that stained it beforehand, as if it had been always already soaked in blood shed 'from the foundation of the world', as he stood before humanity to protect it against God's wrath against the sinfulness in which humanity had become steeped. The veil, as it were, had always separated the sin from the sinner, enabling Jesus himself to become sin precisely in order to save his prospective brothers and sisters.

The conjunction of red and violet can lead in another direction, however, one not connected directly with the sacrificial ritual whereby, paradoxically, red makes clean, makes white. It concerns the status of red and violet as the colours framing the rainbow, marking the edges of the split body of light. As James Elkins notes,

> To us, the two extreme ends of the spectrum look very similar: red on one end seems to blend well with violet on the other. In terms of wavelengths they are opposites, but in our perception they seem like a good match. That is the reason why artists have been able to bend diagrams of the spectrum into color circles, connecting the red to the violet to make a continuous (and unscientific) cycle of color. If you think of what happens when you mix the deepest red with the deepest violet, you can only imagine a color very much like red or violet.[28]

The circularity attributed to colours in the colour wheel actually belies their progression along a line of ascending and descending wavelengths. That circularity, however, spells out a feature of colour concealed by the linearity of wavelength, but revealed by the rainbow red and violet hold in place: the fact that colour is both bent, like a circle, an arch built of hues calling out for their complements, and straight, like a line. When the red and the violet meet they are images of the alpha and omega that themselves image the all-encompassing nature of Jesus as God. They also suggest a fulfilment of the promise of the rainbow, that sign of future safety sealing God's covenant with Noah after the Flood. Under the covenant it sealed, God undertook never again to destroy humanity by water. This 'old' covenant is in a sense a version of the new covenant established by the breaking of the body of light that belonged to Jesus: the rainbow's appearance anticipates that breaking, and shows that the God who inhabits eternity views the future as established already. And inasmuch as Jesus is anticipated typologically by the patriarch Joseph, the rainbow is the heavenly 'coat of many colours'. Joseph, however, is spared the death that strikes Jesus: only his coat becomes red (to be displayed to his father as a sign of his ostensible demise), not his body. If red and violet meet in the death of the regally dressed King and blood-bearing priest who is Jesus, it indicates the unity of opposites within him – God and Man – that is also the one of red and white whose properties are confounded miraculously when blood washes clean.

NOTES

1. Stanley Cavell, *The World Viewed: Reflections on the Ontology of Film* (enlarged edn) (Cambridge, MA, and London: Harvard University Press, 1979), p. 81.

2. Ibid., p. 82.

3. Ibid., p. 85.

4. Pauline Kael, *Going Steady* (Boston and Toronto: Little, Brown and Co., 1970), p. 121.

5. Aldous Huxley, *The Doors of Perception and Heaven and Hell* (London: Flamingo, 1994), pp. 75–6.

6. Ibid.

7. David Batchelor, 'Chromophobia', in Angela Dalle Vacche and Brian Price (eds), *Color: The Film Reader* (New York and London: Routledge, 2006), p. 74; Salman Rushdie, *The Wizard of Oz* (London: BFI, 1992), p. 16.

8. Batchelor, 'Chromophobia', p. 74.

9. Peter Van Gelder, *Onscreen Offscreen: The Inside Stories of 60 Great Films* (London: Aurum, 1990), p. 283.

10. Laura Mulvey, 'Visual Pleasure and Narrative Cinema', in Leo Braudy and Marshall Cohen (eds), *Film Theory and Criticism* (6th edn) (New York and Oxford: Oxford University Press, 2004), pp. 837–48.

11. Donald Spoto, *The Art of Alfred Hitchcock: Fifty Years of His Motion Pictures* (Garden City, New York: Doubleday/ Dolphin, 1979), pp. 316–17, and Ornan Rotem, 'The World as One Whole: The Syntactic Role of Colour in Film' (*Kinema*, Spring 2003), <www.kinema.uwaterloo/rotem031.htm> (accessed 29 May 2009).

12. Steve Neale, *Cinema and Technology: Image, Sound, Colour* (London: BFI/Macmillan, 1985), pp. 151–5.

13. Richard Allen, 'Hitchcock's Color Designs' in Dalle Vacche and Price, *Color*, p. 141.

14. Rotem, 'The World as One Whole'.

15. Jason Swiderski, 'Colours of Obsession, the Supernatural, and the Past: Chromatic Definitions in *Vertigo*', mid-term essay for Film 311F, Department of Film Studies, University of Western Ontario, 2007, pp. 9–10.

16. Rotem, 'The World as One Whole'.

17. Ibid.

18. Quoted in Susanne Marschall, *Farbe im Kino* (Schüren: Marburg, 2005), p. 145.

19. Tobin Siebers, *The Mirror of Medusa* (Berkeley, Los Angeles and London: University of California Press, 1983), p. 24.

20. Huxley, *The Doors of Perception*, p. 75.

21. Ibid., p. 76.

22. Blaise Pascal, *Pensées*, trans. H. E. Stewart (London: Routledge and Kegan Paul, 1950), p. 11.

23. Derek Schilling, *Eric Rohmer* (Manchester and New York: Manchester University Press, 2007), p. 33.

24. Ibid.

25. Slavoj Žižek (ed.), *Everything You Always Wanted to Know about Lacan (But Were Afraid to Ask Hitchcock)* (London: Verso, 1992), pp. 235–6.

26. Eric Rohmer, 'Reflections on Color', in Dalle Vacche and Price, *Color*, pp. 121–2.

27. Jerusalem Bible version.

28. James Elkins, *The Object Stares Back: On the Nature of Seeing* (New York: Simon and Schuster, 1996), p. 65.

D : BETWEEN MONOCHROME AND COLOUR: SUFFERING AND THE UNREPRESENTABLE

8 Colour and Suffering

The gold of your hair Margarethe
The ash of your hair Sulamith. (Paul Celan)

A MATTER OF LIFE AND DEATH

Sometimes, shockingly, the properties of film technology – its powers and inadequacies – can make the difference between life and death. Thus movies, and the way the qualities of Technicolor could be seen as shortcomings, form a leitmotif in the Holocaust survival of Dina Babbitt, giving her a life-line out of a labyrinthine dark. Asked by Freddie Hirsch to liven up with paintings the children's barracks at Auschwitz, she followed the children's requests and painted *Snow White and the Seven Dwarfs* (1937) – the last film they had seen (and one she herself had seen seven times) before deportation. When summoned to an interview with the SS, she assumed it was for painting without permission, and feared the worst. She was taken to the Roma camp, to see Dr Josef Mengele. Having heard of her painting talent, he asked if she could provide accurately coloured portraits of the Roma, particularly their skin tone and eye-colouration, as Technicolor was inaccurate. As she herself would say subsequently – 'too garish'. The perceived deficiencies of Technicolor saved her life.

(Shortly after the war, Dina Babbitt married the former chief animator of *Snow White and the Seven Dwarfs* – the animator, in fact, of Dopey, with whom she had always identified. Later still, she became an assistant animator at Warner Bros. Movies, whose technical shortcomings had saved her life, would pervade it thoroughly.)

DISCOLOURED REALITY: *AMATEUR PHOTOGRAPHER*

How can one understand the meaning of this coloured vision of the ghetto in the colours of Genewein?
(Arnold Mostowicz, soundtrack to *Fotoamator*)

The perceived inadequacies of colour technology circa 1943 are central also to an archive that came to light in 1987, and has been documented and interrogated in a remarkable film by the Polish film-maker Dariusz Jabłoński, *Fotoamator* (*Amateur Photographer*) (1998). The archive had belonged to Walter Genewein, chief accountant in a garment factory the Nazis set up in the Łódź ghetto, and comprised colour slides he took using an expropriated Movex 12 camera. When writing to IGFarben Agfa to request 'the most up-to-date colour film' he stated that such film would 'better show the achievements of [his] unit'.

On various occasions, however, Genewein conveys to Afga his discontent with the accuracy of the colours on the developed slides. A practiced amateur photographer, he states that his own developing of the images cannot be to blame. One complaint concerns images assuming a reddish-brown hue, while a later one notes with exasperation, and in greater detail, that white areas are coming out pink, blue ones appearing purple, and green becoming brownish. The bluish tinge of his earlier films makes this reddish tonality all the more surprising.

Although Genewein's complaints suggest an accountant's irritation over the failure of a project of reproductive perfection homologous with the National Socialist quest for perfection in biological reproduction, other motives seem relevant also. The montage of images that accompanies the reading of the letter of complaint suggests that they may reflect the connotations and associations of this reddish-brown tonality, a greater commitment to aestheticisation than to truth, and a denial of death. Thus red-brown may disturb because it can recall blood, and the inexplicable distortion of the image may function in the same uncanny manner as the disappearance of Jews from pre-war photographs taken by a fictional character in Krzysztof's Zanussi's *Wherever You Are …* (1988): as a mystical anticipation of their deaths. The primacy of the aesthetic for Genewein (of which the concern for colour is symptomatic) reflects a denial, as he describes the red-brown tonality as 'ugly'. The form of words he employs embodies the particular form of negation and fastidious evasion known as euphemism, as he does not say 'häßlich' (ugly) but 'unschön' (not pleasant; literally, 'unbeautiful').

The return of red thus suggests one of the repressed. In an illuminating reading, Tomasz Majewski sees Jabłoński's juxtaposition of Genewein's letter of complaint with images of death as defining Genewein's disturbance as one by the uncanny indeed: by the surfacing of that which should have remained hidden.[1] In this context, the absence of blood Paul Monaco described as a recurrent feature in representations of death in Weimar-period German films may be a relevant precursor of this repression.[2] Jabłoński's sequence begins by associating red with death through the animal ribs seen outside a Jewish slaughterhouse; proceeds to show a Jewish corpse in binding cloths carried through the streets; and concludes with a Jew seated beside gravestones in a Jewish cemetery. This train of images mirrors a possible dreamlike displacement of the initial one in Genewein's mind. First, the montage of animal and Jewish death encodes the Nazi belief in Jewish subhumanity, even as the red that renders death disquietingly visible is partly repressed by the body's enshrouding. Since the body is clearly Jewish, the denial of death persists in the drive to associate death only with the Jews: that which was projected onto animals at first is now projected onto 'the Jew' (a displacement whose rails are greased by Nazi associations of Jewishness with animality). The solitude of the Jew in the cemetery makes him indeed 'the Jew', the singular figure into which the diversity of the Jewish community is absorbed in order to boil it down into a stereotype. The degree to which this process entails annihilation is apparent from his placement at the site of consummated destruction: the graveyard, that new home. The music drifting beneath this montage facilitates an associative movement the film seems to present as a diagram of the workings of Genewein's unconscious.

Arguing that Genewein's complaints about colour inaccuracies indicate his belief in the possibility of a precise photographic rendition of reality, while noting that Arnold Mostowicz – whose interviews, shot in monochrome, punctuate the film – had stated his inability to situate himself in the time and place depicted by the accountant's slides, Tomasz Łysak concludes that 'one has to ask what reality Genewein believes in'.[3] One might rephrase this to ask whether he sees the reality before him, even though it is one he himself has framed, irrespective of his degree of awareness of realities not included in the image. Jabłoński's stylistic strategies imply that Genewein failed to perceive properly even what lay before him. (Whether or not this simply made him 'a typical Nazi' is an issue that falls outside the frame of the film, though it circulates insistently *between* its frames.) Thus Jabłoński's camera delves repeatedly into Genewein's images, viewing them not from the distance of the slide-taker but floating within them. In this respect it may be deemed an alter ego of Mostowicz himself, possibly seeking on his behalf to find a place within images that exclude him, that refuse acknowledgment of the ghetto he knew from his work as a doctor. Jabłoński's project, which involves doing justice both to the frame's individual components and to the individuals herded together within it, often starts not with Genewein's 'establishing shot' (the round-up) but rather with details of images seen in full only later, if at all. In one example, the camera discovers a figure at a window in the background of a street scene and approaches the person, only to halt, and thereby end this particular investigation, when the figure becomes too blurred for identification. This procedure substantiates Łysak's suggestion that 'Genewein's slides "see" more than he does'.[4] For Jabłoński, the very presence of colour is a marker of misreading, all the positive associations of colouration being belied by the situation. An initial determination to question the presence of colour, along with notions of veracity as superficial verisimilitude, is enacted in the early movement out of colour, as a camera traversing snow-sprinkled cobblestones finds them become both snowless and monochrome. The Janus-faced quality of snow, which is both real and indicative of the possible mediation of monochrome, permits a telling transition, as the presence of whiteness within a 'coloured' world itself puts colour into question, perhaps even 'under erasure', as if asking where truth may lie. Monochrome shots of present-day Łódź follow. Repeatedly black-and-white images of present-day sites bleed and fade into colour slides of the same places in wartime Łódź, as if enacting a process of 'finding oneself' in the slide by suggesting that there is a hidden reason why the camera has held on this particular image: because it catches on the subterranean presence of one from the past. If such present-day images function as screens lifted aside to reveal past ones, there is a suggestion of a traumatic repetition compulsion recurrently placing the viewer in a position like that of Mostowicz. Once again, the camera acts as if it were his representative or alter ego, roaming streets, haunted both by the slides and their double alienation, both from current realities and those of the past.

One consequence of such disparities is that the word 'image' needs redefining to incorporate the aural. Thus Mostowicz describes an image (obraz) that has haunted him, but that almost defies visualisation, suggesting a tainting of the realm of the visual by the operations performed upon it by a Genewein. This image cannot be fixed: first, because the date of its occurrence is uncertain (it was probably 1943) and, second, because it occurred at night, albeit just before dawn. What remains in Mostowicz's mind is less a visual image than an aural one itself out of sync with the visual: a sound akin to hammering then became decipherable as that of the clogs of the ghetto's inhabitants walking to work. If one source of the inadequacy of an image is its stasis, Jabłoński counters this in two ways. One involves adding ambient noises appropriate to the activities the slides depict, creating an hypothesis about the aural dimension of the depicted world, and suggesting a desire to reanimate that sunken world. Another involves the above-mentioned movement within the image. In other words: reality is not given or self-evident but requires reconstruction or unearthing. Even when it exists in the present visible in colour to the film-maker himself, the possibility that colour is not necessarily the best mode of access (after all, colour hardly made the reality of the ghetto accessible to Genewein) may be why all the interviews with Mostowicz are filmed in monochrome. The shadows cross-hatching his face underline the thesis that there may be no direct access to reality, as does Jabłoński's documentarist commitment to the labour of montage and imagination. By way of contrast, Genewein's complaints about the unexpected metamorphoses of colour fail to understand their testimony to the partial, and possibly misleading, nature of any representation.

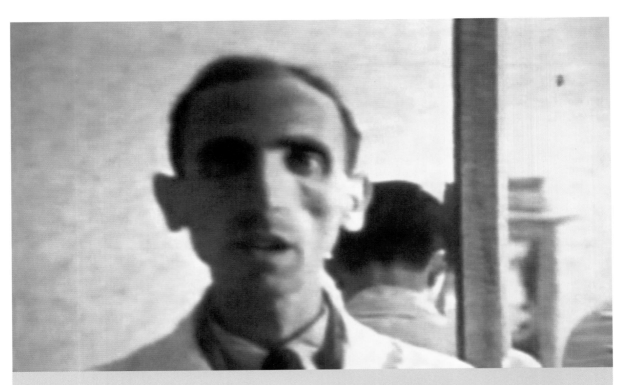

Amateur Photographer: Jabłoński focuses on the imminent death Genewein buried under distracting detail

In this context, the development of the Afga colour process becomes as much an experiment as the Nazi project within which IG Farben was embedded, the failure of the one in Genewein's present anticipating that of the other in his near-future. It is fitting, ironic and tragic that the final slide in Genewein's collection should be the one modern viewers will see as most unlike the reality identified in its accompanying caption: 'Jewish bath house'. It shows rows of showers, and naked men standing beneath them. If, as Roland Barthes argues, truth is what comes last,[5] here it comes in the form of a reality that, in becoming a metaphor, turns against the Nazis themselves the mendacity they practised systematically upon the Jews. For, of course, the image prophesies the gas chambers in which these men would shortly stand beneath false shower-heads. Both the final placement of the image and its contents reveal 'the final solution' for those who 'have eyes to see'. (One might want to compare the different, and rather controversial, play with the image of the shower at a key point in Spielberg's *Schindler's List* (1993).) Since this image comes last, does it show the unconscious of Genewein talking back to him, convicting him of guilty knowledge, for all his protestations of innocence? If, as many would argue, colour is inappropriate to images of horror, his colour slides become the false façade concealing the Nazi and Wehrmacht images of naked figures awaiting execution; his own private equivalent of the decorated, sanitised Theresienstadt the Nazis were happy to have the Red Cross visit.

'THE PAST IS NOT PAST': *NIGHT AND FOG*
Faced with a juxtaposition of colour and monochrome film stocks, our awareness of the historical succession of their periods of hegemony prompts us almost automatically to say: 'that was then, this is

now', 'now' being coded as more 'our time' than the one embalmed in monochrome. Alain Resnais' *Nuit et brouillard* (*Night and Fog*) (1955) works with and against this assumption, strategically letting it stand for much of the film, but subverting it in the end. That end is anticipated implicitly, however, in the first movement of the opening sequence: although the camera begins with a pastoral landscape in colour, it slides down very slightly to reveal barbed wire framing the fields, registering the ease with which the ordinary, the everyday and the present can metamorphose into the monstrous (and can place one imaginatively on a transport to the past). This initial minimal reframing shows how the colour that carries so many positive connotations, including those of designating a present separated as formally and apparently absolutely from the past as the concept of 'democracy' is from that of 'tyranny', adjoins horror: how, indeed, a focus on colour alone can repress awareness of the afterimages of horror. In terms of the colour/monochrome contrast, the first and last images of fields correspond to a statement made by the author of the commentary, Jean Cayrol, in one of his *Poèmes de la nuit et du brouillard*, that 'c'est maintenant le temps des herbes sur les ruines' (now is the time of the grass on the ruins). The encroachment of green upon ruins is one of colour on a reality whose nightmarishness involves its having been in a sense *really* black and white – 'in this world but not of it' (of a different, infernal, order). Thus the coming of grass is a veiling of horror, not its ending. (If the quotation of the beginning of Resnais' film, *in black and white*, in Godard's *Une femme mariée* (*A Married Woman*) (1964) prompts his female protagonist and her lover to walk out, is this because they reject the monochrome in which Godard's own film is cast, or the idea that colour and negativity might be associated? In any case, they differ significantly from Nana in Godard's earlier *Vivre sa vie* (*My Life to Live*) (1962), who is riveted by the image of the suffering face of Maria Falconetti in Dreyer's silent *La passion de Jeanne D'Arc* (*The Passion of Joan of Arc*) (1928).)

   As Resnais' film, having documented the development of the *univers concentrationnaire*, considers at its end the possibility of a return of darkness, its final import resembles the starting point of Christa Wolf's *Patterns of Childhood:* 'the past is not past'. Rather, its possible recurrence becomes conceivable, as the roles it assigned its participants – victim, hangman – still remain in history's repertoire, awaiting redistribution. Its account of the past has left many things – many horrors – to the imagination, defining them as horror by relegating them to a space inaccessible to the image, like the off-stage scene of horror in Classical Greek tragedy. Monochrome film stock has arguably served at points to indicate that certain things require the extra work known as imagining in order to be grasped. After all, a monochrome image of reality is one from which something is missing recognisably, by definition. As Ewout van der Knaap notes, '[i]n part four, all in black-and-white, the perfected method of extermination is depicted with images of the gas chambers and the stacks of bodies'.[6] Imagination, which has been enjoined up to this point to work to understand an incomprehensible past, and to link it to the present, now turns to the future, meditating, for instance, on the identity of the prospective hangmen currently moving among us. If death made a selection in the past, it may do so again. One cannot know who will be selecting, who will be selected, nor why: not only because in the world of the camps, as Claude Lanzmann would maintain, quoting the saying of a Kapo, 'hier ist kein Warum' (there is no why here), but also because a 'next Holocaust' may not necessarily be motivated by anti-Semitism, or anti-Semitism alone. Since Resnais wished the work to be taken in the context of the French-Algerian war underway at the time, this is no simply hypothetical notion. As we will see in the next section, and as Resnais well knew, other groups may, or may also, be affected.

RACE REFLECTED (AND NOT REFLECTED) IN COLOUR

Once, when teaching a course on colour in film, I learned that one of the registered students had a conflict with another course, on Blaxploitation. Because several meanings inhabit the term 'colour', I contacted her to ensure that she knew my course was not concerned centrally with racial issues, since in case of a misapprehension she could simply drop it and escape the conflict easily. There was no misapprehension, however – and the conflict was not resolved so simply. If issues of race and filmic colour were connected more accidentally in the life of Dina Babbitt, their connection within the semantics of the word 'colour' is less accidental. Consider the following, instructive passage from Brian Winston:

> The makers of *El Pueblo Vincera* (sic), a colour film, must have been aware of the limitations placed upon them by colour when filming black people. All professionals fully understand that colour films, despite continuous improvements in performance, do not render black skin tones as easily as they do white and that, when filming blacks, it is often necessary to augment lighting, by bouncing reflected light back into the face from a low angle, for instance, so as not to lose details. Were these stocks to offer 'a direct ... registration of colour in the natural world', we could simply attribute the difficulties of filming black people to a natural racial disadvantage – somewhat like, say, sickle-cell anaemia. But colour film, and colour television systems, do *not* directly register the world; 'a whole technology' intervenes. As the comedian Geoffrey Cambridge once hyperbolized – but only slightly – African-Americans look green on American (NTSC) television; no amount of knob-twiddling changes their colour (unless one makes the whites orange); and he for one was not surprised. The history and ideological implications of these technologies, technologies created by whites which best reproduce Caucasian skin tones, offer a good case study in technological agenda-setting at the stage when a technology is transformed from idea to existence.[7]

However, when Winston adds that colour film's 'supposed objective qualities are seductive enough to convince many (for whom Diego de la Texera, the director of *El Pueblo Vencera*, can stand), who in different circumstances would be more on the *qui vive* as to the ideological forces with which they are dealing',[8] his condescension may be misplaced: the Sandinista director might retort that lauding the usefulness of film in radical struggle did not entail a naive belief in its cultural neutrality, but rather one that it is *sufficiently* neutral for the extent of its non-neutrality not to matter. After all, much politically radical film has eschewed the realism that appears best served by any technology that is thought to reproduce the surfaces of reality exactly. Winston's overall point is important, but its formulation is too simple.

THE COLOUR OF BODILY SUFFERING

> [T]he funeral pyre of Hercules continues, like a natural symbol, to portray to us the destiny of mankind.[9]

On 8 September 1968, during a Harvest Festival celebration at the Stadium of a Decade in Warsaw, Ryszard Siwiec, aged sixty-eight, immolated himself amid 100,000 people in protest against the policies of a Polish regime he saw as displaying an oppressiveness, hypocrisy and hatred threatening to spread across the world. As his body burned, he uttered statements surely resembling the following ones he had tape-recorded, perhaps as rehearsals, a few days beforehand, and which Maciej Drygas plays at this point on the soundtrack of his film about Siwiec, *Usłyszcie mój krzyk* (*Hear My Cry*) (1981): 'Every country that subjugates others must fall'; 'there is no price that would not be worth paying to prevent such a system dominating the world'; and 'hear my cry, the cry of a grey and common man, the son of a nation who loved his and everyone else's freedom more than anything else, more than his own life. Come to your senses!'

A key element in Drygas's film, and in its dramatisation of the possibility and morality of the representation of suffering, is its treatment of colour. Colour appears only as an idea, inaccessible directly to the black and white of the film, and occupying two contrasting contexts in its verbal discourse. Like the most interesting filmic meditations on colour, that of Drygas is well aware of its ambiguity. On the one hand, there is the world of the Harvest Festival dances whose colourfulness represents a key element of popular attraction, being mentioned often by the ex-state radio commentator when discussing the event. This is not colour as an element of liberation, able to rupture the web of officially imposed signification, as described by Julia Kristeva. It can serve mystification equally well, belonging to a folklore whose preservation by the totalitarian world is intended to indicate not its own contradictoriness, the incompatibility of folklore and the industrialised 'radiant future', but rather its putative ability to preserve the best of the past, discarding the worst. Only some elements of the past are to be branded poisonous. Colour is shown not to be the special preserve of capitalism, with its billboard-lit streets, but compatible with construction of the socialist future. Analysis of the political unconscious of the culture of socialism may indeed assign symptomatic status to this policy, but totalitarian officialdom refuses any such insight. Milan Kundera, of course, would argue that the culture of folklore is completely compatible with that of the socialist administered world, being equally unreal. No wonder Drygas eschews colour throughout his film.

On the other hand, however, is the metamorphic colour of the flame that engulfed Siwiec. It can no more be controlled than could his righteous, prophetic anger. As described by a man who sought to extinguish it with his coat, it changed 'from purple to red to green, like a chameleon'. Elias Canetti might well have seen the eruption of this metamorphic colour within the self-proclaimed 'grey and common man' as reason to identify Siwiec with the Proteus who seeks to elude the threat of spiritual death by constantly transforming himself.[10] The constant transformation itself results in a real death that is the only true escape. It is as if the self-immolation belongs not in the Buddhist tradition but in that of the *auto-da-fé*, destroying the body trapped in an oppressive state in order to save – and release – the exasperated spirit.

The power of Siwiec's action rests upon the identification of flame with purification. In killing himself thus, he symbolically projected the possibility of a national self-purification through a mortification that has to be truly deadly, the disease having progressed so far within the body politic. His rejection by the nation clearly reflects a refusal to accept so radical a diagnosis, reinforced by fear of trauma: if '[m]odern psychiatry … has brought to light the serious traumatism that a psyche can suffer from the spectacle of a roof or haystack that has been set on fire',[11] how much greater is the trauma of viewing a human's self-immolation? Siwiec's image would be deeply troubling in its fusion of a positively charged patriotism with a suicide classified negatively: the two identities most Poles took as mutually reinforcing components of the hyphenated 'Polak-katolik' (Pole-Catholic) become uncoupled. What could be classified as an example of 'the Empedocles complex' disturbingly unifies 'the instinct for living and the instinct for dying'.[12] Thus the problem of Siwiec's action was not just one for the censorship apparatus of the Polish United Worker's Party. At some level of malign consciousness, moreover, the possible persistence of the mythology of a spontaneous combustion linked to alcoholism[13] may have facilitated its dismissal as less a martyrological symbol of a self-purifying Poland than the embodiment of a besetting national sin. The flame intended to redeem could aid a blaming of the victim in accordance with the scapegoating mechanisms studied so extensively by René Girard.

COLOUR AND ABJECT IDENTITY: *CYCLO* AND *THREE COLOURS: BLUE*

The pursuit of an abject identity has been a key strand in recent cinema. In a penetrating analysis and theorisation of this trend, John Orr cites such films as *Trois couleurs: bleu* (*Three Colours: Blue*) (1993), *Nil By Mouth* (1997), *Sans toit ni loi* (*Vagabond*) (1985), *Under the Skin* (1997) and *Morvern Callar* (2002). Had the focus of his essay not been European cinema, he might also have cited Anh Hung Tran's *Xich lo* (*Cyclo*) (1995), a film whose status he recognises elsewhere as that of 'possibly the most complex and challenging film of the decade' (the 1990s).[14] For Orr, this cinema, one of abjection, displays a 'traductive realism' that 'instantiates something against nothing, substance against the void' and involves 'the choice to be stranded as protection against the void'.[15]

Orr's 'something' may be described as a social death that is felt magically to preclude actual or existential death, and yet risks such death by cutting away support networks in the name of liberty; it is closer than it knows to the void it seeks to elude. The embrace of this form of 'death', however, may embody two errors: the assumption that one can know and avert a 'worst' whose contents one is allowed to determine in advance, a tactic whose efficacy is undermined by Edgar's assertion in *King Lear* that 'the worst is not/ So long as we can say "this is the worst"'; and an inability to perceive the extent to which the abjection clutched as a talisman against the void threatens to grant the abyss entry. Sometimes, though, the pursuer of abject identity may indeed realise this. His or her identification with the aggressor may be a strategy to protect the self from a feared Other by offering a part of the self instead of the whole: a strategy of sacrifice and appeasement. What is more, he or she can even figure this social death as a form of life: the hollowness of society's central identities – patriarchal, selfish and exploitative – may make true life seem achievable only at its periphery. In the aftermath of the collapse of belief in the feasibility of social revolution, abjection becomes the only form of liberation on offer: the individualistic one of Beckett's tramps: outside society, they become free. The choice to plunge into the abyss can forestall a reality one fears may give one no choice. In *Cyclo* and *Three Colours: Blue*, I will argue, it immerses the protagonist in the bath of a single colour. In each case, this colour functions as Deleuze says it does in Antonioni: it 'elevates space to the power of the void, when that which can be realised in the event is [or, if one likes, 'has been' – P. C.] accomplished'.[16] The foregrounding of colour represents, as it were, the afterlife of the protagonist, just as a colour continues in abstract form the object from which it has been squeezed. The film then tracks what persists of life (often simply physis, the body (Orr's 'substance')) in the aftermath of existential death. It may show a single colour engulfing the character's body from without, as painting or lighting (*Cyclo*), or suffusing the mind from within (the black-, blue- and whiteouts of what Bruce Kawin might term Julie's 'mindscreen' in *Three Colours: Blue*). In each case, though, the total subordination to a single colour accompanies a moment of maximal abjection, overwhelming suffering.

In Tran's film, as Orr rightly notes, the inspiration for the body's immersion in paint may well have been the ending of Godard's *Pierrot le fou* (1965).[17] Tran establishes the identification of total colour immersion with abjection very early on, when the simple-minded son of the Boss Lady whose machi-nations will devastate the life of Kien and his sister simultaneously (the theft of his cyclo takes him out of circulation, allowing his sister's recruitment as a prostitute) pours yellow paint all over his body, as he does frequently. The Boss Lady becomes the allegorical embodiment of a Vietnam in which lulling is killing, as it is for 'the Lullaby Man', who coos songs to his victims just before slitting their throats, releasing blood like a jet of paint. Her son's fish-like gulping prompts children to mock him as 'fish-face', and, near the film's end, a Tet celebration firecracker they have placed in his toy lorry explodes, sending him reeling into the path of a fire engine. Finding him covered with blood, his mother echoes Godard's equation of paint and blood, cradling him and saying: 'What is this thing you've got about paint? Where did you find this paint? It's not a colour we've used at home.' Indeed, the Boss Lady's banishment of red paint from her house is of a piece with her desire to ensure that the bloodshed her businesses cause occurs well away from home.

The fire engine that crushes the Boss Lady's son had been on its way to a blaze at the apartment of the Poet. His remorse over complicity in the rape of Kien's sister, who loves him and whom he had given to a client seeking S and M satisfactions, makes him torch his own apartment, where he writhes and dies. Earlier, as he left the club where he had handed over the key to her handcuffs, he had been immersed in a red light suggestive of his self-tormenting sense that, in selling her, he had sold himself. It is as if the red has followed him, making him recreate it as self-immolating (self-destroying, self-puri-fying) flame. When, the next day, the sister weeps for him before a religious street fire, it is as if she is staring into a place he has vacated. Since she was a virgin, the red that engulfs him on leaving the club may be linked to her sacrificial blood, as well as his own sacrificial death.

Cyclo and abject red 1: the Poet-Pimp walks away after giving Kien's sister to an abusive client

Cyclo and abject red 2: the Boss Lady's son now red with blood and not paint

The film's cataclysmic climax, which links the deaths of the Boss Lady's son and the Poet to the near-death of Kien, is also the elegant moment at which Tran adds the abjection of blue to those of yellow and red (see the illustration at the end of Chapter 5), rescoring the theme of colour abjection in terms of the only painter's primary omitted hitherto. It is as if such triangulation signifies the totality of experience, its exhaustion of the palette allowing him to end his film. Here Kien, having performed a series of killings and outrages for the Boss Lady, drugs himself, pours blue paint over his head and body, then shoots himself. His first shot hits his aquarium, and its fish land on the floor and gulp for air, sealing his identification with the abject 'fish-faced' son. Montage juxtaposes the gun's barrel with a fish's mouth just before he fires.

If Kien survives, and is not then killed by his gangster cronies, it is surely because his painted appearance reminds the Boss Lady of her own son – though, unsurprisingly in a film whose reality is both cruel and inscrutable, no reason is given. Any thought that the idyllic, high-end apartment blocks, tennis court and swimming pool across which the camera finally pans mean an end to the suffering is dispelled as the pan ends in the street, where the cyclo is pedalling his whole family, to the dissonant score that had been the signature tune of the work's most abject moments.

Given the centrality to this 'cinema of abjection' of the yearning for liberty and its denial, perhaps the most self-aware such film is the one that takes the French Revolution's watchword of 'freedom' as its keyword (reserving 'equality' and 'brotherhood' for the remaining parts of a trilogy): Krzysztof Kieślowski's *Three Colours: Blue*. *Three Colours: Blue* also foregrounds the lure of a void, as described both by Deleuze and Orr, through its repeated verbal references to a 'nothing' (an intriguing indicator of proximity to *King Lear*, whose theme of total loss is underpinned by a verbal texture in which 'nothing' also figures prominently) – as well as through its inundations of the screen with blue, white and black. The

fact that emptiness can appear as a colour, and as 'something' other than (emerging out of?) the black
or white that are recognisable forms of 'nothing', corresponds both to Julie's initial failure to recognise
its danger and her final ability to elude it, as she resumes composition. But if Julie is able to survive
the déclassement she chooses as a companionable form of the abject identity forced upon her by
bereavement, she is haunted by the spiritual, artistic and even material resources of a past she cannot
entirely abandon. Here both she and Kieślowski's film are unusual. If Julie temporarily embraces the death
whose shadow threatens to crush her life, most others never realise the extent to which the abjection
assumed as an alternative to the void threatens to suck one into it. Their position embodies the fantasy
around which Mathieu Kassovitz organises his *La Haine* (1995): that of the man plunging from a
building who states repeatedly, as he falls, 'so far so good'.

For Orr, the patron philosopher of this new existentialism (for which 'freedom' was also a keyword)
is not Sartre, however, but Kristeva.[18] In arguing thus, though, he overlooks the relevance of the Sartrean
analysis of the grounds of Jean Genet's choice of abjection. Branded a thief, Genet subsequently chose
that identity in the spirit of the mockery whereby so many political and artistic movements adopt as
names ('Tories', 'Impressionists') the would-be destructive taunts of their enemies. This manoeuvre, of
course, satisfyingly mocks and enrages the mocker, whose negative naming is shown merely to have unified his opponents. The case of these movements suggests nevertheless that individuals unable to find
strength in numbers by joining a group so constituted may well be destroyed by the potency of its
poison.

Embracing abjection means embracing a sense that humanity has fallen irrevocably, and is inca-
pable of self-redemption. It is post-ideological and post-theological. Ideologies are excluded because the
twentieth century had rendered their possibly devastating consequences all too evident. Theology –
the hand that opens our prison from without – is excluded because the invisibility of that hand is con-
flated with its non-existence. All that remains is the ambiguous materialist negative of theology: negative
theology. The place outside society, the possible site of identification with the redemptive crucifixion
beyond the city walls, becomes merely the no-place where Godot never arrives: a black or a blank,
colour as colour's negation.

SCHINDLER'S LIST: CANDLES IN THE DARK

Two sequences assume prominence in most discussions of the use of colour in Steven Spielberg's
Schindler's List. The most widely noted instance, featured on the cover of Franciszek Palowski's book on
the film,[19] involves its use to separate a little girl from the crowds of Jews being rounded up by the
Nazis as the Kraków ghetto is cleared. The red of her coat embodies the capacity of her image to leap
out representatively and catch the eye of Oskar Schindler, sitting on horseback, and looking down help-
lessly. Given the centrality of children to Spielberg's *oeuvre*, and the optimism pervading most of his earlier
films, a first-time viewer might be forgiven for thinking she might survive. After all, she attracts the
attention of Schindler, who is able to save so many. It is almost as if the redness of her coat indicates the
kindling of his attention. To quote Bachelard: '[w]hat I recognize to be living – living in the immediate
sense – is what I recognize to be hot'.[20] The redness of her coat symbolises the fullness of life within her,
rendering her a Red Riding Hood who might just experience a fairy tale and escape the ogre-filled
Nazi wood. The dashing of the hopes the image raises gives the measure of the mercilessness of the
Shoah, intensifying our sense of its perversity. Although Spielberg spares us the worst cruelty, refraining

from showing her death, we are able to identify her body among ones later exhumed for incineration, all the specialness of life snuffed out even as, in a bitter irony, that of red persists. That identification of red with life is cemented by the female camp inmates pricking their fingers to obtain blood to rub on their cheeks before a selection, as if responding to age-old folk beliefs in such an association, reflected, for instance, in the fact that the Russian word for 'red' can also signify 'beautiful' (similarly, lipstick on cheeks is considered beautifying by the little Afghan schoolgirls of Hana Makhmalbaf's *Buda as sharm foru rikht* (*Buddha Collapsed Out of Shame*) (2007)).

The other commonly discussed use of colour involves the ending, set in modern Jerusalem. Its appearance here indicates the contemporary, documentary status of the scene in which the Jews Schindler saved lay commemorative stones on his tomb. The advent of colour here draws a line under the darkness of the nightmare that preceded it: a move some viewers would see as placing the Shoah too definitively and safely in the past, with none of the sense of a possible recurrence of catastrophe found at the end of *Night and Fog*.

The relative rarity of the mentions accorded the work's third major use of colour, however, may be surprising, given its highly visible position at the film's start. Like the death of the little girl, it involves a 'snuffing out of red' that is both literal and metaphorical. The opening shot shows a match being struck, then lighting two candles. A chanting voice and the appearance of a solemnly assembled Jewish family indicate celebration of the onset of the Sabbath. Montage then removes the family. The candles burn down until the final one gutters, its flame becoming smoke. That smoke inaugurates the black and white that will prevail through almost all the film. The montage rhyme between the candle smoke and the steam of a train, thrusting into the sky, poetically matches the dying of an object associated with one people with the onset of another force: inevitably, the train recalls, and so anticipates within the film's chronology, the means by which most such families were despatched to the concentration camps. Heart-breakingly, it also anticipates their own rendition into the smoke of the crematoria. Montage is so recurrent a feature of the film that it is clear that, for all its Americanism, it has also been to school with Eisenstein, adding extra justification to Miriam Hansen's reference to Spielberg's 'popular modernism', which she correlates with his indebtedness to Welles[21] – this time with the word *modernism* underlined. In a rhyme that accords rather with the vocabulary of classical cinema than that of modernism, however, the small coloured flame on candles returns when the rabbi first celebrates the Sabbath at Schindler's transplanted, Brinnlitz plant. The celebration is muted by the monochrome of the candles below the flames.

Andrzej Wajda reports suggesting that Spielberg shoot in black and white:

> When Steven Spielberg was preparing *Schindler's List* I met him in Cracow. Earlier, Lew Rywin had told him that I thought *Schindler's List* ought to be a black-and-white film. Spielberg asked me why I thought that. I used an argument I believe convinced him. I said: if you have decided to make a film about the tragedy of the Jews in Europe it must set itself apart from all your previous films. Only then will spectators understand that you have something different to say.

Wajda adds that Spielberg asked him whether he knew that Schindler's eyes were blue (Wajda did), adding that he was considering colouring those eyes throughout the film.[22] Such a move would doubtless have been motivated not by a desire for realism, as it would have disrupted the monochrome visual

Schindler's List: colour gutters prophetically in a Sabbath candle

texture, but by the film's pervasive irony, which in this case would have concerned the correspondence between a key element of the racist Nazi physical ideal and the appearance of a man who would rescue Jews. Spielberg's eventual rejection of this possibility may have reflected a fear that this blue, while serving a more superficial purpose, might distract from, clash with, or reduce the impact of, the red of the poignant image of the little girl.

Thus colour, and its contrast with monochrome, is integral to *Schindler's List*. It may appear at its margins, but those margins set the tone and frame the context. Colour marks a normality violated by the Shoah, and re-established at the work's end. Its brief flicker on a red coat reminds one both of that normality, and of how little normality was present in the camps and the ghettoes. Identifying such normality as persistent is, of course, part of the hopefulness of Spielberg's film, the optimism that prompted him to address the Holocaust through the tall tale of that unlikely redeemer, the entrepreneur Oskar Schindler. The indirectness in addressing the Holocaust is not entirely unlike that of Claude Lanzmann's *Shoah* (1985), with which it has been compared and found wanting – not entirely justly – in academic debate. The separation of darkness and light, black and white and colour, is constitutive of the universe established by Spielberg, who argues that although the Shoah must never be forgotten, at a certain point its echoes simply, mercifully, cease to resound.

A MONOCHROME PALETTE: *THE HOURGLASS SANATORIUM*

If using black-and-white film can signal recognition of the suffering of the inhabitants of a filmic world, it may seem paradoxical that Wojciech Has's *Sanatorium pod klepsydrą* (*The Hourglass Sanatorium*) (1973), which is strewn with Jewish tombstones, should employ colour throughout. This may be all the more surprising for a reader of the Bruno Schulz story that furnishes its title, whose primary tonality is monochrome. The following sentence is typical: 'The mournful semidarkness of an undefined time descended from a sky of interminable grayness.'[23] The use of colour stock in Has's film, which records Schulz's vivid, fantasy-riddled inter-war world in the light of its violent demise in the Holocaust, may therefore seem doubly strange. Given Has's artistic seriousness and long-standing enthusiasm for Schulz's work, explanations in terms of the normative status colour had acquired by the early 1970s, or its inseparability from fantastic spectacle, would be trivial and even insulting. Gradually, however, it becomes clear that using colour, and this story as its main frame, allows it to place in brackets the multi-hued world of Schulz's other stories, with its exotic birds and armies, which it can thus be seen as 'quoting' in its mid-section. Since, as Konrad Eberhardt noted, Schulz's fictional world is founded upon continual metamorphosis, to which death is inimical,[24] choosing this particular story enables Has in a sense to mobilise Schulz 'against Schulz',[25] as the theme of death nestles naturally into its monochrome palette and sanatorium setting. The title story becomes a pair of pincers used to pick up the coloured world, examine it gently, then put it down in a manner that marks its expiry. The central section's saturation with colour permits one to measure the significance of its draining away in the opening and closing sections, which echo the frame placed around the story by history. Their drab tonality is appropriately sepulchral; and the train transporting its protagonist Józef to the sanatorium at the beginning, whose blind conductor he has become at its end, belongs in the imagery of the Holocaust. No wonder its passengers are Surrealist dolls foreshadowing arrival at a place of dehumanisation. To quote Eberhardt: 'The dim interior of the carriage is full of objects and household effects that are somewhat unnecessary, such as people take with them when forced to leave their place of abode forever.'[26] The disparity between a richly coloured world and another, deathly one seeps even into the film's mid-section, as if the emergence of that other world is only a matter of the time that forms one of Has's obsessions. Thus, at one point, Józef stands in

The Hourglass Sanatorium: Holocaustal imagery as the darkness of Schulz's palette pervades Has's sanatorium-bound train

sunshine outside a wall, peering through a gap to view a desaturated garden, where a dead woman walks. What he sees suggests both a flashback and a flashforward. The gap, a crack in time born both of hope and relativity theory, suggests the possibility that a death that has supervened in one place may not be definitive, as it has not arrived elsewhere. As Dr Gotard tells Józef, in words that acquire a particular resonance in a film made after the Holocaust and set in a defunct inter-war Jewish small town: 'You know as well as I that from the point of view of your home, from the perspective of your own country, your father is dead.'[27] If death is a matter of perspective, even of the difference between countries, it is possible that – as L. P. Hartley suggested at the start of *The Go-Between* – past and present are indeed simply places where 'they do things differently'. Gotard, however, adds, both realistically and grimly euphemistically: 'This cannot be entirely remedied. That death throws a certain shadow on his existence here.'[28] Simultaneously, it throws one upon the vivid colouration of the majority of Schulz's stories. The shadow renders their existence a mixture of fantasy and recollection, Eliotic memory and desire, Bergsonian lag between reality and its perception. Has's film registers death at work, consuming the brightness of its middle world. In the end, as the blind Józef walks away through a cemetery studded with votive candles, the camera slides downwards into darkness. Memory gutters, unconsciousness envelops sleep-born fantasy and the viewer becomes like Józef himself, seeing nothing.

POSTSCRIPT

At this point one might venture some more general reflections concerning colour and suffering. Almost notoriously, Theodor Adorno argued after World War II that to continue writing poetry after Auschwitz would be barbaric. His critique of poetry was not obviously pointed (as if he felt other arts could carry on regardless), but it could well have been deemed such, given the liability of poetry's native distortions of diction to commonsensical classification as varnishings of bare facticity: as if truth-telling meant removing such patent decoration – as it had for the Romantic opponents of late-eighteenth-century poetic language. It is surely relevant that one stereotypical image of art's failure to humanise the 'nation of musicians and poets' manning the concentration camps depicts an SS man reading Rilke in the evening: the failure of civilisation becomes one of poetry (and, characteristically, of a poet often deemed self-absorbed and mannered, the example seemingly contaminating the genre it represents; though a reading of the diaries of Etty Hilsum, a Dutch Jew steeped in Rilke, who herself died in the camps, would shake such stereotypes). If an art that makes no difference is merely decorative, it is worth remembering the frequency with which 'decoration' is deemed synonymous with colour, even though colour and suffering are in one sense intimately related: most dyes emerge through the destruction of an object (or even creature – as in the 'blooding' of a child's cheeks at their first fox-hunt). Meanwhile, of course, the whiteness neo-classicists associated with Greek statues of the gods, even if, in fact, it resulted from their colours' fading, seemed a fitting indicator of Olympian distance from earthly sorrow. The hegemony of pale-skinned ethnic groups over the last few hundred years does indeed seem to bolster the view that whiteness suffers less.

Where cinema is concerned, the aesthetic and ethical prohibition issued 'after Auschwitz' might well be seen as one of colour. If Adorno could argue later, in his *Aesthetic Theory*, that the signature 'colour' of those modernist works most strongly resistant to unthinking affirmation is black, colour would seem to be proscribed: it implies that life goes on undisturbed. However, the coloured images of the deserted camps in Alain Resnais' *Night and Fog* are framed to indicate how life went on and yet still nourished the danger of disaster's recurrence. If the task of the artist faced with the camps is both to speak and remain silent – as Claude Lanzmann would define the project of his own *Shoah* – then monochrome can represent a dialectical necessary acceptance and contravention of Adorno's *Bilderverbot*, that secularised version of the old covenant proscription of graven images (a contravention Adorno himself would later concede might be justified). Monochrome can manifest solidarity with a vanished past: in this case, that of the form of film that began to disappear, however coincidentally, about the same time as the Jews, in the 1930s. Nevertheless, the vow of visual poverty monochrome seems to exact is more ambiguous. After all, neither *Night and Fog* nor *Shoah* – the two films usually viewed as virtually alone in beginning to take the measure of the problems of representation posed by the Holocaust – employ monochrome, as if its use would throw up questions of style and stylisation that would distract from the documentary task. (Jean Renoir notes, with his usual acuity, albeit in another context, that '[t]here's an element of surprise in black and white that you don't have in color. Black and white also gives the director and the cameraman an infinite number of possibilities for special effects.'[29]) Both Resnais and Lanzmann recognise colour as not 'poetry' but the prose of the modern filmic world, where monochrome may be less a renunciation than a luxury. After all, few modern film-makers would be able to compel from producers a non-use of the expected colour stock. Renunciation of one form of spectacle may be possible only at the cost of preserving another, as may well occur in *Schindler's List*, which mobilises masses none-too-distant from the proverbial 'cast of thousands', and whose black and white often has a noirish lusciousness. It may be, though, that a gesture such as Spielberg's constitutes, in the realm of fiction, a necessary, legitimising replication of documentary's traditional founding vow of poverty: that of maximal fidelity to historical records. (This is why Andrzej Wajda reverted to black and white in his *Korczak* (1990).) If there is a justification for Spielberg's red-colouring of the coat of one little girl among those of so many, it may lie not just in its individualisation of the unimaginable fate of that mass, underlining its poignancy, but also in its implicit acknowledgment that, in an era in which colour film is normative, no film can cease entirely to be a colour film.

At the same time, though, as Drygas's *Hear My Cry* indicates, a genuine sense of horror can render the use of colour problematic, particularly in any fictional dramatisation: coloured recreations of blood-letting can so patently showcase special effects as to evoke an obscenely connoisseurial delectation. Spurts of coloured blood evoke baroque spectacle, Grand Guignol and distracting reflections on the precise variety of animal blood – or ketchup – employed. As so often, the presence of colour is read as one of distraction, which not everyone is as prepared to deem as constitutive of the cinematic as was Walter Benjamin, or gloss as positively as he did. Monochrome may even be a mode of rendering reality that allows room for the hope that suffering may spiritualise – not just embody the transformation of subject into object sought by the Nazis or slip into the simulated preterition of a vanished, superseded world. (The monochrome of Martin Scorsese's *Raging Bull* (1980) both suggests the obtuse passion of its subject, Jake LaMotta, and reproduces the loss of colour vision head-blows can induce in a boxer.[30])

Rendered monochromatically, reality is already being translated out of this world, into a shadow-spectrum. Monochrome can embody hope that such suffering is not all this world amounts to. And if art can indeed claim to be the 'antenna of the race' envisaged by Ezra Pound, then the shaven head of Falconetti in Dreyer's *Passion of Joan of Arc* prefigures the suffering multiplied just over a decade later, in the camps. Perhaps because it was a one-time role for Falconetti, her image may be one of the very few fictional ones able to survive the truth-test of comparison with those of the camps. It never suffered that form of falsification, the repetition (and suggestion of immortality) constitutive of stardom, while the muteness of silent film itself embodied a form of suffering, a speechlessness compelling the eyes to implore. In this context, the askesis of monochrome can be (though it need not; there are no guarantees) a form of tact. If cryptic colouration is the creature's road to survival, colour's absence may be the best simulation of death, underlining soberingly just how few survived.

NOTES

1. Tomasz Majewski, 'Getto w kolorach Agfa, Uwagi o *Fotoamatorze* Dariusza Jabłońskiego', in Andrzej Zalewski, Beata Lisowska, Ewa Rewers *et al.*, *Między słowem a obrazem* (Cracow: Rabid, 2005), p. 328.

2. Paul Monaco, *Cinema and Society: France and Germany During the Twenties* (New York, Oxford and Amsterdam: Elsevier, 1976), pp. 130–3.

3. Tomasz Lysak, 'O niemożliwej wierze w dokument. *Fotoamator* Dariusza Jabłońskiego', *Kwartalnik filmowy* 43 (Autumn 2003), p. 71.

4. Ibid.

5. Roland Barthes, *Mythologies*, trans. Annette Lavers (St Albans: Paladin, 1973), p. 84.

6. Ewout van der Knaap (ed.), *Uncovering the Holocaust: The International Reception of* Night and Fog (London: Wallflower, 2005), p. 9.

7. Brian Winston, *Technologies of Seeing: Photography, Cinematography and Television* (London: BFI, 1996), p. 41.

8. Ibid., p. 40.

9. Gaston Bachelard, *The Psychoanalysis of Fire*, trans. Alan C. M. Ross (Boston: Beacon Press, 1968), p. 20.

10. Elias Canetti, *Crowds and Power*, trans. C. V. Wedgwood (London: Gollancz, 1962), pp. 344–6.

11. Bachelard, *The Psychoanalysis of Fire*, p. 13.

12. Ibid., p. 16.

13 Ibid., p. 96.

14. John Orr, *Contemporary Cinema* (Edinburgh: University of Edinburgh Press, 1998), p. 31.

15. John Orr, 'New Directions in European Cinema', in Elizabeth Ezra (ed.), *European Cinema* (Oxford: Oxford University Press, 2004), p. 306.

16. Gilles Deleuze, *Cinéma 1: L'Image-Mouvement* (Paris: Les Editions de Minuit, 1983), p. 168, and *Cinema 1: The Movement-Image*, trans. Hugh Tomlinson and Barbara Habberjam (Minneapolis: University of Minnesota Press, 1986), p. 119.

17. Orr, *Contemporary Cinema*, p. 109.

18. Orr, 'New Directions in European Cinema', p. 306.

19. Franciszek Palowski, *Witness: The Making of* Schindler's List, trans. Anna and Robert G. Ware (London: Orion, 1998).

20. Bachelard, *The Psychoanalysis of Fire*, p. 111.

21. Miriam Bratu Hansen, '*Schindler's List* is not *Shoah*: Second Commandment, Popular Modernism, and Public Memory', in Yosefa Loshitzky (ed.) *Spielberg's Holocaust: Critical Perspectives on* Schindler's List (Bloomington and Indiana: Indiana University Press, 1997), p. 97.

22. Andrzej Wajda, *Kino i reszta świata* (Cracow: Znak, 2000), p. 253.

23. Bruno Schulz, *Sanatorium Under the Sign of the Hourglass*, trans. Celina Wieniewska (New York: Walker and Company, 1977), p. 121.

24. Konrad Eberhardt, *O polskich filmach* (Warsaw: Wydawnictwa Artystyczne i Filmowe, 1982), p. 343.

25. Ibid., p. 345.

26. Ibid., p. 347.

27. Schulz, *Sanatorium Under the Sign of the Hourglass*, p. 116.

28. Ibid.

29. Jean Renoir, *Renoir on Renoir: Interviews, Essays, and Remarks*, trans. Carol Volk (Cambridge and New York: Cambridge University Press, 1989), p. 50.

30. For a description of this phenomenon of the loss of colour-perception, see Oliver Sacks, 'The Case of the Colorblind Painter', *An Anthropologist on Mars: Seven Paradoxical Tales* (Toronto: Alfred A. Knopf, 1995), p. 31, n. 22: 'Mr I, fond of spending time in sports clubs and bars, did some research here himself and told us that he had spoken to a number of boxers who had transient, and sometimes persistent, losses of colour vision following blows to the head.'

Acknowledgments

My thanks to Lloyd Michaels for his support of some of the work incorporated into this book, namely one section of 'Le Mépris: Women, Statues, Gods' (*Film Criticism* vol. 22 no. 3 (1998), pp. 38–50) and the whole article 'On the Dialectics of Colour (in general) and Red (in particular): *Three Colours: Red*, *Red Desert*, *Cries and Whispers* and *The Double Life of Véronique*' (*Film Criticism* vol. 32 no. 3 (Spring 2008), pp. 2–23). Particular thanks are due to Charlie Egleston, whose patience and technical expertise extracted the precise split-second forms of the illustrations to this book.

Thanks also to the anonymous readers of the BFI, who made many useful suggestions regarding directions into which to take portions of the typescript, and to Brian Price, who bravely came out of the shadows of that anonymity.

Index

LIST OF ILLUSTRATIONS

While considerable effort has been made to correctly identify the copyright holders, this has not been possible in all cases. We apologise for any apparent negligence and any omissions or corrections brought to our attention will be remedied in any future editions.

Une femme est une femme, Rome-Paris Films/Euro International Films; The River, © Oriental International Films; Red Desert,Film Duemila/Francoriz; Opus 1, Walther Ruttmann; Two or three things I know about her, Anouchka Films/Argos-Films/Films du Carrosse/Parc Film; The Lives of Others, © Wiedemann & Berg Filmproduktion; Solaris, Mosfilm; Europa, Nordisk Film/Gunnar Obel Films/Gérard Mital Productions/Telefilm/Svensk Filmindustri/Sofinenergie 2/Eurimages Conseil de l'Europe; Three Colours: Red, © MK2 Productions/© France 3 Cinéma/© CAB Productions/© Zespol Filmowy 'Tor'; Cries and Whispers, Cinematograph/Svenska Filminstitutet; The Double Life of Véronique, Sidéral; Cyclo, Productions Lazennec/ARTE/Canal +/SFP Cinéma/Lumière/Sept Cinéma/Salon Films (H.K.) Ltd/Giai Phong Film Studio; The Curse of the Golden Flower, © Film Partner International Inc.; Marnie, © Geoffrey Stanley Inc.; The Flight of the Red Balloon, © 3H Productions/© Margofilms/© Films du Lendemain; Three Colours: Blue, © MK2 Productions/© CEO Productions/© France 3 Cinéma/© CAB Productions/© Zespol Filmowy 'Tor'; The World, © Office Kitano/© Lumen Films/© Xstream Pictures Ltd; Le Mépris, Rome-Paris Films/Films Concordia/Compagnia Cinematografica Champion; Moulin Rouge, © Romulus Films; All that Heaven Allows, © Universal Pictures Company; The Wizard of Oz, Loew's Incorporated; Vertigo, © Alfred J. Hitchcock Productions; Amateur Photographer, Apple Film Production/Broadcast AV/Telewizja Polska/Polska Korporacja Telewizyjna Canal/Mitteldeutscher Rundfunk/ARTE; Schindler's List, © Universal City Studios, Inc./© Amblin Entertainment; The Hourglass Sanatorium, Polish Corp.